Excavating Nauvoo

Critical Studies in the History of Anthropology

Excavating Nauvoo

The Mormons and the Rise of Historical Archaeology in America

Benjamin C. Pykles

Foreword by Robert L. Schuyler

University of Nebraska Press • Lincoln and London

Portions of the introduction have been published as
"A Brief History of Historical Archaeology in the United States,"
SAA *Record* 8, no. 3 (May 2008): 32–34.

Manufactured in the United States of America

Library of Congress Cataloging-in-Publication Data

Pykles, Benjamin C.
Excavating Nauvoo: the Mormons and the rise of historical archaeology in America /
Benjamin C. Pykles; foreword by Robert L. Schuyler.
p. cm. — (Critical studies in the history of anthropology)
Includes bibliographical references and index.
ISBN 978-0-8032-1893-2 (cloth: alk. paper)
ISBN 978-1-4962-0224-6 (paper: alk. paper)
1. Nauvoo (Ill.)—Antiquities. 2. Mormons—Illinois—Nauvoo—Antiquities.
3. Excavations (Archaeology)—Illinois—Nauvoo. 4. Historic preservation—Illinois—Nauvoo. 5. Archaeology and history—United States—History—19th century. I. Title.
F549.N37P95 2010
977.3'43—dc22
2009039045

Set in Quadraat & Quadraat Sans by Kim Essman.
Designed by Ray Boeche.

Contents

Illustrations

Foreword

ROBERT L. SCHUYLER

Historical archaeology is the archaeology of the modern world, the last five or six centuries of global cultural development. In light of its subject matter, it is not surprising that it emerged as an organized discipline last in the sequence of appearance of the various specialized archaeologies. Classical antiquarianism emerged as early as the Italian Renaissance, prehistoric archaeology with the mid-nineteenth-century geological revolution, and the study of various ancient civilizations in the later nineteenth or early twentieth century. Historical archaeology's roots in North America go back to the Great Depression. By 1960 it was a fully recognized if small topic of research among fieldworkers in both the United States and Canada. The following decade saw the successful establishment and professionalization of this new field, which today is equal in importance to North American prehistory and, unlike that older specialization, is rapidly expanding as a discipline around the world.

Historians of science and archaeologists themselves have only recently begun a full investigation of the discipline's origins and development. The pioneers in the field fortunately preserved at least an outline of their own oral histories, as exemplified by Stanley South's fine edited collection, *Pioneers in Historical Archaeology: Breaking New Ground* (Plenum Press, 1994), a collection of oral histories compiled in 1977. A few brief historical syntheses have also appeared. It was not until 2005, however, that the first book-length study of the subject, based on primary sources and using standard historical and contextual analysis, was produced. Donald W. Linebaugh's *The Man Who Found Thoreau: Roland W. Robbins and the Rise of Historical Archaeology in America* (New Hampshire, 2004) is an excellent first such study because it outlines in detail the career of a famous avocational fieldworker who helped build the field but who was in turn eventually marginalized by the discipline's growing professionalism.

Benjamin Pykles's book, the second serious, extended study, affords a fascinating exploration of a key episode in the development of historical archaeology in America. *Excavating Nauvoo: The Mormons and the Rise of Historical Archaeology in America* not only convincingly adds a chapter to the discipline's history, it also has implications for the history of general archaeology and, more broadly, for the history of all the human sciences. Human history, and the histories of individual professions and specializations, follow broad developmental patterns, but the history of any individual society or any discipline is also highly controlled by specific elements in its cultural setting.

As we look at the record of the human past we see both the determined patterns of cultural evolution and the much more chaotic and unpredictable factors that are to be found in any given historical sequence.

Pykles recounts the chance coming together, late in his career, of the ultimate pioneer in American historical archaeology, Jean Carl Harrington, and a singular institutional setting for the growth of the discipline in the 1960s. The normal pattern during the decade of the 1960s, the period during which the events in this book took place, was characterized by a series of predictable steps: (1) the recognition of the recent past as a legitimate subject of archaeological research, (2) a successful demonstration of the field's contributions, with case studies, and (3) the acceptance of this new discipline by various institutions, with expanding support for the future. In North America the earliest institutions involved with historical archaeology typically were national governmental agencies, especially the National Park Service (NPS) in the United States and Parks Canada north of the border, or their state or provincial equivalents. Slightly later academia (especially departments of anthropology) provided major support. Finally, in the 1970s private firms engaged in cultural resource management (CRM) emerged as even more powerful and financially solid allies of the field.

The Nauvoo project (1961–84) stood out from other projects under way at the time because its support came from an ecclesiastical institution, the Church of Jesus Christ of Latter-day Saints (LDS), and its counterpart, the Reorganized Church of Jesus Christ of Latter Day Saints (now called the Community of Christ). Because of the senior standing of J. C. Harrington within historical archaeology—with three decades of work in the NPS on some of the most famous historic sites in the United States—and the very strong initial support from the First Presidency of the LDS Church, a normal sequence of steps would have been predicted for this project at its inception. However, the final outcome of the Nauvoo project and the subsequent relationship between the discipline and this institutional setting were both structured and altered by the internal activities of the two Mormon churches, especially the potentially watershed event of succession when a president of the Church dies and is replaced by a new president, prophet, and seer.

Pykles, using primary documentary sources, which he has hunted down in impressive detail, presents the reader with a persuasive study of the interplay of the personalities involved, the growing professionalism of the discipline and its own internal shift from a restoration-preservation purpose to fully anthropological, interpretive goals, and the shifting support of the two separate Mormon churches that own the historical site of Nauvoo. The passing of one president and designation of his predecessor within the Utah LDS Church was a central event, even if one external to the discipline itself, for it had a direct impact on the project and the future relationship between the field and this unusual ecclesiastical sponsorship.

Excavating Nauvoo recounts the story of one of the first nineteenth-century urban settlements to be explored through excavation, a potential "Williamsburg of the West." Equally important is the book's demonstration of the specificity of history itself: how events, personalities, and structures unique to the setting at Nauvoo encouraged, significantly supported, and then truncated the normal growth of historical archaeology as an essential tool for preserving and exploring a major American historic site.

Pykles's well-grounded book sends a powerful message that reaches well beyond the nineteenth-century Mormon city on the Mississippi to make a statement about the history and future of the entire discipline, even all of archaeology. The institutional settings that have supported the growth of historical archaeology in America have themselves changed over the past quarter century of American history. The transition from governmental agencies to the academy to the business world was successfully navigated, but any drastic alteration in one or more of these three contexts could have greatly affected the history of the discipline, and such alterations may indeed occur in the future. The global triumph of neoliberal capitalism since 1990 has already caused major changes in the academic and professional worlds within which historical archaeologists carry on research. The prediction is for a steady global expansion of the discipline building on all these and additional new supportive settings, but history is messy and unpredictable. What will happen to historical archaeology in the future? The history of the discipline is generally optimistic as we use the discipline's past to look forward, but the unpredictability of history as seen in this case study is a strong warning for all of us working in the most successful and expansive type of archaeology practiced in North America today.

Acknowledgments

Numerous individuals unquestionably aid a project as long in duration as this has been. First among these is Robert L. Schuyler, who graciously agreed to write the foreword for the book. He has consistently supported and encouraged me in my research on the history of historical archaeology. I am sincerely grateful for the lasting influence he has had on my career.

The library personnel of the University of Pennsylvania largely made it possible for me to write a book on the restoration of Mormon Nauvoo while living on the East Coast of the United States. I owe particular thanks to the staff of the inter-library loan office and to John Weeks and his staff at the University Museum library. Equally influential have been the number of individuals who have assisted me at the Archives of the Church of Jesus Christ of Latter-day Saints in Salt Lake City, Utah. Randall Dixon, William Slaughter, and Ron Read have been especially supportive and helpful in my research. Truthfully, the book would not have been possible without their assistance. Ted Hild and his colleagues at the Illinois Historic Preservation Agency graciously entertained my questions and requests for documents, as did Susan Escherich and Patti Henry with the National Historic Landmarks programs in Washington DC. Likewise, Christina McDougal at the Torreyson Library of the University of Central Arkansas and Emily Lovick at Fort Smith National Historic Site were incredibly helpful in locating and forwarding information and images relating to Clyde Dollar. I also owe special thanks to the staff and friends of the Community of Christ Archives in Independence, Missouri, who helped track down images of the RLDS excavations in Nauvoo. Especially helpful in this regard were Ron Romig, Ken Stobaugh, and Marvin Crozier.

I was fortunate to be able to discuss the Nauvoo excavations with both Dale Berge and Paul DeBarthe, two of the principal archaeologists who worked at Nauvoo. I am grateful to both for sharing their insights and memories in person, over the phone, and through e-mail. Don Enders of the Museum of Church History and Art in Salt Lake City likewise made time for an oral history interview, in which he revealed important pieces of information about the LDS archaeological program. Wendy Bacon graciously shared her personal photographs and reminiscences of her experiences excavating for the RLDS in Nauvoo.

Thanks to my good friends Jon and Sarah Moyer, I always had a place to stay and stimulating conversation when visiting Salt Lake City. Scott Thomas, another friend, came through at a critical time and helped locate a key source for the book.

Donna Pykles and Hilda Serr went far beyond normal familial obligations and helped photocopy and take notes on hundreds of pages of periodicals and other sources; their shared enthusiasm for my research made it all that more enjoyable. Richard Veit of Monmouth University and two other anonymous reviewers provided useful feedback on the manuscript, and I believe the book is much better as a result of their insightful comments. Last, Elisabeth Chretien, Joeth Zucco, and Marjorie Pannell have been nothing but superb as editors. They each responded patiently and promptly to a myriad of detailed questions while effectively guiding me through the publication process.

Each of these individuals (and probably many more I have unintentionally left out) has contributed something to this endeavor, resulting in something far greater than what I could have achieved if left to my own. I, of course, accept full responsibility for whatever errors there may be in the final product.

Finally, this project would not have been completed were it not for the enduring love and support of my wife, Chelise, and our four children, Emmalyn, Clayton, Jamison, and Lincoln. In addition to enduring many weeks without a husband and father while I was away on research trips, they have regularly expressed unwavering confidence in me at the times when I needed such encouragement the most. Even in the darkest hour, brought on by a catastrophic failure of my computer's hard drive, Chelise selflessly devoted countless evenings to help edit the entire manuscript for a second time! She and our children are the source of true joy in my life. This book would mean nothing without them.

Series Editors' Introduction

STEPHEN O. MURRAY AND REGNA DARNELL

Benjamin C. Pykles provides a remarkably even-handed case study of the history of historical archaeology in the context of excavating and restoring Nauvoo, Illinois, a sacred site for both major Mormon denominations, the Church of Jesus Christ of Latter-day Saints (LDS) and the Reorganized Church of Jesus Christ of Latter Day Saints (RLDS).

Before its founder, Joseph Smith (who at the time was mayor of Navuoo and president of the Church, and was also running for president of the United States), and his brother Hyrum (who was assistant president of the Church) were murdered in the jail in Carthage, Illinois, on June 27, 1844, and the majority of the Latter-day Saints migrated to Utah under the leadership of Brigham Young, the Mormons were gathered at Nauvoo. Pykles effectively makes the case for the importance of the negotiations around the meaning and interpretation of Nauvoo to the practice of historical archaeology in the mutually antagonistic context of LDS and RLDS interpretations of the Nauvoo site. Within both churches, conflict occurred over the scientific versus religious authenticity of the archaeological work even as historical archaeology was professionalizing, a process that generally includes attempting to ensure that professional decisions are made only by certified professionals. In the case of historical archaeology, professionalization involved moving beyond being an adjunct to historical restorations, such as that of Colonial Williamsburg in Virginia.

A tension between the ideology of professionalism and the ideologies of various stakeholders, notably descendants of those who built whatever is being excavated by archaeologists, often arises, and was certain to arise because of the different sacralized histories propounded by LDS and RLDS Church members eager to undercut each other and to garner historical legitimation among nonbelievers.

As Pykles shows, initial enthusiasm for historical authenticity gradually declined into more rigidly sectarian goals. From an archaeological standpoint, the project remains incomplete. Even among the archaeologists, moreover, there was dissent over pursuing long-term scientific goals or providing immediate aid to reconstruction and restoration endeavors, with the latter almost always prevailing. Pykles not only shows what the archaeologists did, he also explores the cross-pressures of religious politics and jockeying for ownership of historical heritage at one important historical site. Such ownership was not only a concern for disputed sacred histories but a more mundane one of revenues from tourism to the partly restored Nauvoo site.

Alongside the story of professionalizing historical archaeology, Pykles tells a story about the Mormons. Heretofore, little attention has been given to the "archaeology" of the Mormons, that is, to how Mormons (LDS and RLDS) pursue scientific goals and why education—as exemplified by Brigham Young University—was and is so important to them. Archaeological discoveries have long been called on as a "scientific" way to buttress sectarian claims to divine destiny. This necessarily has meant that supporters of archaeological work within the two denominations vary in their commitment to scientific methods and in the way they use history for theological and proselytizing purposes.

Excavating Nauvoo

Introduction

On the afternoon of January 5, 1967, J. C. Harrington, "the father of historical archaeology," and twelve other leading scholars in the field gathered in the North Park Inn Motel near the campus of Southern Methodist University in Dallas, Texas. The men had come to Dallas to participate in the International Conference on Historic Archaeology being held at SMU that weekend. The purpose of this exclusive meeting of the Special Committee the day before, however, was to discuss the creation of a professional scholarly society devoted to historical archaeology (the archaeology of the modern world, AD 1400 to the present). Among other things, the participants discussed the need for and purpose of such a society and debated what it should be called. Their deliberations extended into the early hours of the following morning. When the proposal to create the society was presented to the more than 100 conference attendees later that day, the measure was unanimously approved.

Subsequently, officers were elected and details concerning the society's purpose, meetings, publications, and membership were worked out. By the end of the two-day conference the Special Committee had achieved its purpose, and a milestone in the professional development of the field had been reached. The Society for Historical Archaeology (SHA) was officially organized.[1]

The year before this historic conference at which the SHA was founded, J. C. Harrington had retired from the National Park Service after nearly thirty years of service, during which he pioneered the field of historical archaeology. Indeed, it was precisely because of his experience and status in the field that Harrington was invited to be a member of the Special Committee that organized the SHA, and why he was elected to the society's original board of directors. Although retired, Harrington was by no means inactive. In fact, at the time the SHA was created, he and his wife, Virginia, were deeply involved in the archaeology program of Nauvoo Restoration, Inc. (NRI), a nonprofit corporation sponsored by the Church of Jesus Christ of Latter-day Saints to authentically restore the city of Nauvoo, Illinois, as it was during the Mormon period of the 1840s. For four years (1966–69) they spent their summers in Nauvoo, excavating no fewer than five historic sites, including the massive excavation of the Mormon Temple. It was undoubtedly Harrington's association with the restoration of Nauvoo at this time that resulted in NRI becoming one of the original institutional members of the newly created SHA in 1967.[2] In fact, upon his return from the conference in Dallas he eagerly wrote to his colleagues in NRI telling them about the society he had helped organize and about his election to its board. At the end of a long career excavating historic sites, Harrington clearly understood the historical significance of the event. "You will be interested in the meeting at Dallas," he wrote. "Some 120 professional people (mostly archaeologists) gathered there, primarily for the purpose of organizing a new association dealing with historical archaeology. This shows how the interest and active participation in this field has grown, as ten years ago I doubt if we could have garnered a dozen people."[3]

The connections between the SHA and the restoration of Nauvoo do not stop there. Fifteen years after it was founded, the SHA, boasting a membership of almost 2,000, created a medal to recognize "scholars who have made outstanding contributions to the field." Not surprisingly, the award was named in honor of Harrington, acknowledging his significant and lasting contributions as the "founding father" of historical archaeology. Appropriately, the first J. C. Harrington Medal was awarded to Harrington himself at the 1982 meetings of the SHA. Medals have been awarded to qualified recipients at the annual meeting of the society ever since. Significantly, those who designed the award incorporated elements of Harrington's work into the medal itself. In particular, on the back of the medal are stylized depictions of three archaeological sites that represent "both the discipline as a whole and Harrington's individual career." The site chosen to represent the nineteenth-century settlement of the Midwest and the subsequent opening of the Far West was that of the Nauvoo Temple. In this way, the medal symbolically represents and permanently

1. Front (left) and back (right) of the J. C. Harrington Medal of the Society for Historical Archaeology, showing the archaeologically recovered floor plan of the Nauvoo Temple. Courtesy Robert L. Schuyler.

preserves not only the relationship between Harrington and NRI but also the association between the field of historical archaeology and the restoration of Nauvoo (figure 1).[4]

But what exactly does the restoration of Nauvoo have to do with the discipline of historical archaeology? The archaeological excavations carried out by Harrington and others in connection with the restoration of Nauvoo took place at precisely the same time the field of historical archaeology was emerging as a professional scholarly discipline. Indeed, the formation of the SHA was a sign of the discipline's unfolding professionalization at this time. Accordingly, the Nauvoo excavations reflect many important aspects of this critical period in the development of the field. On a larger scale, because they took place during a pivotal and transitional time in the discipline's development, the excavations in Nauvoo serve as an illuminating case study of the history of historical archaeology at large. Indeed, although historical archaeology was born long before the Nauvoo excavations began, and continues to thrive after they ceased, the historical archaeology of Nauvoo remarkably illustrates the principal contours of the field's development over time. Thus, even though Nauvoo's archaeology programs have long since closed down, the story of the excavations at Nauvoo deserves to be remembered for what it reveals about the history of historical archaeology in general.

A Short History of Historical Archaeology

To appreciate why the historical archaeology of Nauvoo is such an excellent case study of the field's historical development, an understanding of the history of historical archaeology in the United States is required. Although there are numerous isolated examples of excavations at historical sites from the seventeenth, eighteenth, and nineteenth centuries, the proper origins of historical archaeology in the United States are linked to the American historic preservation movement of the late 1800s and early 1900s.[5] A crucial element to both the success of historic preservation and, by extension, historical archaeology was the passage of the 1906 Antiquities Act, which was the first law to establish legal protection and public support for the nation's archaeological and historic sites.[6] Private efforts were also instrumental in this process. In fact, the Rockefeller-sponsored restoration of Colonial Williamsburg, begun in 1927, was especially influential in drawing attention to and generating interest in historic preservation and the restoration of historic sites.

Although these events were influential in setting the stage, the true formal beginnings of historical archaeology in the United States can be traced to the government's response to the Great Depression that gripped the country in the 1930s.

Key developments included the creation of relief programs, such as the Civilian Conservation Corps (CCC), the Tennessee Valley Authority (TVA), and the Works Progress Administration (WPA), which put a number of archaeologists to work supervising the survey and excavation of hundreds of prehistoric and historical archaeological sites. Equally significant was the passage of the 1935 Historic Sites Act, which made it an official national policy to preserve the country's historical sites and authorized the NPS (created in 1916) to acquire, preserve, restore, and interpret these sites for public use. It was under these circumstances that historical archaeology had its formal and institutional beginnings, starting with the pioneering work of J. C. Harrington at the site of the first permanent English settlement in America at Jamestown, Virginia.

The NPS offered Harrington a position at Jamestown in 1936 because the archaeology program, begun two years earlier with CCC workers, was faltering. Harrington was at first reluctant to work on a site "only" 300 years old, but the salary was more than he could turn down. Thus, in the fall of 1936, three months after the federal government designated Jamestown and the surrounding area Colonial National Historic Park, Harrington left his graduate studies at the University of Chicago and assumed control of the government-sponsored excavations. Over the course of the next five years, until the breakout of the Second World War, Harrington developed many of the basic field techniques for excavating historical sites, an effort that, in time, earned him the moniker of "father of historical archaeology."[7]

Harrington's work at Jamestown and his later excavations at Fort Raleigh, North Carolina, and Fort Necessity, Pennsylvania, among other sites, are characteristic of the way historical archaeology was originally conceived and practiced. Most excavations in these early years were sponsored by government or private institutions and were specifically oriented toward history and the interpretation and restoration of sites famous in American or regional history. As such, the investigation of architectural remains, necessary for accurate restoration, was frequently emphasized over the study of artifacts. In fact, artifacts, if incorporated at all, were primarily used to help date particular features and to illustrate the types of objects uncovered at a site. At the same time, the display and interpretation of excavations to the visiting public was frequently a component of this early work.[8] This emphasis on history and historic site restoration and interpretation dominated the field in its early years. Indeed, up until the 1960s, the majority of archaeologists involved in this kind of work used the term coined by Harrington himself to describe their activities: "historic site archaeology."[9]

Things changed in the 1960s, however. This was a decade of professionalization for historical archaeology. During this time the young field outgrew its role as an auxiliary to historic preservation and became a professional discipline of its own. A significant factor in this development was the emergence of historical archaeology in the university classroom. What was probably the first course in the United States to carry the title of Historical Archaeology was taught at the University of Pennsylvania by NPS archaeologist John L. Cotter in the 1960–61 academic year. Over the next few years other courses were introduced at universities across the nation, including the University of Arizona, by Arthur Woodward, Harvard University, by Stephen Williams, the University of Florida, by Charles Fairbanks, Illinois State University, by Edward B. Jelks, the University of California–Santa Barbara, by James Deetz, and the University of Idaho, by Roderick Sprague.[10] From these classes and those that followed there emerged the first generation of professionally trained historical archaeologists in North America.

A second key event in the professionalization of the field was the 1966 National Historic Preservation Act. By requiring all federal agencies to be responsible stewards of the historic properties within their jurisdictions, this mandate created new jobs in government agencies outside the NPS, many of which were filled by the growing number of university-trained historical archaeologists. Equally significant, the law also provided federal funding for work on historic properties, including archaeological excavations. In short, the National Historic Preservation Act stimulated the professional growth of the field by creating both employment and funding opportunities for the expanding corps of professionally trained historical archaeologists emerging from the nation's universities.

The capstone event for this period of professionalization was the organization of the SHA in 1967. Although preceded by the Conference on Historic Site Archaeology (founded in 1960) and the Council for Northeast Historical Archaeology (organized in 1966), the SHA was the scholarly association that ultimately gave the discipline an independent, professional, and viable foundation in the United States. Indeed, the SHA afforded the growing community of historical archaeologists a professional and autonomous society that represented their unique interests.

Since its establishment as a legitimate and independent professional discipline, historical archaeology has continued to thrive in the United States and abroad. The SHA currently has more than 2,000 individual members, and historical archaeology is the most commonly practiced type of archaeology in the United States. Federal legislation since the 1960s has stimulated this growth by requiring archaeological investigation prior to all government-sponsored building projects. The resulting explosion of cultural resource management (CRM) archaeology has significantly increased the ranks of practicing historical archaeologists in the nation, but it has also thrust the discipline into the foreign environment of a marketplace economy, where its scholarly goals are often muddled. Academically, at least, historical archaeology is theoretically grounded in anthropology. However, much of the actual on-the-ground historical archaeology continues to be motivated by historicalist research goals and objectives. This partly reflects the predominance of nonacademic sources of funding. Recent decades have also witnessed the discipline's growth internationally. Especially significant in this regard are the Society for Post-Medieval Archaeology in Europe, established in 1967–68, the Australian Society for Historical Archaeology, founded in 1970, and the Historical Archaeology Research Group at the University of Cape Town, begun in 1987. At the beginning of the twenty-first century, the discipline continues to grow both nationally and internationally and remains secure in its professional standing.[11]

It is significant that the two beginnings of historical archaeology—its formal beginnings in the 1930s and its professional beginnings in the 1960s—both coincided with periods of low national morale among American citizens. Whereas the economic hardships of the Great Depression bred feelings of distrust and resentment toward the federal government in the 1930s, the fearful suspicions of the cold war and the nation's involvement in the Vietnam War led many in the 1960s to question the government's authority. Notably, in both cases government officials turned to the nation's historic sites to help remedy the diminishing sense of national unity. In both instances federal laws relating to historic preservation were passed (the 1935 Historic Sites Act and the 1966 National Historic Preservation Act) as part of efforts to revitalize public faith in the federal government and restore national pride among American citizens. Regardless of whether or not these acts were successful in fostering renewed nationalism, by establishing federal sanction and support for work on historic sites, including archaeological investigations, both pieces of legislation had a significant impact on the development of historical archaeology in the United States.

The restoration of Nauvoo was conceived of and carried out amid these events. As a result, the history of Nauvoo's restoration in many ways parallels the history of historical archaeology in the United States; conversely, the rise of historical archaeology in America is duly reflected in the history of the restoration of Nauvoo. Indeed, the archaeological excavations undertaken for the restoration of Nauvoo took place at precisely the same time that historical archaeology was emerging from its institutional roots in the American historic preservation movement and transitioning into a professional and autonomous scholarly discipline. Consequently, the historical archaeology at Nauvoo serves as a window onto important developments in the history of the field.

This book seeks to illustrate the rise of historical archaeology in America by documenting the history of the restoration of Nauvoo. As the primary concern is the history of historical archaeology, particular emphasis is given to the archaeological excavations undertaken in the historic city. The first chapter outlines the historical background for the restoration of Nauvoo, including the early interest of federal, state, and private institutions in restoring the historic city. Chapter two describes the actual restoration of Nauvoo, tracing the efforts of the different parties involved in the restoration projects. Chapter three discusses the decline of the restoration projects in the city and details the conflicts over interpretation that precipitated this decline. Building on the three previous chapters, chapter four tells the story of the Nauvoo excavations, highlighting their origins, rise, and eventual demise within the context of the different restoration projects. Finally, the fifth and concluding chapter discusses the ways in which the Nauvoo excavations characterize the history of historical archaeology as a whole and summarizes their significance in terms of the discipline's development over time.

Altogether, the history of historical archaeology in Nauvoo is an excellent case study in the history of the discipline at large. Indeed, the rise of historical archaeology in America is plainly illustrated in the Nauvoo excavations. What follows is an account of this history, even, in Michael Coe's phrase, "the archaeology of the Mormons themselves."[12]

Chapter 1

The Origins of the Restoration of Nauvoo

Approximately 150 miles north of St. Louis, the Mississippi River bends around a wide and flat peninsula in Illinois. It was here that early members of the Church of Jesus Christ of Latter-day Saints, or Mormons, founded the city of Nauvoo (map). From 1839 to 1846, Nauvoo was the center of the LDS Church. At its height, approximately 12,000 Latter-day Saints lived in the hundreds of brick, frame, and log homes of the city, a population that rivaled Chicago's as the largest in Illinois at the time. In many respects Nauvoo was like any other thriving, bustling, frontier city of the mid-nineteenth century, complete with blacksmiths, coopers, wheelwrights, tinsmiths, shoe makers, brickyards, gunsmiths, printers, postmasters, and store clerks. However, atop the bluff that overlooks the floodplain on which the city grew up stood an imposing temple. Visible from miles away, the temple served as a constant reminder to both inhabitants and passers-by that Nauvoo differed in an

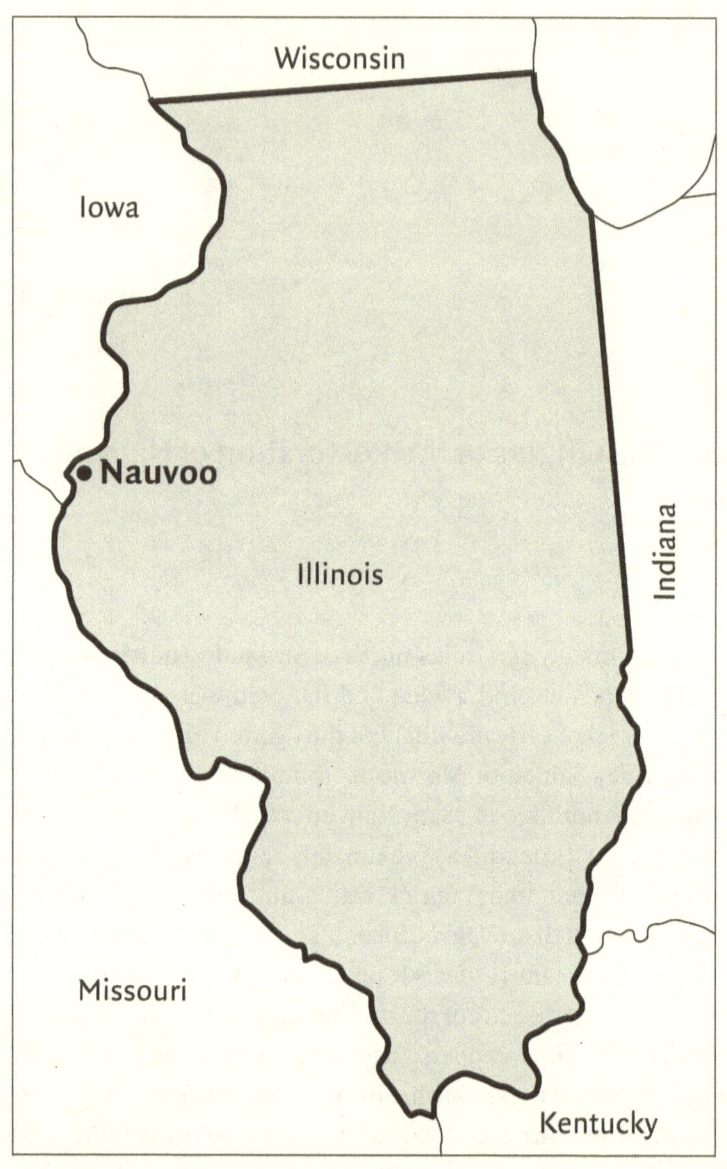

State of Illinois showing the location of Nauvoo.

important way from other frontier settlements at the time. Here was the headquarters of a peculiar and persecuted religious group that had originated some twenty years earlier in the spiritual experiences of Joseph Smith Jr.[1]

Overview of Mormon History

Joseph Smith Jr. was born in rural Vermont on December 23, 1805, to Joseph Smith Sr., a farmer, and Lucy Mack Smith, his wife.[2] One of eight children, Smith was a poorly educated youth when his family moved near the town of Palmyra, upstate New York, in 1816, after having suffered financial hardships in Vermont. With their relocation to New York, the Smiths found themselves in the center of the religious revivalism that characterized the Second Great Awakening of the early nineteenth century. Historians have since described the region at this time as the "burned-over district," a comment on the intense religious fervor that swept the area.[3] This religious excitement troubled the young Smith. He later wrote,

> *During this time of great excitement my mind was called up to serious reflection and great uneasiness . . . so great were the confusion and strife among the different denominations, that it was impossible for a person young as I was, and so unacquainted with men and things, to come to any certain conclusion who was right and who was wrong. . . . In the midst of this war of words and tumult of opinions, I often said to myself: What is to be done? Who of all these parties are right; or, are they all wrong together? If any one of them be right, which is it, and how shall I know it?*[4]

Smith claimed to have received answers to his questions in the spring of 1820 when, while praying in a grove of trees near his home, God the Father and Jesus Christ appeared to him in a vision, instructing him not to join any of the churches then extant. Other heavenly visitors soon followed. In September 1823, an angel identifying himself as Moroni, an ancient American prophet, visited Smith and revealed to him the location of buried records with the religious and secular history of a Precolumbian New World civilization. The records were in the form of gold plates and were buried in a nearby drumlin identified as Cumorah. Although forbidden to retrieve the records until 1827, Smith dutifully visited the Hill Cumorah every ensuing year on the anniversary of Moroni's first appearance, each time receiving further religious instruction from the angel. Persecution and ridicule grew once it was known that Smith claimed to have the records in his possession.

Over the next two years, Smith met and married Emma Hale, moved from New York to Harmony, Pennsylvania, translated the ancient records, published the translation as the Book of Mormon, and moved again to Fayette, New York, because of opposition from his antagonists.[5] All the while Smith continued to claim visitations from heavenly messengers, including John the Baptist and the apostles Peter, James, and John, from whom Smith professed to have received the holy priesthood.

With the Book of Mormon in print and the priesthood in his possession, Smith officially organized what came to be known as the Church of Jesus Christ of Latter-day Saints on April 6, 1830.[6] Early missionary efforts began to produce large numbers of converts soon thereafter. One particularly fruitful locale was the vicinity of Kirtland, Ohio, where more than 120 people joined the Church in less than three weeks. A few months later, Smith and most of his followers migrated to

Kirtland, fleeing mounting persecutions in New York.[7] Shortly afterward, Smith, claiming divine mandate, sent a substantial group of Latter-day Saints to Independence, Jackson County, Missouri, then the far western frontier, to lay the foundations of Zion—the New Jerusalem—the future millennial seat of Christ at the Second Coming. Although seeking religious liberty, this large group of Latter-day Saints, galvanized by millenarian doctrines, posed a political, economical, and religious threat to the residents of Missouri. Consequently, in late 1833 the Missouri state militia forcefully expelled the Latter-day Saints from Jackson County, driving them northward, where they found temporary refuge. Here Church members founded a settlement called Far West in the summer of 1836.

Meanwhile, Smith and the other Latter-day Saints remained in Kirtland, Ohio, where they created an industrious community and constructed their first temple. By early 1838, however, internal and external opposition in Ohio had forced Smith to flee to the Mormon settlement at Far West, Missouri. The remainder of the Latter-day Saints soon followed, only to find the situation in Missouri rapidly deteriorating. As the number of Mormon emigrants swelled, the neighboring populations became increasingly hostile. By late October 1838 the stage was set for the "Missouri War." After a small battle erupted between the Saints and the state militia on the Crooked River, Governor Lilburn W. Boggs of Missouri issued an executive order in which he enjoined, "The Mormons must be treated as enemies and must be exterminated or driven from the state, if necessary for the public good."[8] Three days later a large group of men attacked a small Mormon settlement at Haun's Mill, killing at least seventeen people. Shortly thereafter, Smith and other Church leaders were arrested and incarcerated, while the rest of the Church prepared to leave Missouri. This was the fifth time in less than a decade that most of the Latter-day Saints had left their homes in search of refuge.[9]

Smith and his associates remained in jail over the subsequent winter as more than 8,000 of their followers gathered in western Illinois, where they had found sympathizers. After being allowed to escape in April 1839, Smith quickly reunited with the body of the Church and located a new gathering place on the swampy banks of the Mississippi River, where the Latter-day Saints built the thriving city that Smith named Nauvoo, allegedly a word of Hebrew origin meaning "beautiful place."

The Latter-day Saints remained in Nauvoo for six years. Missionary work abroad swelled the city's population as converts congregated at the new gathering place. As before, their large numbers and untraditional religious, economic, and political practices generated hostile feelings among those living in surrounding areas. These hostilities culminated in the murder of Joseph Smith and his brother, Hyrum, on June 27, 1844, while the two were incarcerated in the nearby town of Carthage. Although their enemies believed the loss of Smith would prove the end of the Church, the majority of Latter-day Saints rallied behind Smith's apostles, chief of whom was Brigham Young. In the following months, under the threat of continued violence, Young directed the completion of the Nauvoo Temple and made preparations to evacuate the city. The massive westward migration began in February 1846, when the Mississippi River was still frozen. By summer, Nauvoo was virtually empty. The majority of its former inhabitants followed Brigham Young to the Salt Lake Valley, where they would build yet another city and temple several years and hundreds of miles later.[10] Significantly, another group, choosing not to follow Brigham Young, remained in Illinois and surrounding areas and formed the nucleus of what later became the Reorganized Church of Jesus Christ of Latter Day Saints (RLDS).[11]

Early Interest in Mormon Historic Sites

Over the past 175 years, various elements of the Mormon past have been commemorated, memorialized, and otherwise ritualized by both the LDS and RLDS Churches through numerous mechanisms of remembering.[12] Central to this process of remembering are various historic sites—the places where significant events of the Mormon past occurred. Although the LDS and RLDS Churches did not begin to acquire and develop these sites until after the dawn of the twentieth century, they were the destination of LDS pilgrimages throughout the nineteenth century. Indeed, even before the LDS Church migrated to the Salt Lake Valley, both missionaries and converts visited sites like Palmyra and the Hill Cumorah to witness the places where they believed Joseph Smith had experienced his remarkable visions.[13] Later on, others came to these and additional important sites on official assignment to collect historical information about the Church's past. Yet none of these nineteenth-century pilgrims expressed interest in acquiring or preserving these places for interpretive purposes. Their visits were primarily motivated by nostalgia or a specific desire for historical information.[14]

In reality, these early pilgrims were the forerunners of a period of heightened interest in the Mormon past that peaked in the years leading up to and immediately following the turn of the twentieth century. This was a time of accommodation and reconciliation for the LDS Church.[15] Threatened with federal legislation that would have effectively disenfranchised its organization, the LDS Church abandoned its long-established practice of polygamy, and in return, Utah was finally granted statehood.[16] Accordingly, the LDS Church purposefully began to reshape its history as less controversial and more unifying aspects of the Mormon past were emphasized over polygamy and other divisive practices and doctrines.[17] At the same time, increasing numbers of Mormon pioneers (many of whom were former residents of Nauvoo) were taking their memories and experiences of the Church's past to the grave. As a result, "[LDS] Church leaders wanted the rising generation to gain an improved collective memory and personal appreciation for Latter-day Saint heritage."[18] Indicative of this desire was the work of the LDS Church Historian's Office, which published numerous historical works during this time.[19] Yet Church publications were only one part of a multifaceted effort to emphasize the Church's history throughout this period. The historic sites associated with key events of the Mormon past came to play an important role in this campaign as they could "provide continuity at a time of great change in the [LDS] Church, and . . . help give the Church the prestige of an established institution with a respectable history and tradition."[20]

Interest in Mormon historic sites coincided with a period of increased concern for the preservation and protection of the nation's historical objects and properties. These sentiments bore fruit in the Antiquities Act of 1906, which gave the president of the United States authority to designate public lands as national monuments. At precisely the same time, LDS

Church officials slowly began acquiring places of historic significance to the Church. Unsurprisingly, the first site acquired was the old Carthage jail, purchased in 1903, where Joseph Smith Jr. and his brother Hyrum had been shot and killed in June 1844. The president of the LDS Church at this time, and the man who secured the purchase of the jail, was Smith's nephew, Joseph F. Smith (son of Hyrum), who undoubtedly had personal reasons for acquiring the site, in addition to more general commemorative motivations spurred by the approaching centennial anniversary of his uncle's birth (1905). The LDS Church purchased additional Smith-related properties over the next several years including Smith's birthplace in Vermont, in 1905, his boyhood home and the Smith family farm near Palmyra, New York, in 1907, the Peter Whitmer farm in Fayette, New York, in 1926, and the Hill Cumorah property in upstate New York, in 1928.

Attention on the LDS Church's past and its historic sites was further focused through centennial anniversary celebrations that took place during key years in the first half of the twentieth century.[21] The first of these was in 1905, with the hundredth anniversary of Joseph Smith's birth, at which time a large granite obelisk was erected at his birthplace in Vermont.[22] Others came in 1923, the hundredth anniversary of the angel Moroni's visit to Joseph Smith; in 1930, the centennial anniversary of the organization of the Church; and in 1944, the hundredth anniversary of Joseph Smith's death.[23] The historic sites at which these key events took place were frequently the setting for these commemorative celebrations. Of particular importance was the 1947 centennial anniversary of the Latter-day Saints' arrival in the Salt Lake Valley, which was celebrated by a commemorative motorcade that drove the length of the historic Mormon Trail, beginning in Nauvoo. Replicating the exact number of the original vanguard company of Mormon pioneers who entered the Salt Lake Valley in July 1847, the 148 reenactors in 1947 traveled in vehicles decorated to resemble covered wagons, complete with white canvas tops and cardboard oxen fastened to the front fenders.

As a result of these and other activities, the number of Mormons visiting the LDS Church's historic sites dramatically increased during this time. Accordingly, the development and interpretation of these sites became more sophisticated as the LDS Church constructed visitors' centers at key sites, in addition to erecting monuments and markers at others.[24] Overall, throughout the first half of the twentieth century, the LDS Church looked to its historic sites as a way to promote its history and doctrine and, at the same time, solidify the religious identity of its members.

Preliminary Interest in Restoring Nauvoo

Given its prominent place in the Mormon past as the city built from the swamps of the Mississippi, the last mortal abode of Joseph Smith, and the launching point for the great westward migration to the Salt Lake Valley, Nauvoo never retreated from Mormon historical consciousness. Like other of the LDS Church's sites, the historic city was a popular destination for Mormon pilgrims at the turn of the twentieth century. Despite its historical significance, however, Nauvoo lay in a state of ruin as the twentieth century dawned. "The whole place has a half-deserted, half-dilapidated appearance," wrote LDS official B. H. Roberts of his 1885 visit to Nauvoo; the site "seems to be withering under a blight, from which it cannot recover," he concluded.[25] Unbeknownst to most observers at the time, however, things were to drastically change in Nauvoo over the next several years. By the end of the twentieth century the deteriorating Nauvoo that Roberts and others had observed a century earlier had been transformed into one of Mormonism's most popular historic sites.

Strangely enough, the story of Nauvoo's restoration does not begin in Nauvoo. Rather, its origin lies in the historic preservation efforts of the LDS and RLDS Churches around the turn of the twentieth century. In particular, it is in a conflict over Joseph Smith's birthplace site in Vermont where the restoration of Nauvoo has its beginnings.

The hierarchy of the RLDS Church had good reason to be concerned when the LDS Church purchased Joseph Smith's birthplace site in 1905. Although both churches looked to Joseph Smith as the founder of their religion, the two diverged sharply when it came to later teachings and practices of the prophet. Primarily at issue was the doctrine and practice of plural marriage, along with related doctrines underlying the performance of special temple ordinances, all of which publicly emerged while the early Latter-day Saints resided in Nauvoo. Whereas the LDS affirmed that these teachings and practices originated with Joseph Smith through direct revelation from God, the RLDS adamantly denied Smith's involvement, placing the burden of their origin instead on a corrupt and beguiling Brigham Young. Although a source of contention between the two churches since the years following Smith's death, the dispute was magnified with the activities of the LDS Church at the prophet's birthplace in 1905.

Fifteen years prior to its purchase of Joseph Smith's birthplace, the LDS Church was forced, under threat of disfranchisement by the federal government, to renounce the practice of plural marriage. Although the LDS Church's manifesto on plural marriage, issued in 1890, was a major catalyst in the Americanization of the Church at the turn of the century, practicing Latter-day Saints did not easily surrender their belief in "the principle." In fact, while the granite monument marking Joseph Smith's birthplace was being assembled in Vermont, LDS apostle Reed Smoot, recently elected to represent Utah in the U.S. Senate, was under investigation in the nation's capital, as there were still serious suspicions about the LDS Church's continued practice of plural marriage. Over time, the Smoot hearings expanded beyond an inquiry into the life of the senator (who was not a polygamist) into an investigation of the LDS Church itself, during which the president of the Church, Joseph F. Smith (Joseph Smith's nephew), was called on to testify. The scrutiny to which the LDS Church was subjected at this time resulted in a second manifesto declaring again the end of LDS plural marriage.[26]

The enduring suspicion that the Utah church was continuing to practice plural marriage only exacerbated the conflict surrounding the LDS's acquisition and development of Joseph Smith's birthplace in Vermont. Like the jailhouse in Carthage, Illinois, where Joseph Smith was murdered, the site of his birth was perceived as a significant place to commemorate the prophet's life and legacy. Aware that the Utah church had purchased the Carthage jail two years earlier, RLDS members were deeply troubled that the birthplace site would now also be subject to LDS interpretation. In a public attempt to halt its construction, Frederick M. Smith, son of RLDS president Joseph Smith III and counselor in the Church's First Presidency, called the birthplace monument "unfair" and a "great discredit to the memory" of his grandfather.[27] Despite the RLDS protest, however, the LDS finished the monument and dedicated it "to the memory . . . of Joseph Smith, the great Prophet and Seer of the nineteenth century."[28]

The tension over the birthplace monument centered on a single question, one that would continue to shape RLDS-LDS interactions at historic sites for years to come: Whose interpretation of Joseph Smith would prevail? Would the world remember Joseph Smith as the progenitor of the LDS Church, complete with its heritage of plural marriage and temple ordinances, or would the prophet be remembered as the monogamous visionary whose legacy was inherited by the RLDS Church? As the identity of both churches rested on their individual interpretations of the prophet's history, the answer to this question was perceived as a matter of institutional life or death.

Early RLDS Restoration Efforts

As the conflict surrounding the birthplace monument reached its height in late 1905, the friction over interpretive control spread to Nauvoo, prompting the RLDS to take action. Earlier that summer, a large group of Latter-day Saints had gathered in Nauvoo for a special two-day missionary conference. Among the group was eighty-six-year-old Lorin Farr, who had his photograph taken in front of the deteriorating remains of the brick home he had built and subsequently left behind some sixty years earlier. Of this occasion, Farr stated, "All of the people I talked with were anxious to have our people come back. . . . I told them most of the people that were men and women when we left 60 years ago were not living, but I thought some time in the near future many of the Latter-day Saints would come and assist in the building of a beautiful city, as I consider that Nauvoo is one of the prettiest sites or locations for a city on the Mississippi river."[29]

Although Farr was not likely imagining a historical restoration of the city when he made this statement, his words reflect a sentiment that incited rumors about the LDS Church's plans in Nauvoo. Heman C. Smith, RLDS Church historian and apostle, visited Nauvoo shortly after the 1905 LDS conference and became aware of the Utah church's alleged efforts to acquire property in the city. Writing to RLDS Presiding Bishop E. L. Kelley, Smith reported on the rumors circulating in Nauvoo at the time. "The Brighamites [LDS]," he wrote, "have recently been here over fifty strong and held a conference. We are following them with a series of meetings in City Hall. They have made quite an impression on those who want to sell property by giving out the impression that they are coming back to build up the place within two years."[30]

In reality, it would be nearly sixty years before the LDS would return to reconstruct a city on the bend in the Mississippi. Nonetheless, the RLDS were rightfully suspicious that Nauvoo would be the next object of the growing LDS historic site campaign that had already secured possession of the prophet's place of birth and death. In his letter, Smith expressed specific concern over the Nauvoo House, a large brick structure across the street from Joseph Smith's homestead. A rumor the LDS Church had already acquired the structure was discovered to be false, but Smith still advised the RLDS bishop to take preemptive action in Nauvoo. "If they [LDS] have not secured the [mortgage] note," he wrote, "perhaps we better look after that."[31]

Fearful of losing additional opportunities to put forward their interpretations of the prophet and his legacy, the RLDS leadership began acquiring the Nauvoo properties historically associated with Joseph Smith. Between 1909 and 1917 they purchased the Nauvoo House, the Smith Homestead, and Joseph Smith's Mansion House. Facilitating these purchases was the fact that these properties had remained in the possession of relatives of the Smith family, who had close ties with the RLDS Church. By 1918, early preservation work had prepared the three properties for exhibition to the public, and guided tours of the structures began in May of that year. Additional improvements were made in 1939–40, when the structures' interiors were decorated with period furnishings (many of which were donated by RLDS Church members) and the grounds on which the buildings sat were landscaped.[32] Enthusiastic over the potential of the site, Bishop C. A. Skinner wrote to RLDS Church officials in 1941, expressing an early desire to develop a comprehensive interpretive program for Nauvoo. "Every time I visit Nauvoo," he reported, "it gives me a broader vision of the possibilities there. No doubt, it will pay to work out a long time program for that place."[33]

Early LDS Restoration Efforts

The LDS Church, on the other hand, did not begin to acquire property in Nauvoo until 1937, when a portion of the lot on which the Nauvoo Temple originally stood was purchased.

This relatively late start in Nauvoo was undoubtedly due in part to the fact that the RLDS Church had already secured title to the significant Joseph Smith properties more than two decades earlier. In reality it was the work of a few interested and enthusiastic individuals that encouraged the LDS Church to become involved in the city's preservation and restoration at this time.

Foremost among these was Lane K. Newberry (1896–1961), a young artist from Chicago and descendant of Nauvoo pioneers, who had visited Nauvoo periodically since the early 1930s to paint the scenes of the deteriorating yet picturesque city. During this time, Newberry became convinced that "the World should honor men and women who accomplished what the Mormons accomplished in Nauvoo," as "There was a spirit back of the building this city that the World needs today, and it can only be attained by honoring those who had it yesterday."[34] As an individual struggling to survive the crisis of 1930s America, Newberry personally believed in Nauvoo's potential to uplift and heal the broken morale of those suffering through the Great Depression. As an artist, he desired to see Nauvoo restored, especially the Temple, as it "would give the State of Illinois one of the finest examples of primitive art in America."[35] Finally, the year 1939 marked the hundredth anniversary of Nauvoo's founding and the commemorative date was fast approaching, providing Newberry with additional motivation and rationale to support his vision of a restored Nauvoo.

Thus, in April 1938 he traveled to Salt Lake City, where he met with LDS Church president Heber J. Grant and his counselor, the former ambassador to Mexico, J. Rueben Clark Jr., to whom he presented his expansive ideas for the city. Newberry believed that ownership of the entire Nauvoo Temple lot should be transferred to the LDS Church so the Church, in turn, could reconstruct the Temple on the property. In addition, he proposed that the old Mormon structures, of which he was enamored, be restored and that the entire area be dedicated as a state park. The Church leaders responded positively to Newberry's presentation, expressing appreciation for his vision and enthusiasm while pledging their support for his restoration project. "It will indeed please us to cooperate with you in the project and help work it out," they wrote, adding, "We shall be glad to erect in the future such memorial on the Temple Block, if secured by the State of Illinois, as will fittingly carry out your project."[36]

Having successfully garnered the cooperation of the LDS Church, Newberry set out to promote his vision of a restored Nauvoo to various prominent citizens of Illinois. These efforts culminated on May 21, 1938, when Newberry escorted a group of individuals on a pilgrimage from Chicago to Nauvoo with the intent of gaining additional support for his project. Included on this tour was the chairman of the Illinois State Planning Commission, the secretary of the Illinois Historical Society, various railroad officials, and the travel editors from a number of the state's major newspapers. The trip was a huge success, providing the guests with a favorable impression of the project's potential. As a result, Newberry's vision of a restored Nauvoo began to circulate among the public and between top Illinois state officials, who likewise professed their support.

Another key figure who enthusiastically supported Newberry's vision was Bryant S. Hinckley (1867–1961), then president of the LDS Church's Northern States Mission, based in Chicago

2. Bryant S. Hinckley (center) standing on the Nauvoo Temple lot with Lane K. Newberry (left) and Thomas Judd (right). Courtesy of the Church History Library, the Church of Jesus Christ of Latter-day Saints.

(figure 2). Having heard of Newberry's ideas for a reconstruction of the Temple and a restoration of the city, Hinckley eagerly did what he could to further promote the project. Writing for the Church's periodical, *The Improvement Era*, Hinckley endorsed the commemorative restoration of Nauvoo in terms that resonated with the depressed times in which he was writing. "The completion of this extraordinary project," he wrote, "will be a matter of far-reaching significance. It will bring into relief one of the most heroic, dramatic, and fascinating pioneer achievements ever enacted upon American soil. It will reveal a record of fortitude and self-reliance; of patriotic and courageous endeavor, that should stimulate faith in the hearts of all men, in a day when the strongest hesitate and falter."[37]

Hinckley's enthusiasm for the restoration project took him to Nauvoo and the surrounding area more than fifteen times during his three-year tenure as mission president. The climax of his efforts, however, came at the end of his presidency, when he helped organize a major pilgrimage to Nauvoo on June 24–25, 1939, in commemoration of the centennial anniversary of the city's founding. More than 700 members of the LDS Church made the trip and collectively took part in the celebrations, which included a special Sunday service held on the Temple lot, at which both Hinckley and Newberry made speeches and promoted the proposed restoration of the Temple and all of Nauvoo.

Early Government Restoration Efforts

The federal government was also aware of historic Nauvoo and interested in its development at this time. Although it is not clear how much influence the efforts of Newberry and others had on the government's interest in the restoration potential of the site, whatever motivation the private sector provided was paired with that supplied by the Historic Sites Act of 1935, which authorized the secretary of the interior, through the National Park Service, to "Make a survey of historic and archaeologic sites, buildings, and objects for the purpose of determining which possess exceptional value as commemorating or illustrating the history of the United States."[38] In compliance with this mandate, regional historians of the NPS set out in search of the nation's most significant historic sites. Nauvoo was quickly identified as a site of national, state, and religious historic significance.

A 1940 report issued by the NPS's History Branch described Nauvoo's significance by asserting "it was the domain of a group of people destined to play an important part (as an organized group) in the opening up and development of the Far

West."[39] The report also maintained that Nauvoo was important because it was representative of numerous other communities in the upper Mississippi River Valley during the middle of the nineteenth century. Adding to Nauvoo's appeal and significance, the report argued, was the fact that much of the old city had remained virtually unchanged, leaving several of the original Mormon structures still standing at this time. Further, Nauvoo's location on the banks of the Mississippi River presented favorable scenic and recreational possibilities. Having established the site's potential, the report recommended that the State of Illinois acquire all the land formerly part of old Nauvoo and restore the city as a cultural memorial. The report also recommended that the state secure ownership of a suitable area for recreational purposes. Places for picnicking and camping would be necessary, as would areas for more active types of recreation, but the report suggested these not adjoin the restoration area. "A midwestern city as it was in 1840 could be reborn at Nauvoo effectively," declared the report, adding that "Virginia's 'Williamsburg' . . . seems no more representative of a formative period in the development of the State of Virginia than is old Nauvoo of early Illinois."[40]

The comparison to Colonial Williamsburg seemed appropriate, as the situation in Nauvoo in 1940 was in many ways similar to the conditions of Williamsburg in the 1920s, before the massive Rockefeller-sponsored restoration program got under way.[41] Both places were recognized as having national historical significance, and many of the original structures of both towns were still standing. Moreover, the obvious popularity of Colonial Williamsburg as a recreational tourist attraction served as prime justification for proposing a similar restoration project in Nauvoo. Citing Williamsburg's success, the NPS report argued that a restoration of Nauvoo would likewise be received with popular appeal and be an effective means of teaching others about the past:

Obviously the most interesting recreational activity possible at Nauvoo will be highly cultural, consisting of perception and contemplation, with the aid not of models but of original structures and authentic reproductions of buildings, gardens, industries, and commercial, social and religious establishments such as were used by the early settlers of the upper Mississippi valley—our great, great grandfathers or their contemporaries. An understanding of the physical aspects of that period of our national history in the Upper Mississippi valley can be better taught and more thoroughly comprehended in that way than in any other. The throngs which every year visit Williamsburg, Virginia demonstrate the tremendous popular appeal of that very elaborate restoration and . . . show beyond a doubt the public reaction to be expected.[42]

The NPS report also emphasized the importance of creating a master plan before commencing any construction work toward the proposed restoration. Such a plan would be created and approved by competent administrators, who would also supervise the restoration work. The report likewise stressed the need to have "the best talent (in many fields of study and technical knowledge) that the State and other interested agencies can supply."[43] These and other professionals would help ensure the restoration work be "first carefully studied and later carefully executed in an authentic manner," as "only *authentic* restoration is justifiable."[44] Although there are different definitions and uses of the word "authentic," it appears that the author of the NPS report was using the term to signify a restoration that was credible, convincing, and believable to the general public.[45] Qualified professionals with specialized knowledge and expertise in restoration work stood at the center of this quest for authenticity. However, at the time the report was issued, in 1940, few such specialists existed in the United States. The majority had received their training by working on the Colonial Williamsburg restoration, which literally set a standard for "authentic" restoration that would be followed by other restoration projects for years to come.[46] Finally, the report surmised that the proposed restoration of Nauvoo could be financially supported by an endowment, taxes, revenue, or some combination of the three.

Conflicting Interpretive Interests

These early interests in the restoration of Nauvoo shared a similar enthusiasm for the city's potential to memorialize the past. Where they differed, however, was in which past was to be memorialized. For the RLDS Church at this time, Nauvoo was the place where the Church could memorialize the prophet Joseph Smith. Not having access to other historic sites associated with Smith, RLDS members took advantage of the Nauvoo properties in their possession to interpret the prophet's history in a way consistent with their beliefs. The LDS Church, on the other hand, stirred by the enthusiasm of a few visionary individuals, believed a restored Nauvoo would stand as a great monument to the idealized Mormon pioneers, who, through great sacrifice and faith, built the impressive city in just six years. As such, it would "forever challenge the sympathy and admiration of the thoughtful of mankind; and . . . quicken the pride, stimulate the faith, and strengthen the resolution of Latter-day Saints."[47] Finally, the U.S. government, represented by the NPS, conceived of Nauvoo's potential in terms of memorializing a romanticized period of national history "when culture was struggling to gain a foothold, where the enterprising 'early settlers' were trying to bring order and civilization to a virgin country."[48] Nauvoo, in the eyes of the government, was representative of a typical antebellum community in the upper Mississippi River Valley, and to restore it would be a way to memorialize the perceived ideals and values of that time and place. Government officials also saw in Nauvoo a way to meet the recreational needs of their constituents. Finally, somewhere in between were individuals like Lane K. Newberry, who envisioned a restored Nauvoo as a shrine to both the cultural and aesthetic ideals of a bygone era.

Despite these differences, however, each group saw Nauvoo as a powerful, physical symbol of particular values and ideals that had the potential to bolster group identity at a time when this was badly needed. The sufferings and spoils of the Great Depression had seriously challenged the public's trust in the American government and its belief in the American Dream. Additionally, the heavy influx of immigrants leading up to this period contributed to expanding divisions and instability within American society. National identity, like the economy, needed a "new deal." Faced with the sagging national morale and the disintegrating sense of national unity, government officials were quick to capitalize on the country's historic sites as resources to restore and unify public faith in the values and ideals that underpinned America's self-imposed greatness. Nauvoo fit the bill perfectly. Here was a place that seemed to symbolize the very ideals—hard work, individualism, and progress—that typified America's past and future success. Visitors to a restored Nauvoo, it was imagined, would come away not only with a greater respect and appreciation for the nineteenth-century Americans, who through hard work, freedom, and sacrifice were able to erect a city from the swamps, but with an increased hope and belief that they too, as Americans, could succeed, given the same formula of ideals, regardless of present trials. In this way, a restored Nauvoo had the potential to teach cherished American principles, instill a love of country, and provide hope for the future, all at a time when national identity was suffering a period of crisis. Correspondingly, at a time when everything took on a shade of gloom and despair, beautiful Nauvoo, situated as it was on the banks of the majestic Mississippi, was seen as a potential escape, no matter how temporary, from the dreary strictures of the Great Depression. Thus, government officials believed that both the cultural and the recreational needs of the American people would be met by a trip to the restored city.

The LDS Church likewise saw Nauvoo as a powerful physical symbol of certain values and ideals that could aid in solidifying LDS identity at a time when this identity was rapidly changing. Throughout the first decades of the twentieth century, the LDS Church altered its self-presentation to the American public. Legislatively forced to abandon or otherwise deemphasize some of its unique and most cherished religious practices and teachings (including polygamy and theocracy), the LDS Church was coerced to take on a more distinctively American appearance at this time.[49] This compulsory shift in identity was a difficult process that took at least a generation to complete. Yet, similar to the way government officials approached the crisis facing the American people at the close of the 1930s, Mormons turned to their historic sites for help in solidifying their transition of identity. Although not the first site to be developed by the LDS Church, Nauvoo was unique in that, in addition to its capacity to memorialize important religious persons and values, it also represented certain ideals that appealed to an America that was emerging from the Great Depression. Whereas the scope of other contemporary Mormon historical sites was restricted to the commemoration of Joseph Smith Jr. and significant spiritual events of the Mormon past, Nauvoo presented an opportunity to go beyond this and memorialize what was truly American about the LDS Church. Of course, the commemorative perspective was not fully lost on Nauvoo, as members of the LDS Church pictured it first and foremost as a shrine to the Mormon pioneers. But coupled with the strictly religious significance of the site were values and ideals that could appeal to all Americans, especially in a time of depression and despair. LDS Church leaders did not lose this opportunity to hold up the Mormon pioneers as inspirational examples of what Americans had achieved in the face of hardship. Writing of the Mormon pioneers of Nauvoo, Bryant S. Hinckley declared, "No depression could defeat, no adversity conquer a people animated with the hope and sustained with the faith that warmed their hearts." "Relying upon their Creator," he continued, "and their own resourcefulness they fought every foe, conquered every enemy, and won a place among the good and great of all time."[50]

Even if the Mormon pioneers who left Nauvoo in the 1840s intended to remove themselves from the United States of America and the reaches of its government, the interpretation a century later was that they represented the hard-working, diligent class of Americans who, through great sacrifice and faith in God, achieved great things while overcoming great obstacles, and opened the western regions of the country to civilization. This shift in interpretation was captured nicely by Hinckley when he wrote, "As time lifts the clouds of prejudice that enveloped this great drama, it reveals a piece of work so fine in character and of such significance and magnitude as to reflect great credit upon the people who did it and upon the state where it took place."[51] A restored Nauvoo, therefore, would stand as a symbol of something all Americans could appreciate and emulate, while portraying the LDS Church as a significant, if not exemplary, group of Americans who played a key role in the nation's history. By thus interpreting the importance of Nauvoo, the LDS Church solidified its American identity in the eyes of the recovering nation, and at the same time promoted this explicitly American self-presentation to Church members.

The "Americanization" of the LDS Church at the turn of the century created an unusual dilemma for RLDS identity as well. Until this time, the RLDS Church easily distinguished itself from its Utah counterpart by rejecting key theological principles upheld by the LDS Church, including the practice of polygamy and the observance of temple ordinances (such as baptisms for the dead, sealings, endowments, and the like). Some members of the Church did not accept these practices and the doctrines underlying them when Joseph Smith introduced them in Nauvoo during the final years of his life. This was a primary reason why many did not follow Brigham Young, who clearly intended to continue these practices, into the intermountain West. These individuals remained behind in Nauvoo and outlying areas and later formed the nucleus of the RLDS Church. By the early twentieth century, however, the LDS practice of plural marriage had virtually ceased, and the LDS Church had begun to reshape its history by calling attention to less controversial aspects of the Church's past. This reevaluation of LDS Church history, which in particular deemphasized the practice of polygamy, left the RLDS Church with less ecclesiastical differentiation on which to base its identity. Furthermore, the enthusiasm in the late 1930s over the proposed reconstruction of the Nauvoo Temple, generated by individuals like Lane K. Newberry and Bryant S. Hinckley, must have been of great concern to RLDS members, who unequivocally denied the validity of LDS temple theology. Consequently, the RLDS, like the others, looked to its historic sites for ways in which to solidify its religious identity. Nauvoo was central to this effort, as it was where the RLDS possessed the most significant base from which to tell its story. Even though the LDS Church owned the historic sites in New York where Joseph Smith's earlier spiritual experiences took place, giving it complete control over the interpretation of the events fundamental to the religious tradition shared by both churches, the RLDS owned all of the significant Joseph Smith properties in Nauvoo, which it used to its advantage in telling its version of the prophet's story. Unsurprisingly, the RLDS interpretation included a refutation that Joseph Smith ever practiced polygamy or instituted temple ordinances, together with the charge that it was really Brigham Young who instituted the practices after he and his followers had settled in Utah.[52] "These doctrines," proclaims a 1938 RLDS publication entitled *The Early History of*

Nauvoo, "were never tenets of the original church during the lifetime of Joseph Smith but were a departure from the early faith and doctrine."[53] Nauvoo was the ideal place in which to make such claims, as it was where polygamy and the temple rites were first widely practiced. Thus, by continuing to emphasize the fundamental doctrinal differences with its religious counterpart, the RLDS tried to offset the Americanizing shift in LDS identity and keep the LDS skeletons out of the closet and in full view of the visiting public. In this way, the RLDS sought to maintain its identity, which was cast in terms of what the members did not believe during this time of change.

The Disruption of the Second World War

Whatever plans there were for the restoration of Nauvoo came to a halt with America's entry into the Second World War in December 1941. Both churches and the NPS diverted their energies and efforts elsewhere. For example, in a March 1942 letter to Secretary of the Interior Harold Ickes, President Franklin D. Roosevelt stated his opinion about the survey of historic sites undertaken by the NPS in compliance with the Historic Sites Act of 1935. He wrote, "While I favor the preservation for public use of historic sites, buildings, and objects of national significance, and while a designation as an historic site frequently requires no Federal expenditure, it seems inappropriate, when the Nation is at war, to utilize the time of Government employees in conducting investigations looking to the designation of such sites. I believe that such employees could be assigned duties more closely related to the war effort."[54]

The response to America's entry into the war was similar among those leading the restoration campaign in both the

LDS and RLDS Churches. Although the vision of a restored Nauvoo remained a reality in the hearts and minds of the early proponents, essentially all preservation work and restoration plans ceased until the war was over. There was the rare pilgrimage during this time, as was the case on June 27, 1944, when a number of Latter-day Saints gathered in Nauvoo for a centennial memorial service in honor of Joseph and Hyrum Smith's deaths.[55] But except for these special occasions, visitors to Nauvoo sharply decreased during the war as peoples' attention was diverted elsewhere.

Postwar Resurgence of Restoration Activities

Just prior to America's entry into the Second World War, an author writing for the federal government's Works Progress Administration speculated about Nauvoo's future. He observed, "there is a move on foot to convert the entire Flat into a State Park, so that it may be preserved for the future, much as New Salem of Lincoln's day has been preserved. Whether or not the plans are consummated," he continued, "Nauvoo is in little danger of extinction. Its importance to both branches of the church, and its citizens' knowledge of their heritage, assure the zealous guarding of Nauvoo's landmarks."[56]

It is doubtful this author knew that in less than three years America would be at war, and that plans for the restoration of Nauvoo would be shelved until peace was restored. Nonetheless, he astutely observed that Nauvoo's preservation was virtually assured, regardless of the final outcome of the state's plans, because of the city's vital importance to both the LDS and RLDS Churches. In this the author manifested remarkable foresight, as restoration plans resumed following the war, with the churches leading the way.

War spending had revived the American economy and ushered in a period of unprecedented prosperity in the 1950s. One result of this favorable situation was a postwar surge in tourism. With money in their pockets and shorter working hours, more and more Americans packed up their new automobiles and traveled along the new interstate highways to get to their various vacation destinations. Increasingly, the country's national parks and historic sites were among the favorite stops.

Representative of this national trend, visitors to Nauvoo greatly increased after the war. People came for various reasons, but most arrived with a desire to commemorate and memorialize their past. Some were motivated by genealogy, to honor and remember a revered pioneer ancestor. Others came to celebrate the Mormon past at large, stopping in Nauvoo as part of an expansive tour of the LDS Church's historic sites. Each summer, busloads of LDS Church members arrived in Nauvoo on their way to the Church-sponsored pageant staged annually at the Hill Cumorah, in upstate New York. Others, especially young LDS missionaries returning from their assignments in the East, stopped at Nauvoo while journeying home to Utah. Meanwhile, students from Church-sponsored schools arranged field trips to Nauvoo, and both churches hosted reunions, special conferences, and other commemorative festivals in the city throughout this time.[57]

A visitor to Nauvoo in 1950, however, saw a place that was very different from what tourists experience today. At that time, the only "restored" sites open to the public were the Joseph

Smith properties owned and operated by the RLDS Church. The LDS Church, on the other hand, only had portions of the Temple lot in their possession, but no formal system of interpretation at the site. Finally, the State of Illinois had done little following the war to satisfy the recommendations for restoring Nauvoo put forward in the 1940 NPS report. Nevertheless, as the 1950s dawned it was evident that all three parties maintained their individual interests in a restored Nauvoo. By the time the decade drew to a close, however, it was clear that one of the three was poised to play the major role in the years ahead.

With the Joseph Smith properties already in its possession, the RLDS Church devoted its energies and monies to improving these Nauvoo sites at this time. In all, the RLDS spent just over $50,000 on its Nauvoo properties in the 1950s, making them an even more appealing destination for the increasing numbers of postwar tourists. The Joseph Smith Homestead, for example, underwent major renovations at this time, which included the construction of a new foundation and replacing the logs that made up its exterior walls. Joseph Smith's Mansion House was also completely refurbished at this time. In fact, the firm of Sidney Moore, a member of the RLDS Church and an alleged expert on early American furniture, outfitted the home with period furniture consistent with historical descriptions of the interior. Fire suppressant systems and furnaces were also installed in the structures, and the grounds of both sites were newly landscaped, which involved the removal of certain buildings that did not date to the Mormon period of Nauvoo. Finally, the Nauvoo House was also extensively renovated at this time, resulting in an overall more comfortable, safe, and visitor-friendly environment. These improvements in part reflected a greater preservation maturity among those responsible for the RLDS properties at this time, but they also illustrate an attempt to better market Nauvoo and the Joseph Smith sites to the burgeoning numbers of postwar tourists. Indeed, more than 6,000 visitors were recorded at the RLDS properties in 1956. Impressively, the number of tourists more than doubled the following year, exceeding 15,000.[58]

Although the RLDS Church was engaged in giving guided tours of its Nauvoo properties since 1918, it was not until 1951 that the LDS Church began an official interpretive program in Nauvoo. In June of that year, the LDS added to its Nauvoo holdings by purchasing a structure on the northwest corner of the Temple lot, which was subsequently converted into an information bureau and staffed with LDS missionary guides, who interpreted the Temple site and the city to visitors.[59] Although destroyed by fire in 1848 and toppled by a tornado a few years later, the Nauvoo Temple was an integral part of the LDS program of interpretation at this time, a fact highlighted by the location of the information bureau on the Temple lot. The perceived importance of the Temple, however, overshadowed other historical dimensions of the site. For example, at various times throughout the ensuing years, LDS officials oversaw the destruction of a number of non-Mormon historic buildings on the Temple lot. Although some of these structures had their own significant histories—one of the oldest continuously operated businesses in Nauvoo and French Icarian apartments that were partially constructed of Temple stone—they were razed in order to landscape, beautify, and otherwise transform the Temple site so the LDS story could be told. Additional transactions before the end of the decade placed three-fourths of the entire Temple block in the possession of the LDS Church, cementing the site as the centerpiece of the LDS presence in Nauvoo.[60]

Many of these early LDS acquisitions in Nauvoo were made by Church member Wilford C. Wood (1893–1968), a furrier from Woods Cross, Utah, with a keen interest in Mormon history. Over many years, Wood acquired historical properties in Nauvoo and elsewhere that he thought the LDS Church should own, often purchasing them with his own money before turning them over to the Church without remuneration.[61] In addition to acquiring much of the Temple lot, including the first parcel in 1937, Wood was instrumental in securing LDS possession of a number of other structures and properties in Nauvoo throughout the 1950s. Of particular note was the acquisition of the buildings that had housed the Latter-day Saints' printing plant, which Wood subsequently renovated (placing plasterboard over walls and ceilings, laying new floors, and erecting new partition walls) so an LDS couple could occupy the structures and serve as additional guides for the increasing number of visitors to Nauvoo. With the purchase of these and other Mormon-period structures and the procurement of more than three additional blocks of land within the historic section of the city, Wood did a great deal to firmly establish an LDS presence in Nauvoo in the 1950s.[62]

Among the visitors to Nauvoo throughout the first half of the twentieth century was another young LDS member who would later play a central role in the restoration of Nauvoo—J. LeRoy Kimball. In 1930, on his return trip to resume study at Northwestern University's School of Medicine, Kimball passed through Nauvoo and saw the brick home of his great-grandfather, Heber C. Kimball, one of the Church's original twelve apostles. Enamored of this relic of his personal heritage, Kimball diligently persuaded the home's owners to promise him first option to purchase the structure in the future. The opportunity to acquire the home came in March 1954, and Kimball, now a practicing cardiologist in Salt Lake City, seized the chance and purchased his great-grandfather's former Nauvoo residence, intending to renovate it for use as his family's summer vacation home. Not long after, Kimball also acquired the former home of Orson Spencer, early missionary and educator in the Church, which sat across the street from the Nauvoo Temple lot. Like his contemporaries, Kimball was mesmerized by Nauvoo for both scenic and historical reasons. He envisioned a restored Nauvoo as a monument to the prophet Joseph Smith and the hard-working Mormon pioneers who followed him. Predictably, his interest in Nauvoo and the structures he purchased was limited to the original Mormon inhabitants, and as a result, the buildings' significant post-Mormon histories were frequently excluded from consideration and interpretation. Nonetheless, with the purchase of these two structures, Kimball began what would burgeon into a multi-million-dollar program of property acquisition in Nauvoo that would last for the next several years.

Aware of the nationwide surge in tourism, Illinois state officials also sought ways to attract visitors to the state. One of the projects undertaken to accomplish this was the creation of a state park in Nauvoo. Dedicated by Governor Adlai E. Stevenson in September 1950, Nauvoo State Park was a partial fulfillment of the recommendations made in the NPS report a decade earlier. Visitors to the historic and scenic town now had a beautiful area in which to satisfy their recreational needs. State officials, however, recognized that most visitors to Nauvoo did not come for purely recreational reasons. It was primarily the town's historical dimension that was the real draw for the thousands of tourists making the trip to Nauvoo each year. However, perhaps due to insufficient funds or to the apparent desire of other interested parties to undertake the restoration of the city, the State of Illinois did not get directly involved in restoration plans for Nauvoo after the war.

Instead, state officials took measures to encourage such development by those groups that were also interested in restoring the city. For example, on April 27, 1949, the Illinois House of Representatives adopted a resolution encouraging both the LDS and RLDS Churches to collaborate on the reconstruction of the Nauvoo Temple. The new Temple, they believed, "would serve as a fitting memorial to the courageous band of pilgrims who here acquired the heroic determination to found a new state in the West." In addition, the rebuilt Temple "would add immeasurably to the attractiveness of historic Nauvoo and would create on the part of many Illinois citizens a new interest in the great movements which have played so prominent a role in the history of our State."[63] Not surprisingly, however, although the idea to rebuild the Nauvoo Temple had been circulating among members of the LDS Church for several years, the RLDS Church had absolutely no interest in reconstructing the edifice. Apparently ignorant of the fundamental difference in temple theology between the two churches, the House's resolution became a cause of great concern among RLDS officials, who felt that a reconstructed Temple would give the LDS Church "a preferred position in Nauvoo." Soon thereafter, leaders of the LDS Church made it clear they had no intention of rebuilding the Temple at that time, effectively diffusing the tensions generated by the misinformed resolution.[64]

Interpretive Tensions Continue

The dispute over the reconstruction of the Nauvoo Temple, set off by the resolution adopted by the Illinois House of Representatives, again brought to the fore some of the doctrinal differences between the two churches. Given that most of the divisive doctrines and practices were fully developed in Nauvoo, it is easy to understand why the historic site would be the subject of competing interpretations between the two churches. These differences also help to explain the RLDS emphasis on the Joseph Smith properties, which allowed them to tell their version of the Prophet's experiences in Nauvoo, and the early LDS focus on the Nauvoo Temple lot, which stressed the beliefs that clearly set them apart from their religious counterparts.

The magnitude of these differences was manifest in the ways the two groups interpreted Nauvoo. Each church took advantage of its Nauvoo sites to support and legitimize its own respective theological agendas and historical claims. For example, one RLDS observer noted that the apparent purpose of the RLDS guided tours at this time was "to spoil some [LDS] Mormons' vacations." He recalled that when a tour reached the place where Joseph Smith Jr. and some of his family were buried, the RLDS guide would subtly deny Smith's, and subsequently Brigham Young's, practice of polygamy by declaring, "We are now standing at the graves of Joseph and Hyrum and of Joseph's only wife, Emma."[65] With that statement, the RLDS guide effectively rejected not only the practice of polygamy, which had been a hallmark of LDS identity for many years, but also implicitly rebuffed Brigham Young as Smith's successor, who unabashedly continued to promote polygamy in the Church after Smith's death.

Other tensions were manifest in 1952 when the RLDS requested that LDS officials remove the plaque they had earlier placed on RLDS property to commemorate the founding of the LDS Women's Relief Society. The commemorative marker had stood for nearly twenty years at the site of Joseph Smith's Red Brick Store, where the prophet organized the women's organization in 1842. When the plaque was installed in 1933, RLDS-LDS relations in Nauvoo were apparently benign enough to allow for such joint interpretation. In 1952, however, sentiments had changed, and the RLDS asked that the plaque be removed. The likely source of this contention was the fact that, in addition to being the location of the founding of the Women's Relief Society, the Red Brick Store was also the place where Joseph Smith first introduced the temple ordinances that are central to LDS identity and theology. The possibility that the LDS would appropriate the RLDS site for the purpose of promoting its own pro-Temple interpretation was all too palpable at this time. The 1949 state resolution concerning the reconstruction of the Nauvoo Temple and the opening of the LDS Bureau of Information on the Temple site in 1951 had moved the issue of temple theology to the front burner at Nauvoo. In light of these developments, RLDS members sought to distance themselves from the competing LDS claims and interpretations, which unsurprisingly resulted in their 1952 request for the LDS to remove its plaque from the site of the Red Brick Store. Accordingly, the commemorative marker was removed and appropriately relocated to the site of the Nauvoo Temple, where it remained for several years.[66] The plaque's removal, like the implicit denial of polygamy at Joseph Smith's grave, was a way in which the RLDS asserted and protected the legitimacy of its own historical claims and interpretations in the face of LDS advances.

Desiring to promote its own theological claims and historical interpretations, the LDS Church also found ways to affirm its unique identity at this time. For example, in 1959 the LDS Church erected a large billboard just outside the city alerting visitors to the "Historic Mormon Country" of Nauvoo. The sign itself would have been rather benign except for the full-body portrayals of Joseph Smith Jr. and Brigham Young, who were conspicuously identified as early Mormon leaders of Nauvoo, an assertion that directly contradicted the RLDS Church's nonbelief in Brigham Young as Joseph Smith's successor.[67] Similar tensions were reported later when one LDS observer noted that "On several occasions recently our traveling [tourist] Mormons have been very offensive to the R.L.D.S. here [at Nauvoo]," adding that "Some of the guilty L.D.S. have bragged to us how they have 'put the Josephites in their place' while visiting their properties."[68] Finally, not having access to the Joseph Smith properties in Nauvoo, the LDS took advantage of other sites available to them and from an early stage concentrated their efforts on the development of the Nauvoo Temple lot and the restoration of the Brigham Young Home, which was still standing. Given that the RLDS rejected both LDS temple theology and the spiritual validity of Young's leadership, both sites were ideal settings for asserting LDS identity by promoting the Church's own theological claims and historical interpretations.

As the 1950s drew to a close, both churches had firmly established their respective interests in a restored Nauvoo, albeit for competing reasons. Within as little as three years, however, the LDS Church became the dominant player in plans for a restoration of the city. This was partly due to the greater financial resources available to the LDS Church at this time. But it also had much to do with the support of the federal government, whose own interests in Nauvoo allied more closely with LDS claims than with those of their RLDS counterparts.

Chapter 2

The Rise of Nauvoo Restoration, Inc.

Early in 1956, Conrad L. Wirth, director of the National Park Service, submitted a proposal for a ten-year development program to improve the facilities of America's national parks in time for the fiftieth anniversary of the Park Service in 1966. The program was called Mission 66, and was soon approved by President Dwight D. Eisenhower and Congress. Included in the proposed program was a revitalization of the Historic Sites Survey, mandated by the Historic Sites Act of 1935 but brought to a halt with America's entry into the Second World War. To jumpstart the survey after the war, NPS officials stressed its importance to historic preservation in light of the accelerated rate of urban development, highway construction, and river basin projects in postwar America.[1] This explicit preservation objective led NPS officials to devise a plan by which sites deemed to possess exceptional value to the country's history would be designated as Registered National Historic Landmarks. The secretary of the interior would award each of the owners of such properties a certificate and a bronze plaque if they would sign an agreement to maintain the property's historical integrity and allow a biennial inspection by NPS representatives. This new category of historic sites satisfied the government's need to promote and encourage the preservation of the nation's most significant historic places, and at the same time freed them of any obligation to financially support such preservation efforts.

Nauvoo: National Historic Landmark

The NPS had been aware of Nauvoo since the prewar days of the Historic Sites Survey, when it identified Nauvoo as a site of national significance and issued a report outlining a restoration and recreation plan for the city and surrounding area. It is not surprising, then, that on January 20, 1961, Nauvoo became one of the country's first sites to be designated a National Historic Landmark. A short time later the city of Nauvoo was given a bronze plaque, still on display today, stating, "Nauvoo has been designated and registered as a National Historic Landmark. Under the provisions of the Historic Sites Act of Congress, August 21, 1935, this site possesses exceptional value in commemorating and illustrating the history of the United States."

Nauvoo's "exceptional value" was explained in a 1959 NPS report in which it was identified as meeting particular criteria established by the NPS for the evaluation of historic sites and buildings. Specifically, Nauvoo was recognized for its remaining structures that embodied the distinguishing characteristics of the architectural styles of the Mississippi River Valley in the mid-nineteenth century (Criterion 4). Equally important, if not more so, was that Nauvoo was perceived as a site "in which the broad cultural, political, economic, military, or social history of the Nation is best exemplified, and from which the visitor may grasp the larger patterns of our American heritage" (Criterion 1).[2] In particular, and similar to the prewar report issued nearly twenty years before, the 1959 NPS report acknowledged that Nauvoo was a natural base from which to tell the story of the nation's westward expansion, as it was the starting point for the great migration that took the Latter-day Saints to Utah. "This journey," declared the report, "was one of the most significant mass movements in the advance of white settlement to the Pacific."[3] The NPS further explained that

> *The movement of the Mormons to the valley of the Great Salt Lake was one of the most dramatic events in the history of American westward expansion. With the Mormon migrations, not only the motivation of westward movement shifted, but the character of the emigrant also changed. No longer were the migrations composed solely of an agrarian people, but shopkeepers, artisans, mechanics, and skilled persons of all types made the trek. The economic motive, so dominant among the earlier emigrants, gave way to the desire to worship in peace and live in isolation from those who would deny this right.*[4]

The designation of Nauvoo as a National Historic Landmark implicitly sanctioned the LDS position in Nauvoo by emphasizing the westward migration from the city, an event inextricably tied to Brigham Young and, hence, the LDS Church. In doing so, the National Historic Landmark designation was reminiscent of the adopted resolution of the Illinois House of Representatives a decade earlier, in which state legislators encouraged the reconstruction of the Nauvoo Temple. In both cases, a governmental body took legislative action that resulted in the promotion of LDS views over those of the RLDS in Nauvoo. In the case of the state resolution, which was never more than a passive and self-serving expression of support for the restoration activity of both churches, the RLDS Church was able to effectively point out the misinformed bias in the government's action and restore balance to the interpretive scales in Nauvoo. The National Historic Landmark designation was on a different order, however. Whereas the state resolution, by focusing on the Temple, limited Nauvoo's importance to a relatively small scale, the NPS designation elevated Nauvoo to national significance by placing it squarely within the drama of the country's westward expansion. No longer was Nauvoo only of interest to members of the LDS and RLDS Churches; now it was important to all Americans, as it represented a fundamental part of a crucial chapter in our country's history. Ultimately, Nauvoo's designation as a National Historic Landmark was at once a major reason for and a testament to the success of the LDS Church in mainstreaming its identity during the first half of the twentieth century. What was once a haven for so-called religious fanatics of the nineteenth century was now the launching point for one of America's most dramatic and important overland migrations.

Given that the rejection of Brigham Young as Joseph Smith's successor was one of the central tenets of RLDS identity at this time, it is easy to see why the National Historic Landmark designation was a blow to RLDS interpretive efforts. Nonetheless, there was still reason for the RLDS to be optimistic about its program in Nauvoo. With the major restoration and preservation work on its Joseph Smith properties completed during the last half of the 1950s, RLDS efforts in the 1960s were focused on utilizing these structures in carrying out its interpretive program.[5] As early as 1963 the newly finished restorations were generating noteworthy results. In November of that year it was reported that the RLDS properties had received more than 35,000 annual visitors, a new record for the Church.[6] While the RLDS concentrated on using what it had already developed, however, the LDS was busy making plans for a massive restoration project that would take shape and become firmly established in this same decade. With greater financial resources and the support of various levels of government, the LDS Church was able to take significant steps during the 1960s toward fulfilling the restoration dream that had been envisioned for decades prior.

J. LeRoy Kimball's Vision of Restoring Nauvoo

Nauvoo's designation as a National Historic Landmark came at a critical moment in the development of LDS restoration plans, providing a vital boost of support and sense of validation, which gave the Church confidence to move forward with its grandiose project. In the months immediately prior to and following the January 1961 designation, the LDS Church began to slowly acquire additional property in Nauvoo—a cautious and inconspicuous start to what would become an enormous, multi-million-dollar campaign of land acquisition. At the center of this activity was Dr. J. LeRoy Kimball (1901–92), the cardiologist from Salt Lake City who had purchased the home of his great-grandfather, Heber C. Kimball, in 1954. Intending to use it as a summer vacation home for his family, Kimball spent more than $35,000 to have the structure remodeled and refurbished. An architect and an interior decorator were hired and substantially modified the interior of the house "to make the place livable."[7] By July 1960, the home was finished and ready to be dedicated (figure 3). Thus, on July 3, 1960, during a Kimball family reunion attended by several hundred descendants of the early Mormon apostle, the remodeled Heber C. Kimball Home was dedicated by one of Heber's grandsons, Elder Spencer W. Kimball, then apostle and future president of the LDS Church. It is believed that more than 1,500 people toured the home that day, including three members of the Quorum of the Twelve Apostles of the LDS Church. So great was the public interest in the historic house thereafter that Kimball never once used the structure for its intended purpose as a family vacation retreat. Instead, at his own expense, he hired an LDS couple to offer guided tours of the home during the tourist season. In this way, the Heber C. Kimball Home joined the LDS Church-owned Times and Seasons printing building and the Church's Bureau of Information on the Temple lot as one of the few LDS places in Nauvoo open for public tours.[8]

As news of the historic structures spread, the number of tourists wanting to take tours increased. Many of the more than 30,000 people that visited Nauvoo State Park each summer wandered across the highway and onto the flats, where they were given tours of both the LDS and RLDS sites. It was not long before local entrepreneurs, aware of the burgeoning numbers of tourists congregating in Nauvoo, sought to take advantage of the situation. As one historian later described the scene, "Some man set up a little kiosk across the street [from the Heber C. Kimball Home] to sell beer, soda pop,

3. Renovated Nauvoo home of Heber C. Kimball, dedicated July 3, 1960. The original structure is on the left with a later addition to the right. Courtesy of the Archives of the Church of Jesus Christ of Latter-day Saints.

tobacco, popcorn, and stuff like that," and as a result, the people "were scattering and littering the ground." Naturally, Kimball disapproved of the situation and ended up purchasing the lot on which the kiosk was located, forcing the man to move elsewhere. When Kimball learned that the man planned to move his kiosk across the street to the west, he bought the entire block. Hearing of others' profiteering plans to open businesses nearby heightened Kimball's concern over further encroachment. His solution to the impending threat was to purchase three additional blocks, those immediately to the east, north, and northeast of the Heber C. Kimball Home, creating a protective barrier of land around most of the property once owned by his pioneer ancestor. Thus, in a relatively short period of time Kimball became one of the largest property owners in Nauvoo, having acquired more than four complete blocks of land.[9]

Although he felt compelled to purchase these properties to protect the integrity and value of his great-grandfather's home, this unintended buying spree helped Kimball solidify a more expansive vision for Nauvoo. Of particular interest was the immediate restoration potential of the block on which his great-grandfather's house was situated. Nauvoo's block 106 was unique because, in addition to the Heber C. Kimball Home, it contained two other original brick Mormon structures—the Wilford Woodruff and Winslow Farr homes—and provided what Kimball saw as an opportunity to restore an entire Nauvoo block. With a real estate buffer zone already in place, Kimball believed he could restore the whole four-acre block to its 1840s appearance and recreate a microcosm of the historic city. Even though it was never fully realized, this desire to restore all of block 106 and interpret it as exemplary of the city's original character would remain a significant component of Kimball's personal restoration ambitions for many years.

J. Reuben Clark: An Ally of Restoration

As Kimball expanded the scope of his efforts in Nauvoo, he had the support of important allies in the LDS Church hierarchy. Of particular significance was his close relationship with J. Reuben Clark Jr. (1871–1961), former U.S. ambassador to Mexico and long-time friend and patient of Dr. Kimball.[10] When the Heber C. Kimball Home was dedicated in July 1960, Clark was there as one of the senior members of the LDS Church's Quorum of the Twelve Apostles. More important, as counselor to then LDS Church President David O. McKay,

Clark was a member of the Church's First Presidency, a position he had occupied for more than twenty-five years prior. His tenure in the highest ranks of the Church hierarchy made him a powerful ally to Dr. Kimball. Bolstering this relationship was a shared interest in Nauvoo. Like Kimball, Clark had genealogical ties to the city—his grandfather, Edwin D. Wooley, had lived in the city—which motivated him to visit Nauvoo on numerous occasions over many years. Kimball accompanied Clark on at least one of these visits in 1957, and restoration enthusiast Wilford Wood escorted the apostle during other trips to the city. It is little surprise, then, that Clark developed his own personal appreciation of Nauvoo's restoration potential.[11] In fact, Kimball later recounted how Clark recorded "his enthusiastic support of such a [restoration] project and outlined certain steps to follow" in his personal notebook, allegedly affirming that "if it were in his hands, he would give a yearly budget to the program."[12] With the help of others, Clark also accumulated a wealth of knowledge about Nauvoo's Mormon history. For example, hoping to identify the land on which his ancestors settled, Clark asked his personal secretary, Rowena J. Miller, to conduct a study of Nauvoo properties. In response, Miller conducted a meticulous survey of land ownership in Nauvoo, successfully tracing the title of numerous lots back to their original Mormon owners. Miller also made a detailed study of the Mormon-period Nauvoo newspapers, compiling data on the shops, business establishments, trades, professions, and manufacturing in the city during the 1840s. This information was of inestimable value not only to Clark's family history but also to the later restoration effort in Nauvoo. It was also a major reason why

Miller was employed as the restoration's secretary following Clark's death in 1961.[13]

President David O. McKay: Major Advocate of Nauvoo Restoration

Before his death, Clark was Kimball's access to David O. McKay (1873–1970), president of the LDS Church. It was through Clark that President McKay kept abreast of Kimball's restoration efforts, and it was undoubtedly Clark who helped persuade the president to support the idea of a restored Nauvoo. One inside observer downplayed Kimball's role in the restoration's beginnings when he later recounted that it was really Clark "who fed President McKay's interest" in restoring Nauvoo.[14] Despite such influences, however, McKay had developed his own abiding interest in Nauvoo. Significantly, his interest was not rooted in a personal genealogical attraction, as none of his ancestors had ever resided in Nauvoo. What motivated McKay, rather, was Nauvoo's historical significance, and "he was interested in having the LDS Church participate in getting that importance before the world, the nation, [and] before the members of the Church."[15]

President McKay's desire to "showcase" the LDS Church by highlighting its history was not original to the discussions concerning the restoration of Nauvoo.[16] Even before he became president of the Church, McKay was actively involved in efforts to commemorate and memorialize the history of the Mormon pioneers. For example, from 1939 to 1948, McKay was the chairman of the Utah Centennial Commission that planned the 1947 pioneer centennial celebration. The commission's primary responsibility was to plan and carry out celebratory events commemorating the pioneers who settled Utah. Among other things, the commission oversaw the placement of a centennial float in the 1947 Tournament of Roses Parade and encouraged the LDS Church's production of a special musical drama entitled *Promised Valley*, in which the Mormon pioneer trek and early years in Utah were depicted through word and song. The commission also organized centennial parades in Salt Lake City and initiated and sponsored a number of other cultural, educational, and athletic events held throughout the state to celebrate the special anniversary year. One high point of the anniversary celebration was the dedication of the This Is The Place Monument. Situated at the mouth of Emigration Canyon in Salt Lake City, the monument—a massive granite structure sixty feet high and eighty-six feet long—memorializes with a bronze sculpture the Mormon pioneers and other figures who played important roles in the early development of the West.[17] This impressive monument was the product of many years' work by another state commission, the This Is The Place Monument Commission, also headed by prominent LDS leaders. Indeed, two presidents of the Church, George A. Smith and Heber J. Grant, served as chairmen of this commission at one time, which may help explain why the LDS Church made substantial financial contributions to the construction of the monument and why Mahonri M. Young, a grandson of Brigham Young, was awarded the contract to create the bronze sculptures that adorn the imposing granite structure. Once the monument was dedicated in 1947, the Monument Commission maintained responsibility for the care and future development of the site until the state legislature turned the site over to the newly created Utah State Parks and Recreation Commission in 1957. Significantly, it was McKay's counselor,

J. Reuben Clark Jr., who served as the Monument Commission's chairman during this time.[18]

Thus, when J. LeRoy Kimball gathered his friends and family in Nauvoo for the dedication of the Heber C. Kimball Home in July 1960, both Clark and President McKay—the two highest officials in the LDS Church at the time—were already well acquainted with the advantages and possibilities of historic preservation and presentation as these related to the LDS Church. Further, with Clark's endorsement of Kimball's efforts, on the one hand, and McKay's own personal appreciation of Nauvoo's potential on the other, it was not long before Kimball found himself in "numerous conversations and conferences with Church officials in which [they] . . . discussed the possibility of restoring other old Mormon homes and making Nauvoo more attractive and interesting as a site of historic importance to the Church, as well as to the nation."[19] On a number of occasions after the fact, Kimball recounted a dialogue that purportedly occurred between himself and President McKay during one of these meetings. "I met with President McKay," he related, "and after I told him this story and my reason for being involved in it, President McKay asked, 'How many homes are there?' I answered that there were about forty, and stated I knew what I would do if I had the money. He asked, 'What?' I said, 'I would buy them all.' His reply was, 'you have the money. Go ahead and buy them.'"[20]

Soon thereafter a $350,000 account was made available to Kimball, who began purchasing additional historic Nauvoo homes and lands on behalf of the LDS Church, taking the properties in his own name, "so that people would not become unduly aroused."[21] Among the properties acquired at this time was the Brigham Young Home, which Kimball purchased in

1961. The Catholic Church's Parish Hall and parochial school, both of which sat on the southwest corner of the Nauvoo Temple lot, were also purchased, giving the LDS Church ownership of the entire Temple block, with the exception of a single house (the Datin House), which was still in the possession of the RLDS Church.[22]

It is not clear what exactly President McKay envisioned as the ultimate objective in Nauvoo at this time. However, his unilateral decision to begin bankrolling the acquisition of property did not go unnoticed by others in the upper councils of the LDS Church. One individual later observed that President McKay's failure to consult members of the Quorum of the Twelve Apostles concerning developments in Nauvoo resulted in negative sentiments that had lasting effects on the restoration project. According to this observer, the restoration project "had the enmity or the antagonism of . . . most of the men in the quorum as a result of it." Apparently, this was especially true of the senior apostle and quorum president, Joseph Fielding Smith, who became president of the LDS Church following McKay's death in 1970.[23] Adding to these frustrations was the fact that this was not the first or the last time that President McKay committed significant amounts of Church resources without first consulting members of the LDS Church hierarchy.[24]

Harold P. Fabian: Gentile Champion of Nauvoo's Restoration

Although he did not seek the advice of the Twelve Apostles, President McKay did solicit the opinion of one professional with respect to the envisioned restoration of Nauvoo, Harold

P. Fabian (1885–1975).[25] Although born and raised in Salt Lake City, Fabian was not a member of the LDS Church.[26] After graduating from Yale in 1907 and receiving his law degree from Harvard in 1910, he returned to his birthplace and began to practice law, eventually becoming a senior partner in the firm of Bagley, Fabian, Clendenin, and Judd. In this capacity Fabian developed positive relations with powerful men in the LDS Church hierarchy, as his firm was frequently enlisted to provide legal services for the Church.[27] President McKay's association with Fabian went beyond his law practice, however. The two had formed a deeper relationship through their common interest in history and preservation.

More than a decade before McKay became the chair of Utah's State Centennial Commission in 1938, Fabian had become involved in an ambitious preservation program financed by oil magnate John D. Rockefeller Jr., which eventually resulted in the creation of Grand Teton National Park near Jackson Hole, Wyoming. His involvement in this project had its roots in his military service during the First World War, when he met his future law partner Beverly Clendenin. Around 1920, Fabian was introduced to one of Clendenin's old college classmates, Horace Albright, future director of the NPS (1929–33), but at the time employed as superintendent of Yellowstone National Park. Fabian shared Albright's love for the outdoors, and the two established a lasting friendship. It was thus unsurprising that, in 1926, Fabian and Clendenin's firm was contacted for legal assistance after Albright had convinced Rockefeller of the value of preserving the Teton Mountains and surrounding area. The following year, Fabian was named vice president of the newly incorporated Snake River Land Company, formed for the purpose of purchasing "large quantities of land in the Jackson Hole Valley so that these could at a later time be turned over to the federal government for preservation and conservation."[28] At the time, Fabian was unaware of Rockefeller's involvement, but it was not long before it became clear to him and others that he was the oil magnate's representative for the project. By 1933, Fabian had orchestrated the purchase of more than 32,000 acres in the valley, spending $1.5 million in Rockefeller money. This land was subsequently turned over to the federal government and became part of Grand Teton National Park in 1950. Having acquired all of the proposed land, the Snake River Land Company was converted to Jackson Hole Preserve, Inc., which was charged with the responsibility to preserve, develop, and overall improve the quality of the acquired lands for the growing numbers of tourists to the area.[29] Fabian and his wife, Josephine, carried out one of the most successful projects at this time by reconstructing Menor's Ferry and the ranch buildings with which it is associated. In undertaking this project, the Fabians not only desired to physically rebuild the historic structures, they also wanted to commemorate the pioneers who had built them, while memorializing the history of Jackson Hole Valley. Through his work on the Grand Teton project, Fabian won the confidence, respect, and amity of the Rockefeller family, who, as a token of their friendship, permitted Fabian and his wife to use the family's cabin near Jenny Lake, at the base of the Teton Mountains, for the rest of their lives.[30] This enduring relationship resulted in Fabian's lifelong association with and connection to other Rockefeller-sponsored projects, including Colonial Williamsburg, which later proved vital to the restoration of Nauvoo.

Although Fabian formally retired in 1954, his more than twenty-five years of preservation and restoration experience launched him into an incredibly active post-retirement civic life. In 1957, for example, he was asked to serve as one of the original members of the newly created Utah State Parks and Recreation Commission, charged with the responsibility of creating a state parks system. Although Utah was the last state in the nation to establish a parks and recreation program, the commission wasted no time in performing its work. Before 1957 was over, Utah had designated its first four state parks, all of which were associated with significant events in the state's history.[31] Further, by January 1959 the commission had submitted a report in which an additional 118 potential state park areas were identified, with the recommendation that some of these areas be immediately acquired and developed.[32] One member of the commission later stated that these early efforts were supported and encouraged by officials in the NPS, who were engaged in park improvement programs across the nation as part of their project Mission 66.[33] Fabian's relationship with the NPS did not end there, however. His service and experience in the field of preservation and restoration resulted in his 1958 appointment to the Advisory Board on National Parks, Historic Sites, Buildings, and Monuments. The advisory board was established under the provisions of the Historic Sites Act of 1935, which authorized the secretary of the interior to appoint no more than eleven members (later twelve), "competent in the fields of history, archaeology, architecture, and human geography," "to advise the Secretary [and later the director of the National Park Service] on matters relating to national parks . . . and to the restoration, reconstruction, conservation, and general administration of historic and archaeologic sites, buildings, and properties."[34] By 1956, with the inception of Mission 66 and the postwar renewal of the Historic Sites Survey, the advisory board was further charged with the explicit responsibility of providing recommendations on the designation of National Historic Landmarks.[35] Significantly, Fabian was a member of the advisory board when Nauvoo was awarded National Historic Landmark status in January 1961. It was in his role as a member of the advisory board that Fabian formulated his earliest opinions of Nauvoo's significance. In subsequent years he repeatedly reaffirmed what NPS historians had written about Nauvoo: that it was the launching point of "one of the most dramatic events in the history of American westward expansion."[36]

Fabian's legal service to the LDS Church, in addition to his service to the state and nation on matters of historic preservation, were well known by President McKay. Thus, in May 1961—five months after Nauvoo's designation as a National Historic Landmark—President McKay solicited Fabian's professional expertise with respect to Nauvoo. Specifically, he asked him if he would visit Nauvoo with the purpose of forming a professional opinion about the restoration possibilities in the historic city. Knowing of Nauvoo's significance to American westward expansion but never having visited the place, Fabian agreed to make the trip. Dr. J. LeRoy Kimball met him there and gave him a grand tour of the city, its old Mormon buildings, and the surrounding area, an experience that left Fabian deeply impressed. Before an audience of LDS Church officials three years later, he recounted his experience in Nauvoo at this time:

I stood on a hill in Nauvoo and I looked down over those old Mormon homes that were standing up above the trees in the fields there, homes that were beginning to go into disrepair, the shutter was off, the door was off, bricks were falling out and one thing and another, but still they stood up there as momentos of one hundred and twenty years ago. As I stood there I looked out across the flats there, across the Mississippi River to Montrose on the other shore and I could see Brigham Young in February and his little band of followers crossing over the ice to Montrose and I could feel—and that is what I mean by contact history—I could feel the drama of that movement. I could feel the sorrow and the pathetic sense that those people must have felt when they took everything that they could in their wagons, left all the rest, turned their faces resolutely to an unknown Rocky Mountains. And as I stood there I thought that we have here in Utah now, what we have in what we call the Intermountain Empire, Idaho and Utah and all our valleys here, all of that we owe to the faith of those people who left Nauvoo that day, to their faith in their religion, to their faith in their destiny, to their courage, to their endurance and to their submission to the discipline of an able and inspired leadership.[37]

Upon returning to Salt Lake City, Fabian again met with President McKay to report on his visit. He later related his recommendation at this time: "I said, 'President McKay, I think not only that you should restore Nauvoo, but I think it is an obligation on the part of your people to themselves and to their forbearers and to the people of America that Nauvoo be restored and that its cultural contribution and its history to the development of the United States and to the development of the American character be perpetually made of record in its restoration.'"[38]

An "Outline for the Restoration of Nauvoo"

President McKay took Fabian's recommendation to restore Nauvoo seriously. Throughout the next several months McKay and his counselors repeatedly met with Fabian and Dr. Kimball to discuss further plans for the city. By December 1961, Fabian, in consultation with Kimball, had created a document titled "Outline for the Restoration of Nauvoo," which they subsequently presented to the First Presidency of the LDS Church on January 4, 1962. The "Outline" set forth their vision of a restored Nauvoo, beginning with a review of the city's status as a National Historic Landmark, calling it "a strategically important base from which to interpret most effectively one of the great western migrations of American history." The text continued with a summary statement of the purpose of the restoration that again emphasized Nauvoo's national significance, but also highlighted the intended role of the Nauvoo Temple as the centerpiece of the restored city. The threefold purpose of the restoration, as declared by Fabian and Kimball in this document, was as follows:

(1) To restore the Mormon Temple at Nauvoo as a shrine to those whose perseverance and faith built it, and to establish and re-dedicate it as a present day place of religious worship; (2) to provide an historically authentic physical environment for awakening a public interest in, and an understanding and appreciation of, the story of Nauvoo and the mass migration of its people to the valley of the Great Salt Lake; and (3) to dramatize the interpretation of that story, not only as a great example of pioneering courage and religious zeal, but also as one of the vital forces in the expansion of America westward from the Mississippi River.[39]

According to the "Outline," the overall plan to accomplish these three objectives included four major phases. First, the entire Temple block would have to be acquired before the Nauvoo Temple could be reconstructed in its original location. Second, all of the land and properties associated with the Mormon occupation of Nauvoo would have to be purchased and restored. Third, a suitable visitors' center would need to be constructed on a section of land purchased for that purpose. Finally, it would be necessary to acquire land on which visitors' accommodations could be built and maintained.

In scope, the restoration project set forth in the 1961 "Outline" was no different from the restoration proposals that had preceded it. Indeed, both the 1940 NPS report and Lane K. Newberry's envisioned restoration in the 1950s had essentially the same structure and goals as Fabian and Kimball's "Outline." All three plans called for the reconstruction of the Nauvoo Temple and restoration of the city on the flats where the Mormons had settled. Likewise, the "Outline" echoed the NPS report's call for visitors' accommodations, financial planning, the employment of a capable administrator, and the work of specialized professionals—historians, architects, archaeologists—to ensure authentic restoration. Fabian and Kimball's Outline was unique in its plan for a "Visitors' Orientation Center," but in this they were influenced by recent developments at places like Colonial Williamsburg, which opened its new Information Center in 1957, and those constructed by the NPS, which was busy building nearly a hundred modern visitors' centers at this time as part of the Mission 66 program.[40] Given his position on the NPS Advisory Board and his affiliation with the Rockefeller family and their projects,

Fabian was well aware of these developments and sought to emulate these efforts while creating the "Outline for the Restoration of Nauvoo" late in 1961.

President McKay's previous interest in and commitment to the idea of restoring the city facilitated the progress of the proposed restoration. In early May 1962 McKay sent two of his counselors, Hugh B. Brown and Henry D. Moyle, to Nauvoo to further consider the proposal set forth in the "Outline." Arriving on the morning of Friday, May 4, McKay's counselors were escorted on a tour of the city, its sites, and buildings. Joining them on this tour were several other prominent figures, including Conrad Wirth, director of the NPS; Otto Kerner, governor of Illinois; A. Edwin Kendrew, senior vice president of Colonial Williamsburg; J. Willard Marriott, of hotel and food industry fame; the prominent Chicago banker David M. Kennedy; and A. Hamer Reiser, member of the Utah State Parks and Recreation Commission (figure 4). During the tour, the distinguished visitors were exposed to the details of Fabian and Kimball's proposal to restore the city, including an explanation of Nauvoo's historical significance. Fabian was quoted as saying, "[the] proposal being made to the First Presidency [of the LDS Church] is to use Nauvoo and the story of Nauvoo and the story of Mormonism as one of the four major contributing factors in the westward expansion of America," citing the Santa Fe, Overland, and Oregon Trails as the other three major contributing factors. "We propose," he continued, "to restore the historic city of Nauvoo so it can be a proper base from which to tell the Mormon story and the Mormon contribution to the building of the west."[41]

4. Inside the renovated Heber C. Kimball Home, May 1962. From left, A. Edwin Kendrew, J. LeRoy Kimball, J. Willard Marriott, Hugh B. Brown, Otto Kerner, David M. Kennedy, Harold P. Fabian, A. Hamer Reiser. Courtesy of the Archives of the Church of Jesus Christ of Latter-day Saints.

After the tour the men were invited to a special meeting sponsored by the Nauvoo Chamber of Commerce. At this meeting several of the prominent visitors shared their feelings about the projected restoration of the city. For example, Conrad Wirth, director of the NPS, expressed appreciation for the hospitality he had received in Nauvoo and spoke about the importance of preserving heritage for future generations. Although careful not to give the impression that the NPS was to be formally involved in the proposed Nauvoo project, Wirth spoke favorably of the site, its restoration potential, and its historic contribution to American history. In reference to the latter, he commented on the multi-million-dollar project the NPS was then undertaking in St. Louis, constructing the Gateway Arch and a visitors' center to tell the story of America's westward expansion. Nauvoo, he believed, had a part to play in telling this story too.[42]

Following Wirth's remarks, Hugh B. Brown, then second counselor to President David O. McKay, praised "the splendid work that has been done" in Nauvoo and, on behalf of the First Presidency of the LDS Church, expressed "our appreciation, our thanks, and our hope that in some way we may be helpful." Although explicit in pointing out that no final decisions had been made regarding the long rumored restoration of the city, Brown and the other Church officials were clearly impressed with the proposed restoration and eager to "further our fine cooperative effort" with Fabian and Kimball.[43]

Nauvoo Restoration, Inc.: An Institutional Base Forms

It is not clear how influential this special meeting was in persuading the LDS Church hierarchy to accept the restoration proposal and officially sponsor the Nauvoo project. Nonetheless, President McKay was already committed to the idea on some level. Further, his counselors seemed pleased with the presentation they had witnessed in Nauvoo. Thus, it was not long before the men decided to formally sanction the proposed project. In the "Outline for the Restoration of Nauvoo" Fabian and Kimball explicitly stated that if the LDS Church's First Presidency were to authorize the proposed restoration, they had first to determine who would carry out the project. On June 28, 1962, McKay and his counselors resolved this issue by announcing the creation of a nonprofit corporation, Nauvoo Restoration, Inc. (NRI), to direct the restoration of the historic city. President McKay himself officiated at the meeting at which the articles of incorporation were signed (figure 5). He

5. Signing the corporation papers, creating Nauvoo Restoration, Inc., June 28, 1962. Seated, from left, Henry D. Moyle, J. LeRoy Kimball, David O. McKay, Hugh B. Brown; standing, from left, A. Hamer Reiser, Harold P. Fabian, J. Willard Marriott. Courtesy of the Archives of the Church of Jesus Christ of Latter-day Saints.

told reporters that the new corporation was being formed to restore the historic homes of Nauvoo "as they were left when the Mormons evacuated the city in 1846." Evoking Fabian's emphasis on Nauvoo's national significance, President McKay also declared that "the full purpose of restoring Nauvoo is to perpetuate in history the part played by the Mormon Pioneers in the building of the West."[44]

Although the LDS Church was the official sponsor of the corporation, financial contributions from private foundations and government agencies were anticipated to help support the costs of restoration. One participant later remarked that the real reason why NRI was incorporated as an official non-profit organization in Illinois was to allow for such financial contributions. "There's some doubt," he observed, "that the federal government would have helped with anything if it meant giving money to a church. So it had to be an independent corporation." The need to maintain a separation of church and state was also relevant to anticipated relations with the government of Illinois. Finally, with respect to private donations, "The Church preferred to have a non-profit corporation organized . . . rather than to have contributions given directly to the Church." Overall, it was believed that a certified corporate structure would give NRI a "base of confidence so that people who had money would feel secure giving it to an on-going corporation" in place of the LDS Church.[45] Thus, instead of organizing the restoration as part of the established Church bureaucracy, NRI was formed according to state law as an official nonprofit corporation of Illinois.

The creation of a Church-sponsored but independent corporation outside the LDS Church's formal system of government was not necessarily unique.[46] What made the formation of NRI somewhat unusual, however, was that it was independently organized despite an existing and active Historic Sites Committee in the Church. Furthermore, even though the Church's First Presidency legally possessed the nominating power for membership on NRI's board of trustees, no one from the Church's Historic Sites Committee, or any other member of the official hierarchy, was initially appointed to serve as an officer or trustee. On the contrary, the original members of the new corporation's board were men appointed because of the expertise, experience, influence, and prestige they brought to the restoration project.

Predictably, J. LeRoy Kimball and Harold P. Fabian were appointed president and vice president of the corporation, respectively. Their involvement in the project was seen as vital to NRI's success, given their prior input and investment. Completing the original five-man board were three other men, who had been recruited as early as May 1962 when they joined Kimball and Fabian in Nauvoo and, alongside members of the LDS Church's First Presidency, heard the formal restoration proposal. Although all three of these men were members of the Church, and as such shared a pious affiliation with Nauvoo, they were asked to serve on NRI's board of trustees because of their impressive secular credentials.

A. Hamer Reiser: The Insider-Outsider

Along with President Kimball and Vice President Fabian, the third and final member of the new corporation's Executive Committee was A. Hamer Reiser (1897–1981), appointed to serve as NRI's secretary-treasurer. Reiser's experience with similar projects, which he acquired through his service on a number of special commissions for the State of Utah, made him a well-qualified candidate for the job. Moreover, his work on these state-sponsored projects placed him in intimate association with some of the important figures in the developing restoration of Nauvoo. Reiser himself attributed his involvement with NRI to his participation in the production of a religious pageant sponsored by the LDS Church, entitled "The Message of the Ages." The pageant was performed for the first time in 1930, in commemoration of the centennial anniversary of the organization of the Church. At this time, Reiser was the secretary of the Centennial Pageant Committee, which was responsible for the pageant's production. Seventeen years later (1947), Reiser was serving as the chairman of the subcommittee on pageantry for the Utah Centennial Commission and was responsible for the encore performance of the pageant during the celebrations marking the 100th anniversary of the arrival of the Mormon pioneers. Apparently, it was Reiser's experience with such pageantry that first attracted the attention of J. LeRoy Kimball. As Reiser recounted years later: "[Before the formation of NRI] Dr. Kimball first asked me to make some suggestions about what attractions I thought they could develop for Nauvoo that would bring people there." "He asked me, I think," Reiser continued, "on the basis of my experience with the 'Message of the Ages' pageant. He had in mind that an appropriate pageant might be presented in Nauvoo. . . . He talked about it and it was in that way that he first got me into it."[47]

But it wasn't only his experience with LDS Church pageants that qualified Reiser to serve as secretary-treasurer of NRI. His associations with influential members of the Church hierarchy also created opportunities and experiences that ultimately led to his appointment. For example, in 1921 Reiser began service as general secretary of the LDS Church's Deseret Sunday School Union, where he worked alongside future Church president David O. McKay, who was the organization's general superintendent until 1934. The relationship forged during this time was strengthened as the two men served together on the Utah Centennial Commission from 1938 to 1947, McKay as chairman and Reiser as the commission's secretary (in addition to his role as chairman of the subcommittee on pageantry). Then, in 1956, five years after McKay became president of the LDS Church, Reiser was asked to serve as assistant secretary to the First Presidency. This position reflected McKay's trust and respect for his long-time associate. Furthermore, it placed Reiser in direct contact and confidence with the highest members of the Church hierarchy, a situation that led to additional opportunities that further prepared him for the work with NRI. For example, one of his duties as assistant secretary to the First Presidency was to serve as secretary to the This Is The Place Monument Commission, then chaired by J. Reuben Clark Jr., second counselor to President McKay. Then, in 1957, when the responsibilities of this commission were transferred to the newly created Utah State Parks and Recreation Commission, Clark suggested, and the governor agreed, to make Reiser a member of the new commission's five-man board. Significantly, the appointed chairman of the new commission was Harold P. Fabian, future vice president of NRI. Finally, in 1961, after he, Fabian, and the rest of the board had successfully initiated the Utah State Parks system, Reiser took over as chairman of the commission, while still serving as an assistant secretary to the LDS Church's First Presidency.

Thus, by the time he was asked to serve as NRI's secretary-treasurer in 1962, Reiser had accumulated nearly fifteen years of experience in working with various state commissions responsible for, among other things, commemorating and preserving important events in Utah's history. In the process, he had won the confidence and respect of members of the LDS Church hierarchy (including President McKay himself) and of men like Fabian and Kimball, all whom would later be major figures in the restoration of Nauvoo. Ultimately, then, it was the combination of Reiser's experience with similar projects and his associations with influential men that led to his appointment as NRI's secretary-treasurer, a position he gladly accepted and served faithfully in until 1971.

The Marriott Connection

In addition to the Executive Committee, comprised of Kimball, Fabian, and Reiser, two additional trustees were named to the new corporation. The first, J. Willard Marriott Sr. (1900–1985), was an extremely successful businessman and faithful member of the LDS Church whose fame, influence, and wealth profited the restoration project. His involvement with the new corporation can be traced to his college days in the mid-1920s, when he met J. LeRoy Kimball for the first time. Both men were students at the University of Utah and both needed to work to finance their education. To pay tuition, Marriott spent his summers selling woolen goods, manufactured by the Baron Woolen Mills in Utah, to lumberjacks in the Pacific Northwest. His son later described his father's business acumen at this early stage of his career:

> *Dad would go to the Northwest logging camps and sell this [black-wool long] underwear for $20 a pair. That was a lot of money back then, so he developed a special selling strategy. He would find two mean-looking lumberjacks and challenge them saying: "Each of you take a leg of this pair of underwear. If you can pull this underwear apart, I'll give you a free pair. If you can't, you've got to buy it." The loggers would then have a tug-of-war but could never tear the underwear apart. Dad earned more than $2,000 in commissions during a single summer and was the most productive salesman in the company.*[48]

Eventually, Marriott came to manage a sizable sales force of other students who sold the company's woolen goods in several states. A family member later told how Marriott "was always on the lookout for a potential candidate who would make him successful in the eyes of his employer," and how he found just a person in J. LeRoy Kimball. The two men worked well together, and "both were most pleased with the amicable economic outcome." Indeed, when Marriott left the company in 1927 to pursue his own business ventures in Washington DC, he recommended that Kimball take over as manager of the sales force. This new job allowed Kimball to finance his medical degree at Northwestern University, managing the team of salesmen during the four summers of his medical school training. Significantly, it was during his return trip to school at the end of the summer of 1930 that Kimball first saw the historic home of his great-grandfather in Nauvoo, sparking his lifelong interest in the city and its restoration.[49]

By 1962, when he agreed to serve on NRI's board of trustees, Marriott had come a long way since his days selling woolen underwear in the Pacific Northwest. When he left Utah and his sales force in the spring of 1927, he was on his way to Washington DC, where he and his business partner opened a nine-stool A&W root beer stand. Later in the year, hot foods were added to the menu, and the root beer stand was converted into the first "Hot Shoppes" restaurant. This first establishment was so successful that additional restaurants were soon opened, and by 1931 Marriott had reached $1 million in annual sales. Not content to limit his energies to restaurants alone, Marriott expanded his business to include airline catering in 1937, the management of food services in defense plants and other government facilities during the Second World War, and food service for hospitals and educational institutions by 1955.

Sensing the business opportunities connected to the postwar travel boom, Marriott opened his first hotel (really a motel) in Arlington, Virginia, in 1957. Shortly thereafter additional Marriott hotels were opened in Dallas, Philadelphia, and Atlanta, initiating a hotel chain that today is internationally recognized.[50] Thus, by the time he agreed to serve as a trustee for NRI, Marriott was already a tremendously successful businessman. Indeed, in 1964, just two years after joining NRI's board, Marriott's company earned $84 million in revenue, while employing 9,600 employees. Incredibly, this was still just the beginning of his success.[51]

Marriott's wealth and business expertise were important assets to the restoration project. However, when Kimball called on his old friend to lend his services to the newly created corporation, it was not just Marriott's success that was alluring. His experience with food and lodging services filled a crucial gap in Kimball and Fabian's vision of Nauvoo as a major tourist destination, complete with a full array of visitor accommodations. Equally important to the new corporation, however, was Marriott's geographic locale. As a well-established resident of Washington DC he had access to influential officers of the federal government. At the first meeting of NRI's board of trustees, Marriott was asked "to confer with Dr. Conrad L. Wirth [director] of the National Park Service in Washington DC, with a view to learn upon what basis the corporation can secure cooperation and assistance of the National Park Service."[52] Thus, in addition to Marriott's wealth, prestige, and business acumen, his expertise in hospitality services and his proximity to influential government officials contributed greatly to his service as one of NRI's trustees.

David M. Kennedy: NRI's Statesman

The final member of the new corporation's board of trustees was David M. Kennedy (1905–96). Sometime prior to the organization of NRI on June 28, 1962, Kennedy received a phone call from Henry D. Moyle, first counselor to President McKay, inviting Kennedy to serve as a trustee of NRI.[53] At the time, Kennedy was serving as a counselor to John K. Edmunds, president of the Chicago, Illinois, stake of the LDS Church. He was also chairman of the Board of Directors of the Continental Illinois National Bank and Trust Company, the biggest and most powerful bank in Chicago. Prior to this, Kennedy had earned a law degree from George Washington University and a graduate degree in banking from Rutgers University, and had worked for the Federal Reserve in the nation's capital. He and his wife moved to Washington DC in 1929, just as J. Willard Marriott's restaurant business was experiencing success in the city. As there were only a handful of Mormons in the Washington DC area at this time, Kennedy and Marriott interacted frequently during the early years of their careers. In 1946 Kennedy left the nation's capital to take a position at Continental Illinois Bank. A decade later he became the bank's president, and in 1959 he was appointed chairman of the board.[54]

As the highest official of Chicago's most successful bank, Kennedy had tremendous power and influence with prominent individuals at the local, state, and national levels. By the time he was asked to serve on NRI's board of trustees, Kennedy had developed a reputation as one of the premier financial minds in the country. A stint as special assistant to Secretary of the Treasury George Humphrey from October 1953 to December

1954 and other special federal appointments further solidified this reputation, culminating in his service as secretary of the treasury under President Nixon from 1969 to 1971. It was not necessarily his influence among federal officials, however, that was important to Kennedy's service with NRI. Whereas Marriott and Fabian were both sufficiently well connected in Washington, it was Kennedy who had tremendous influence with prominent people in Illinois. Of particular significance was his close relationship with Governor Otto Kerner Jr., Illinois's chief executive from 1961 to 1968. He was also a close associate of Chicago's mayor, Richard J. Daley, who appointed Kennedy to chair the Mayor's Committee for Economic and Cultural Development, responsible for favorably promoting Chicago to the world.

Kennedy's relationships with these and other prominent individuals made him an important asset to NRI. As Kennedy himself recognized years later, the trustees "talked about keeping good relationships in the state, and I think that had something to do with [my appointment to the Board]."[55] The hope was that his influence among state and local officials would facilitate the work of the restoration program. Moreover, as head officer of Chicago's largest bank, Kennedy interacted with some of the wealthiest people in the state, who potentially could be persuaded to help financially support the Nauvoo project. It was also believed that his status in the world of finance could draw the respect and confidence from major foundations, resulting in additional financial contributions for the restoration of Nauvoo. In sum, with Kennedy on board, the new corporation had a powerful ally in the state of Illinois and throughout the nation at large.

Articles of Incorporation

With the addition of Marriott and Kennedy, the original five-man board of trustees was complete, and NRI was poised to begin its work. On the afternoon of July 27, 1962, one month after President McKay authorized and announced the organization of the corporation, the five men gathered in Kennedy's office at the Continental Illinois Bank in Chicago to hold their first meeting. Earlier that day NRI had become legally official when, upon receipt of articles of incorporation, the Illinois secretary of state issued a certificate of incorporation. In addition to formally electing themselves officers and members of the corporation, the five men reviewed and officially adopted the articles of incorporation during this first board meeting.[56]

Article I of the new corporation's by-laws modified and expanded on the statement of purpose originally included in Fabian and Kimball's 1961 "Outline for the Restoration of Nauvoo." At its core, the new statement of purpose was essentially the same as its 1961 predecessor: NRI primarily existed to restore the city of Nauvoo. Despite its fundamental similarity, however, the new statement differed from the old in three ways. First, the new statement did not mention the Nauvoo Temple or its contemplated reconstruction. Second, it significantly broadened the scope of NRI's work to include not only Nauvoo but also sites throughout the United States, and detailed the methodological parameters of such work. Finally, it added a specific public service component to NRI's work. Thus, according to the articles of incorporation, the official purposes of NRI were:

(1) To acquire, restore, protect and preserve, for the education and benefit of its members and the public, all or a part of the old city of Nauvoo in

Illinois and the surrounding area, in order to provide an historically authentic physical environment for awakening a public interest in, and an understanding and appreciation of, the story of Nauvoo and the mass migration of its people to the Valley of the Great Salt Lake in the area which has now become the State of Utah; (2) to interpret and dramatize that story, not only as a great example of pioneering determination and courage, but also as one of the vital forces in the expansion of America westward from the Mississippi River; (3) to engage in historic and archaeological research, interpretation and education and to maintain, develop and interpret historic landmarks and other features of historic, archaeological, scientific or inspirational interest anywhere in the United States and particularly along the Mormon Pioneer Trail from Nauvoo, Illinois to its terminus in the Valley of the Great Salt Lake, in the State of Utah; (4) to acquire, construct, equip and otherwise provide suitable property, facilities and services for the public use, understanding, appreciation and enjoyment of the scenic, scientific and historic features of such areas, and (5) in general to promote, encourage and conduct such other activities as are germane to these general purposes.[57]

With this statement guiding their efforts, the trustees set out to accomplish the work of the corporation. From the beginning, they solicited the advice and counsel of professionals to help them in their work. Many of those who ultimately contributed to the Nauvoo project became involved through personal associations with members of NRI's board of trustees. This was especially true of Harold P. Fabian, whose reputation and professional associations resulted in the support and involvement of some of the country's most prominent figures in the field of historic preservation. From the beginning of his involvement with the Nauvoo project, Fabian took advantage of his connections with professionals in both the private and public sectors to gather support for the proposed restoration, in addition to expert ideas, advice, and examples of what could and should be accomplished in Nauvoo. Much to the new corporation's advantage, in the months immediately preceding the formal organization of NRI, Fabian was elected chairman of the NPS Advisory Board on National Parks, Historic Sites, Buildings, and Monuments, on which he had served since 1958. Remarkably enough, this distinction came on the heels of his appointment to chair the Utah State Parks and Recreation Commission as well. These two high-profile positions added credibility and prestige to the budding restoration project in Nauvoo and opened doors that otherwise may have remained closed. Ultimately, however, it was Fabian's connection to the Rockefeller family, through his involvement with the development of Grand Teton National Park, that introduced an incredible ally to NRI in the person of A. Edwin Kendrew (1903–93), senior vice president of Colonial Williamsburg, the nation's premier historic site restoration.

A. Edwin Kendrew and the Williamsburg of the Midwest

Kendrew's involvement with the Colonial Williamsburg restoration stemmed from his employment with the Boston architectural firm of Perry, Shaw, and Hepburn. In the late 1920s Kendrew was assigned to the project when his firm was hired to create preliminary restoration plans for the city. In time, Kendrew was invited to be the project's resident architect, and eventually worked his way up to be Colonial Williamsburg's senior vice president. By the time he was approached by NRI in the early 1960s Kendrew had developed a reputation as one of the country's leading experts in the field of historic preservation and historic site restoration.[58]

As early as 1961, when Fabian and Kimball were busy preparing their "Outline for the Restoration of Nauvoo," Kendrew's assistance was solicited for the budding Nauvoo project. Over the years, Fabian and Kendrew had developed a deep friendship rooted in their mutual interests and experiences with historic preservation and restoration.[59] Furthermore, Fabian knew that Rockefeller hoped the restoration of Colonial Williamsburg "would be an inspiration to others to do likewise in helping to perpetuate the American heritage by restoring these historic places."[60] Thus, when Fabian approached Kendrew concerning the restoration of Nauvoo, the latter gladly contributed. At Fabian's invitation, Kendrew came to Nauvoo in early May 1962 to participate in the important meeting with LDS Church and government dignitaries, during which the restoration program was first officially proposed. Shortly thereafter, with the permission of Carlisle Hummelsine, president of Colonial Williamsburg, Kendrew was appointed advisory architect to NRI. Then, in September 1965, after acquiring the consent of the First Presidency of the LDS Church, Kendrew was officially elected to NRI's board of trustees.

Given his status as one of the nation's most respected professionals in the field, Kendrew's advice was highly regarded by those involved with NRI. Consequently, his influence on NRI's early developments and plans was extensive. As Fabian later put it, Kendrew came to NRI "to help us set up the proper organization and sort of 'ride herd on us' to see that we don't go astray."[61] As a result, a great deal of NRI's early work was directly patterned after the restoration of Colonial Williamsburg.

In fact, on more than one occasion, NRI's board of trustees held their meetings in Williamsburg, where they could observe and be tutored by their seasoned exemplars. More than once, NRI's architects, historians, and archaeologists visited Colonial Williamsburg and received training at the hands of their employees.[62] Thus, early on NRI came to perceive itself as a "little brother" project to that at Williamsburg.[63] Indeed, as early as 1962, J. LeRoy Kimball told a reporter from the *Chicago Tribune*, "We hope to create here [in Nauvoo] a Williamsburg of the 19th century Midwest"[64] (figure 6).

Kendrew himself identified his role with NRI as that of a mentor. "Perhaps the greatest contribution that I can make to the project," he declared, "is to draw upon the experience which we have had in Williamsburg." Continuing, he said, "We have had so many years of experience. We have learned so many things about the science of restoration, the steps that you have to take to do a proper restoration. . . . So my contribution to this work here is largely in saving you from some of the mistakes that we made at Williamsburg, showing you how we approached these problems, and in really trying to get an organization together that would do a creditable job."[65]

In the months following the incorporation of NRI, Kendrew helped Fabian create an "Operational Outline" for the new corporation. This document was an organizational chart that allocated the major responsibilities of the restoration program among several departments, including administration, property acquisition and management, planning and design, construction, furniture and furnishings, interpretation, purchasing, and visitor accommodations. While each department was responsible for various tasks specific to its institutional role, the

6. NRI Board of Trustees at Colonial Williamsburg, September 1962. From left, A. Hamer Reiser, J. Willard Marriott, Mrs. Marriott, Mrs. Kennedy, David M. Kennedy, A. Edwin Kendrew, Mrs. Kendrew, Harold P. Fabian, J. LeRoy Kimball. Courtesy of the Archives of the Church of Jesus Christ of Latter-day Saints.

entire operation was to be supervised by a general manager. This operational outline reflected Kendrew's forty years of firsthand experience at Colonial Williamsburg, drawing on his accumulated knowledge of the intricacies of a large-scale restoration program. The advantage of having this kind of information and direction from the beginning was apparent to the trustees of NRI, who over the next several years used the outline to organize the work of Nauvoo's restoration.[66]

Guiding Principles

In addition to contributing to the operational outline, Kendrew shared his wealth of experience with historic site restorations by generating a list titled "General Principles for the Restoration of Nauvoo." In all, he outlined seventeen principles that he believed should guide the restoration of the city. The first two principles were statements defining the scope of the project. Temporally, the restoration would be limited to the preservation and reproduction of the Nauvoo environment during the eight-year span of Mormon occupation (1839–47). Geographically, the project would be restricted to predetermined areas within the city's historic boundaries, "since it is not essential nor would it be feasible to recreate the entire layout of the original city." However, another principle advocated the preservation of historic Mormon buildings outside the defined restoration area "because of the possibility of extending this area in the future, and since they will witness the original extent of the city's development." Other principles affirmed that existing buildings of the Mormon period would have priority over those already destroyed, while those structures not related to the Mormon period would be removed unless they demonstrated "unusual architectural merit and are of importance in illustrating the sequence of history of Nauvoo."[67] Further, the principles stated that the preservation and restoration of existing structures and features should always be favored over reconstruction, even when the former might be more costly. However, the reconstruction of certain buildings or auxiliary elements would be undertaken when deemed necessary "to effect an authentic representation of the original appearance of the more important sections of the city."[68]

The document also specified principles dealing with the actual restoration or reconstruction work. One principle acknowledged that such work should not adversely affect the citizens of Nauvoo, but recognized that it might be necessary for city officials to change or make exceptions to building regulations in order to "accurately restore and reconstruct the original layout authentically." Another principle declared that "superior results are preferable to more rapid progress" when it comes to the work of restoration and reconstruction. Thus, for buildings and grounds that were intended to be open to the public, "the highest degree of authenticity will be required with a minimum number of concessions to the present-day use," while those structures not needed for public tours were to be restored or reconstructed "as accurately as possible, but with limited concessions on the interior for other appropriate present-day uses." Moreover, to ensure maximum authenticity, all work was to be based on the careful and skilled examination of historical, architectural, and archaeological evidence, which was to be documented in illustrated reports that recorded the existing conditions of all properties, the plans and specifications for the restoration and reconstruction of the targeted properties, and the reasons and theories employed in executing such work. To further attain the desired authenticity, another principle affirmed that old materials and equipment were to be used where possible, but only when such use "[did] not involve the demolition of buildings having any reasonable prospect of being preserved intact on their original sites." On the other hand, Kendrew affirmed that if new materials were necessary, these were to be as historically authentic as possible without resorting to artificial methods of antiquing, while any necessary modern workmanship was to be concealed so as to not interfere with the "required authentic effects." With respect to the installation of modern equipment, the principles outlined that this was to "be done in a manner that will affect the authentic appearance as little as possible." Overall, "In all restoration and reconstruction work, materials and workmanship shall be used which will not only produce authentic results but will also ensure a high degree of permanence and a minimum of future maintenance work."[69]

Taken together, the seventeen principles represent a remarkably sophisticated philosophical treatise on historic site preservation and restoration. Although not every principle would be accepted today, the document, when viewed in its proper historical context, provides a fascinating window onto the current philosophies and trends of historic preservation at that time, and reflects the true expertise that Kendrew brought to the Nauvoo project. With these principles to guide the work, Kendrew provided NRI with a road map for creating a true "Williamsburg of the Midwest."

Land Grabbing

Before any of these principles could be practically applied, however, the corporation had to complete its acquisition of the historic property in Nauvoo. As Kennedy later said, "The first thing to do was to get control of as much land as possible, before the people realized or knew the full extent of things, because otherwise the price could have escalated out of this world."[70] Prior to the incorporation of NRI, President McKay had unilaterally awarded Kimball a $350,000 budget, with which Kimball purchased a number of the historic homes in Nauvoo for the LDS Church. However, as plans to restore the historic city became more concrete, it was understood that more than just the historic homes would need to be purchased. The threat of encroachment by various commercial interests persuaded Kimball and the others to seek protective land holdings as well. Of course, Kimball's personal experience with encroachment in Nauvoo had earlier impelled him to buy up his own protective ring of property around the historic home of his great-grandfather. Added to this were the negative opinions and stories shared by Kendrew concerning the encroachment at Williamsburg, "where there are some 38 motels which care little about the historic aspects [of the city]" and that "are largely chain type operations bent on making money from the public."[71] The fear that something similar would happen in Nauvoo compelled the trustees to think big when it came to purchasing lands for the restoration project. In general, everyone, including the First Presidency of the LDS Church, agreed with Kendrew, who believed "it was necessary to have protective land holdings and that there was no point in the restoration of the historic area if there was to be a great encroachment of modern development for the tourists, as well as wax museums, billboards and honky-tonk, etc., which would detract from the atmosphere which is to be created."[72]

By September 1962, all but $21,250 of the original $350,000 given to Kimball had been expended. Consequently, the First Presidency increased NRI's land acquisition account to $1 million, acknowledging the need to secure a protective barrier of property around the restoration project.[73] At first, the trustees identified three major areas for acquisition. Area 1, the Historical and Recreational Area, consisted of large tracts of property north and east of the historic city, most of which was situated on "The Hill" or bluff overlooking the bend of the Mississippi River. Area 2, the Restoration Area, encompassed a large portion of the historic flats where most of the surviving structures stood, with the exception of those properties already owned by the RLDS Church. Finally, Area 3 included the block on which the Nauvoo Temple once stood and additional properties adjacent to or cornering that lot.[74] Shortly thereafter the trustees agreed that a fourth area should be added to the list "to provide needed protection to the whole area." Essentially, the proposed addition consisted of the property connecting the Historical and Recreational Area to the Restoration Area, resulting in a revised acquisition area of approximately 1,000 acres that included "the main portion of the original town of Nauvoo and [its predecessor] the city of Commerce." To facilitate the purchase of the expanded area, the First Presidency of the LDS Church allotted an additional $500,000 to NRI's property acquisition budget, bringing the total appropriation for land purchase to $1.5 million. At the same time, the First Presidency granted NRI an additional $250,000 for operating expenses.[75]

Ironically, despite the generous appropriation to NRI, the LDS Church was undergoing a major financial crisis at this time. Beginning in the early 1950s the Church had embarked on an ambitious building campaign, during which the substantial cash reserve that had built up during the Second World War was freely spent. In fact, by the close of 1963 a total of 1,941 new meetinghouses had been constructed throughout the world. As early as 1958, however, the elaborate building program had begun to severely tax the Church's cash reserves. In late 1959 the Church announced that its expenses had exceeded its revenues by $8 million. Nonetheless, instead of curtailing the construction of additional buildings, Church leaders resorted to further deficit spending to maintain the accelerated building campaign. As a result, the LDS Church was faced with "a real liquidity crunch" by 1962. Incredibly, notwithstanding the foreboding financial situation, this was the same year the First Presidency awarded a total of $1.75 million to NRI.[76]

A major player in the LDS Church's building program at this time, and an enthusiastic supporter of NRI, was Henry D. Moyle (1889–1963), who became second counselor to President McKay in 1959, following the death of J. Reuben Clark Jr. Prior to his appointment as an apostle in 1947, Moyle had made a personal fortune in the oil industry and was known as a risk-taker. Upon entering the First Presidency, Moyle was given responsibility for the entire missionary program of the Church. In this role, he teamed up with the Church's building program, and set out to improve the Church's image worldwide (especially in Europe) by improving the quality and grandeur of the Church's buildings. By this time, however, the building program had already depleted the cash resources of the Church. But this did not deter Moyle, who within months of joining the First Presidency was overseas, buying up real estate for the Church. As one historian put it, "Rather than viewing the funding of new chapels as deficit spending, Moyle saw it as an excellent investment. New chapels, he reasoned, would result in new converts who, in turn, would provide new sources of tithing revenue that would service the debt."[77]

Moyle died of a heart attack in September 1963, not living long enough to see the long-term results of his efforts. Although his tenure in the First Presidency was relatively short-lived, Moyle's deficit spending was in large part responsible for the LDS Church's worsening financial situation in the early 1960s. Nevertheless, to a large degree he was successful in achieving his vision of "lifting the image of the church throughout the world, of instilling in members a pride in their church . . . and of using handsome buildings to assist missionary efforts."[78]

Moyle's enthusiastic spending spilled over into the property acquisition in Nauvoo as well. As a member of the First Presidency at the time NRI was organized, Moyle was intimately involved with the decisions of the new corporation until his death in 1963. In Nauvoo, he saw another opportunity to advance the missionary work of the LDS Church by improving the Church's image, and he approached this opportunity with the same vigor as he did overseas, despite the Church's deteriorating financial situation.

The year following Moyle's death, A. Edwin Kendrew spoke retrospectively about Moyle's influence on the Nauvoo project:

I will never forget a meeting that I had in Nauvoo when Henry Moyle was there and we were discussing, "Well, it's going to take a lot of money to buy these properties," and I was pointing out some examples of what had happened in Williamsburg, and we had mentioned the possibility of buying this little farm on top of the hill and perhaps we ought to go further. And the next morning Henry Moyle said, "Why don't we take the whole plateau on top of the hill. We should buy that, I think, Mr. Kendrew. That's an idea. It'll never go any cheaper, and if we don't need it in the future, it's good land, we can always dispose of it." And I think that gave us the courage to go ahead and ask for the larger plan, a far-reaching plan which someday I know we are going to be very happy that we looked forward to the big picture.[79]

The 700 acres that were purchased as a result of this interchange comprised most of the Historical and Recreational Area on The Hill northeast of the historic city. On this property overlooking the Mississippi River, Moyle and the trustees envisioned, among other things, the construction of a golf course and a hotel for visitors to the restoration.[80] In this, the trustees were at once patterning their plans after what had been done in Williamsburg and subscribing to Moyle's vision of improving the image of the LDS Church through the construction of impressive facilities.

With Williamsburg as their guide, and with the enthusiastic support of Moyle and the rest of the First Presidency, NRI's trustees began a massive campaign of property acquisition in 1962 with the $1.5 million authorized for this purpose. Although the large tract of land on the hill that Moyle zealously endorsed was a major component of this campaign, it was only one part of the larger area the trustees had targeted for acquisition. The rest of the land and property, including the majority of the historic flats region where most of the old Mormon homes stood, would have to be purchased as well.

In reality, it was the corporation's president, J. LeRoy Kimball, who was primarily responsible for the successful acquisition of NRI's property. Of all the trustees, Kimball was the only one with experience in purchasing property in Nauvoo. The skills he used in navigating the purchase of his great-grandfather's Nauvoo home in the 1930s served him well years later when he was negotiating on behalf of the corporation. As A. Hamer Reiser later said, Kimball "was a fair, competent, patient, and efficient negotiator," and that "was the reason for his success."[81]

Adding to his success was the fact that he knew the people of Nauvoo and was aware of who owned what parcels of land throughout the city. Helping him in this regard was one of

Kimball's distant cousins, Preston W. Kimball, a long-time resident of Nauvoo and a devout Catholic. Preston Kimball was a lawyer, having served as Illinois state's attorney for Hancock County. He was also a member of Nauvoo's City Council and was elected president of Nauvoo's Historical Society in January 1960.[82] His "considerable influence in the community" made him an important ally for the new corporation. In addition to preparing the legal papers for NRI's property transactions, he helped negotiate with those residents who were less eager to sell their land. He also served as a properties manager for the corporation, overseeing the maintenance of the structures once they were purchased.

The demography and physical condition of Nauvoo in the early 1960s also facilitated Kimball's success in acquiring property for the restoration. As David M. Kennedy later explained, "The timing was right because it was a sleepy town. It was overgrown with weeds and the houses were falling down and needed painting and the people living there had very little source of income. And they were glad to sell if they could get some cash."[83] Thus, it was with relative ease that Kimball began buying up land throughout the designated Restoration Area.

Early on, Kimball wrote to Reiser from Nauvoo informing him that after a week in the city, he had met with some success. "I have a number of deals pending," he wrote, adding, "There is nothing I cannot buy here for a price."[84] Years later Reiser reflected on this period of intense property acquisition. He acknowledged that even though NRI essentially created the Nauvoo real estate market in which they were the only buyers, the land was purchased at reasonable prices. "Dr. Kimball," he said, "established the values at which he would buy property.

. . . He'd negotiate and then bring it to the board for authorization before any of the money was spent." In this way, Reiser declared, the property "was acquired at a fair price." "By that," he continued, "I mean the price has been fair to everybody. It's been fair to the people who had land to sell and it's been fair otherwise. The prices have been, I think, to some degree high. We've had to pay for the property. But when you consider everything it's fair. We were not cheated. We've got the value it's worth. There isn't any other market. Nobody else wants to buy the property. We created the market."[85]

Kimball was also understanding of the different needs of many Nauvoo residents and tried to accommodate individuals as much as possible. For example, as Kennedy later recounted, "There were quite a few older people living there that hated to give up their homes and move. So arrangements were made for them to continue to live in their homes until their passing, so they'd have life estate in it."[86] Thus, instead of moving in with irresistible offers and forcing people out of their homes, Kimball secured options on several properties, giving NRI the legal right to officially purchase the properties when they became available for sale.

Notwithstanding Kimball's attempts to be honest and fair in his transactions, as word of his massive purchasing campaign spread, some residents sought to take advantage of the situation. Knowing that their property had suddenly become highly desired real estate, some landowners set exorbitant prices on their holdings, hoping, as Preston Kimball put it, to "cash in."[87] Dr. Kimball reiterated the same sentiment to the First Presidency, explaining, "There are a few [residents] who have not been very cooperative but most people are interested in what they can get out of it [their property]. The people who sold early are sorry that they sold early but the demand is greater now. . . . Those who own the property are putting a price on it."[88]

On one occasion, as the arrangements for an important property transaction were being finalized, the woman selling the land requested that NRI give her a three-carat diamond ring in addition to the previously agreed-upon sale price for her property. In reply, J. LeRoy Kimball told the woman's lawyer that "she was getting enough money to buy herself several diamond rings" and that he "did not feel this was a proper business transaction."[89] Knowing that Kimball had access to large amounts of money with which to acquire the desired property for the restoration project, not all Nauvoo residents were as eager to sell at fair market values as NRI had hoped.

The truth of the matter is, however, that with the generous financial appropriations from the First Presidency, NRI had the money and hence the power to get their way when it came to land acquisition. Although Kimball did make a conscious effort to be fair and reasonable in his transactions, when reluctant residents refused to give up their property, effectively blocking NRI's restoration plans, Kimball and the others used whatever power or influence necessary to secure the transaction in their favor. On more than one occasion, for example, Kennedy, the prominent Chicago banker, used his influence to push along a real estate deal for NRI. In fact, Kennedy's services were influential in dealing with the woman who asked for the large diamond ring. "She was not about to sell, because she had heirs," Kennedy recalled. However, there was "one in Chicago that had to be cleared," so "We finally got them to sell," he reported.[90] In using their influence, NRI officials believed they were pursuing the greater good. After all, in their minds Nauvoo was destined to become another Williamsburg, a bastion of American ideology and an arena of moralistic living history. In this light, no claim upon Nauvoo's old deteriorating buildings was viewed as more important than theirs.

Thus, with the LDS Church's generous financial support, Kimball's skillful diplomacy, the assistance of influential people, and a sincere belief in the moral value of their objective, NRI's property acquisition moved forward rapidly, despite occasional resistance. By September 1962, NRI had spent $328,750, purchasing or acquiring options to approximately 125 acres of land and fifteen historic Mormon homes and buildings in Nauvoo.[91] But this was just the beginning. An official report dated April 1, 1965, indicated that NRI had acquired 760 acres of land and thirty-one historic buildings, in the principal amount of $1,425,340.45.[92] An additional 34.63 acres and another historic building were also under option at this time, leaving little money in NRI's land acquisition account. Although this constituted the bulk of the targeted property, there were still about 213 acres and nine historic buildings within the approximately 1,000-acre area that NRI wanted to buy.[93] To facilitate the purchase of this extra real estate, the First Presidency authorized an additional appropriation of $500,000 in 1965, bringing the total amount of LDS Church funds dedicated to NRI's property acquisition account to $2 million.[94] Expressing satisfaction with the corporation's success at this time, Kendrew reassured members of the LDS Church hierarchy that NRI was making good progress. "In Williamsburg," he declared, "we have never made the progress you have made in land acquisition in two and a half years

. . . and while we are chafing at the bit to get going [with the restoration of Nauvoo] . . . I think we are on the right track in having the land pretty well assured."[95] In 1974, nearly a decade later, NRI's property holdings amounted to 959 acres of land, thirty-six historic Mormon structures, eight historic Mormon foundations, and thirty nonhistoric homes and buildings in Nauvoo.[96]

In spite of such rapid progress, and indeed partly because of it, Kimball and others had to work hard to convince some residents that the restoration project was a worthwhile endeavor. As Kimball's son later wrote, "Dad was well aware that many feared a big corporate takeover by the LDS Church, and he did not wish to tread heavily on the toes of the townspeople." Nonetheless, there were still some who felt that "NRI was a western carpetbagger coming in to impose its will on the community."[97] In response, Kimball tried to reassure the residents of Nauvoo that NRI had nothing but good intentions for their community. In a meeting with the Nauvoo Chamber of Commerce during the summer of 1963, he explained that NRI was purchasing vast amounts of property so it could "protect the [restoration] project from over-commercialization," not so that the LDS Church could capitalize on the venture. He also expressed regret at the lack of community support for the project and communicated his hope that such support would be forthcoming. In response, the Chamber of Commerce pledged to assist the project, and formed a committee to work with NRI and its plans for the restoration.[98]

Not all the citizens of Nauvoo, however, were as willing to endorse NRI's endeavors. Indeed, some actively resisted the restoration project. In early January 1963 a passerby noticed a fuse burning next to a hall near the Temple block that NRI had recently acquired from the Catholic Church. Fortunately, the spectator grabbed the fuse and threw it into the street before any serious damage was sustained. An explanation of the situation remained a mystery, but NRI officials suspected arson.[99] Additional opposition was expressed when one of NRI's signs was forcefully uprooted in the early summer of 1965. The sign was solidly reinstalled in cement, only to be defaced a week later when someone scratched the word "Mormon" from its front.[100] Incidents such as these were unmistakable reminders that not everyone welcomed the restoration project.

Big Plans

Despite some small-scale local opposition, the project moved forward steadily. Although the total amount spent on property acquisition is not certain, NRI had expended approximately $6 million on land acquisition, the construction of a new visitors' center, and the restoration or reconstruction of thirteen buildings by the end of 1977.[101] In reality, $6 million was far below the original projected expenses for the restoration project. Initially, the price tag was significantly higher, because NRI officials envisioned Nauvoo becoming much more than just a collection of a few restored buildings. "I think in Nauvoo we've got to make big plans," declared Kendrew to a group of the LDS Church's hierarchy, "and I say you are very lucky to have a Board of Trustees . . . who seem to have that vision."[102] Unsurprisingly, much of what NRI's trustees envisioned for Nauvoo was directly patterned after what had been done by their East Coast exemplar, Colonial Williamsburg, which had the financial support of the extremely wealthy Rockefeller family.

Thus, even though NRI's monetary supply was not as robust as that of Williamsburg's, the trustees boldly outlined their grandiose plans for the restoration project. In justification of their ambitious proposals, Kendrew recalled the old adage: "Make no small plans. They have no matching to stir the souls of men."[103]

The plans proposed by the board of trustees were by no means small. Operating on the assumption that their land acquisition program would be fully successful, resulting in approximately 1,000 acres to use and develop, their preliminary plans were tailored for an expansive restoration area. In addition to restoring or reconstructing thirty historic Mormon homes and twelve historic craft shops, the board planned to construct a motel and reception center in Nauvoo to accommodate the hundreds of thousands of visitors they envisioned would come to the restoration. This alone, they estimated, would cost more than $5.25 million. Above and beyond this, however, was the proposal to construct a new temple in Nauvoo. This was not to be a reconstruction of the original Nauvoo Temple but an entirely new edifice that would sit on approximately thirty acres of land on a hill north of the historic flats and cost more than $4 million to build. A Nauvoo bell campanile, complete with a twenty-three-acre mall, would cost an additional $320,000, raising the total estimated price tag to approximately $10 million. Doubling this figure, however, was the proposal to devote an additional 165 acres of the restoration area for the construction of a $10.5 million University of Nauvoo, the campus of which would include, among other things, a full-fledged stadium. To further accommodate visitors to Nauvoo, the trustees proposed building a golf course in the restoration area and constructing an amphitheater in which dramatic presentations and concerts could be performed. Finally, a natural inlet on the eastern shore of the Mississippi River was selected as the location for a proposed marina. In addition to providing space where boaters coming to visit the restoration could dock their vessels, the proposed marina would house a vintage steamboat that would ferry visitors up and down the river while offering a spectacular view of the restored city. All in all, it was projected that well over $20 million would be required to execute the grand plan the trustees envisioned for the restoration of Nauvoo.[104]

By the late 1960s, however, some of the proposed developments had been dropped from NRI's agenda. For example, plans to construct a new temple, a university, and a campanile were put on hold as serious work on the restoration and reconstruction of historic homes and shops began. This was partly due to the realization of how much money and time the actual restoration work required. Thus, as early as 1964, Kimball reported that "The magnitude of a project of this kind, makes wise undertaking restoration of a few of the houses at the present, and these would be the nucleus of the project." "These," he added, "could stand alone, if necessary . . . as a minimal practical restoration of historic Nauvoo."[105] In reality, the attempt to moderately scale down their originally expansive plans resulted in the creation of a multiphase master plan for the restoration in which the restoration and reconstruction of historic homes and shops was broken down into a series of eight progressive yet independent phases. The first stage, for example, involved the restoration of the historic structures on block 106 (the Heber C. Kimball, Wilford Woodruff, and

Winslow Farr Houses) and the restoration of the Brigham Young House, while the second stage called for the restoration of the Times and Seasons Building (a newspaper office and shop), the Lucy Mack Smith House, and an additional shop on Main Street.[106]

By breaking up the otherwise massive project into discrete phases of work, NRI officials were able to maintain their expansive and bold vision for the restoration of Nauvoo, without requiring the complete and long-term commitment of the LDS Church hierarchy from the start. In other words, instead of having to sign off on the entire project up front, the First Presidency only needed to authorize one phase or more at a time, knowing that the program could move as fast or as slowly as circumstances required. Thus, even though the eight stages carried the significant estimated cost of $1.5 million each, this figure was not nearly as overwhelming as the total estimated price of the entire project, which still approximated $20 million.[107]

Funding the Restoration

Although LDS Church funds were made available to finance NRI's land acquisition program, the question of how to pay for the rest of the restoration program was always an issue. With total estimated costs approaching $20 million, the First Presidency wanted to know where Kimball and the other trustees were going to get this money, as there was concern over whether or not the project could be supported entirely from LDS Church funds. From the beginning, NRI officials anticipated receiving financial contributions from individuals and institutions outside the Church. Some early funding came from the NPS in the form of a $15,000 grant to support the historical research of David E. Miller, professor of history at the University of Utah, whom Kimball had recruited to help with the restoration project. Instead of giving the money directly to NRI, however, NPS officials bequeathed the grant to the University of Utah, because they were uncomfortable with the relationship between NRI and the LDS Church.[108] Nonetheless, this early financial support from an institution as prestigious as the NPS increased the confidence of NRI's trustees that similar sources of funding would be available to their project. Indeed, this is one of the principal reasons why NRI was organized as a nonprofit corporation—so that financial contributions, especially those from federal and state governments, would be donated to the corporation instead of directly to the Church.[109]

The hope that funds from outside the LDS Church would be available for the project was greatly increased in 1966, when Congress passed the National Historic Preservation Act. In addition to establishing legal parameters for historic preservation in the country, the NHPA made available federal funds to support both public and private preservation efforts. Central to the law was the threefold mandate given to the secretary of the interior: to conduct a survey of the nation's cultural and historic resources; to develop plans for the preservation and management of such resources; and to execute such plans by restoring, rehabilitating, and otherwise preserving the identified resources. Stewart L. Udall, secretary of the interior at the time the law was passed, immediately sought to decentralize his new duties by asking the governor of each state to appoint a person to carry out the preservation directives outlined by the

NHPA on the state level. Thus, it became the responsibility of each state to survey the cultural and historic properties within its boundaries and to develop and carry out a statewide plan to preserve these resources. Facilitating the implementation of these mandates, the NHPA authorized federal funds in the form of matching grants to be controlled by the NPS under the direction of the secretary of the interior. Congress appropriated $2 million to the NPS for this purpose in 1967 and increased the amount to $10 million for each of the successive four years. Under the law, states were eligible to access these monies through NPS grants that would cover up to 50 percent of the projected expenses of their planned preservation efforts. If awarded, the states could then distribute these funds to private organizations or individuals whose preservation efforts met two qualifying criteria. First, the property targeted for preservation had to be listed on the newly created National Register of Historic Places. Second, the proposed preservation project had to be included in the state's preservation plans.[110]

NRI's trustees were eager to take advantage of the funding possibilities of the NHPA. In a board meeting held in October 1967, Fabian explained to the other trustees what NRI needed to do to qualify for such federal funds. As Nauvoo had already been designated a National Historic Landmark, it was automatically listed on the new National Register of Historic Places. "This," Fabian explained, "opens the way for Nauvoo Restoration to have consideration under the [National] Historic Preservation Act." To qualify for federal funds, however, the Nauvoo project "would have to be adopted as part of the program of the State of Illinois." Thus, as Fabian told his fellow trustees, "Unless and until we get on the Illinois plan we will not be in a position to get any funds." By October 1967, however, a full year after the NHPA was passed, the State of Illinois had done nothing with respect to generating a statewide preservation plan. William T. Lodge, director of the Illinois State Conservation Department, was designated as the state's liaison officer to work with the NPS in developing such a plan, yet, as Fabian explained, "The State . . . has not yet communicated to the National Park Service anything to indicate that it is doing anything to make the required plan." Thus, while Fabian and the others knew "The funds of the National Park Service will probably be substantial," they also understood that "the State of Illinois will have to act before any part of the money apportioned . . . may ultimately be made available to projects such as Nauvoo Restoration."[111]

Although NRI's access to NHPA funds depended primarily on factors outside its direct control, the trustees actively solicited the cooperation of state and federal officials in the affair. On the one hand, Kennedy committed to "follow up this subject" with the governor of Illinois and other state officials with whom he was closely allied.[112] Meanwhile, Fabian, Kimball and Steven T. Baird, one of NRI's architects, visited Washington DC in March 1968 to meet with officers from the NPS and the Bureau of Outdoor Recreation. The latter was seen as another potential source of government funding for the restoration of Nauvoo, insofar as the project had recreational potential. As they met with representatives of the two agencies, Fabian and Kimball presented NRI's plans for Nauvoo, using Baird's architectural sketches to illustrate what they hoped to accomplish. According to Fabian, "As much as could be done in Washington in one day was done to gain the assurance of both of these organizations that they will support us as far as they can." The officials, he noted, "were tremendously interested and said they would do all the law would permit them to do to help with the Nauvoo project." Astutely, Kendrew suggested the trustees write a letter to the men with whom Fabian, Kimball, and Baird met, expressing appreciation for their warm reception of NRI's representatives and asking them "to please summarize in writing their advice to the Nauvoo Restoration Board as to how to best proceed to qualify for participation of federal government in the project."[113]

A month after returning from the nation's capital Fabian reported to the First Presidency of the LDS Church, informing them that "the representatives of the federal agencies said that they will help us," adding, "Their help will not only give prestige to our project, but will give financial help in the historic restoration." Fabian also read a letter from Harthon L. Bill, deputy director of the NPS, who, in reply to the trustees' former letter, "expressed his satisfaction in meeting Dr. Kimball, Mr. Baird, and Mr. Fabian and his willingness to assist in what Nauvoo Restoration, Inc. is doing."[114] The evident endorsement of important government officials reassured the trustees that the restoration project was a legitimate and worthwhile endeavor. Equally important, however, it engendered the enduring support of the First Presidency, which continued to fund the project in anticipation of federal contributions.

Aside from government funds, the trustees also made plans to target various state and national foundations for financial contributions to the restoration project. Central to this effort was trustee David M. Kennedy, who, as his biographer aptly observed, "learned that no matter what area of community service he entered, he always ended up raising funds."[115] In 1966, for example, the LDS First Presidency asked him to organize and lead a fundraising drive for the Church-owned Brigham Young University. In reply, Kennedy counseled that requests for financial contributions from national foundations would have to be based on specific strengths of the university in which the foundations were interested. Otherwise, he warned, such donors would not contribute to a Church-sponsored institution.[116] This echoed what Kennedy had articulated a year earlier, when he informed the First Presidency of NRI's plans to attract donations from foundations to help support Nauvoo's restoration. In addition to approaching national foundations interested in the history and preservation of America's cultural heritage, Kennedy believed substantial capital assistance could be received from corporations "that have a vital interest in the preservation of our way of life." He assured LDS Church officials that "many of my friends are interested" in the project, but he counseled that successful fundraising would depend on keeping the historical interpretation of Nauvoo separate from any proselytizing effort of the Church. "I don't think," Kennedy warned the First Presidency, "we could get the foundations to go in on a completely Mormon project."[117] The day before he had told his fellow trustees that the restoration project "must not be denominational."[118]

Other sources of financial support were also considered, including the possibility of inviting contributions from descendants of the Mormon pioneers whose homes and shops were targeted for restoration or reconstruction. The obvious prototype for this kind of donation was J. LeRoy Kimball himself, who personally financed the restoration of his great-grandfather's

Nauvoo home. It was believed that other individuals or groups of descendants would likewise willingly contribute funds to support work on their ancestors' properties. Beyond literal descendants, however, the trustees also considered inviting entire Mormon congregations to sponsor the restoration or reconstruction of a Nauvoo structure, believing that even those not directly related to a Nauvoo pioneer would still manifest a feeling of shared heritage in the Nauvoo past. Such a proposal was not without precedent, as Mormon congregations at this time were responsible for helping finance the construction of the meetinghouses in which they worshipped. Even though the estimated total cost of restoring or reconstructing a Nauvoo building was between $75,000 and $90,000 per structure, Delbert L. Stapley, one of the LDS Church's Twelve Apostles and a close friend of Kimball who joined NRI's board of trustees in October 1967, confidently declared, "I do not think we have any problem in getting some help financially in this way."[119]

In addition to these potential sources of external funds, the trustees believed that revenues generated by the restoration itself would offset some expenses. They supposed that income from the planned visitor accommodations would help pay for the project's operating expenses. "We are very much alive to the necessity of having operating funds over a long period of time," explained Fabian to the LDS First Presidency in 1965. "To some extent," he reasoned, "it can be done from our own revenues." He added, however, "If we do not have means of doing it from our own revenues, it will have to be done through the foundations."[120] To further reassure Church leaders that costs would be kept to a minimum, the Trustees even discussed the possibility of charging admission to some of the restored homes, similar to what was being done at Colonial Williamsburg and other historic sites throughout the country. Part of an official statement approved by the board of trustees in 1969 effectively illustrates their overall vision for this aspect of the restoration.

[V]isitors will be content to stay only a few hours a day, if there is nothing for them to do but look at some restored shops and buildings. There must be motels, hotels, and dining rooms where they can stay and receive the kind of comforts and service to which they are accustomed today. There must be things for them to do that will add recreation and pleasant hours to make history and old houses welcome and instructive interludes in their time—a marina, a golf course, tennis courts, music and so forth, if we want them to stay long enough to absorb the story of Nauvoo and to take home with them that story, associated with pleasant memories of their stay here. A visit of several days or so will add much to the net operating revenue to be expected from the facilities to be provided.[121]

In general, the trustees believed that financial contributions from outside donors, coupled with revenues generated by services provided by the restoration, would result in a self-sustaining operation. Trustees Marriott and Kennedy, however, the two men with the most experience in business, knew that such a belief was naïve and overly optimistic. They understood that a venture as ambitious as that proposed by NRI would be costly, and they were apparently concerned that Kimball and others were misleading the LDS Church hierarchy in claiming the project could be self-financing. As Kennedy later recounted,

*Bill Marriott and I came out of one of these meetings [with the First Presidency] very much disturbed, because we could see that this [*NRI*'s financial estimation] was just showing the tip of the iceberg and that there would be a tremendous amount of additional costs as you go along, and operating expenses forever almost, because none of the restorations make money. They're not for that purpose, even where they charge admission. . . . So . . . we sat down and made up a budget for five to ten years, just out of our heads, knowing full well that it was not a final, accurate reading. But it was within the realm of reason.*[122]

It is not clear how much money the two men really thought the project would cost, but they wanted the First Presidency to see that the proposed restoration would require substantially more financial support than the small annual appropriations the LDS Church had been providing. They took their estimate back to Hugh B. Brown of the First Presidency, wanting to fully disclose their opinion concerning the financial aspects of the restoration project. However, in spite of their concern, Brown informed the two men that President McKay was already thinking about the long-term financial obligations of the proposed project. In fact, after the meeting with NRI's board of trustees, McKay allegedly announced to Brown and the others members of the First Presidency, "Brethren, we must understand that we're undertaking something that will be beyond our lifetimes, and we're committing our successors for the future, and so we want to be very careful and sure of what we are doing."[123]

It was fortunate that President McKay understood the potential long-term financial commitment involved in the restoration of Nauvoo because in the end, the LDS Church financed most of the restoration project itself. The outside sources of financial support the trustees were depending on never materialized. For example, diligent efforts notwithstanding, NRI never received federal funds under the NHPA. The State of Illinois finally submitted a preservation plan in 1970, and some of Nauvoo's historic structures were included in the plan's "Inventory of Architecturally and Historically Significant Sites." However, actual restoration work in Nauvoo was not a part of the plan's application for federal funds. Instead, for the first five years of eligibility (1970–75), state officials submitted annual work programs almost exclusively devoted to surveying—not acquiring or developing—the historic resources of the state. By the time these statewide surveys were completed in 1975, changes in the operation and management of NRI had effectively terminated all efforts to secure government funds for the restoration project. Consequently, the restoration of Nauvoo was never able to benefit from the federal grants made available by the NHPA.[124]

In reality, however, the belief that federal aid would significantly offset some of the project's expenses was unrealistic, for even if the Nauvoo project had been included in the state's plan, the funds available to NRI through the NHPA would have never amounted to more than a fraction of the total cost of the ambitious restoration program. After all, the funds appropriated to the NPS under the NHPA—only $10 million in 1970—had to satisfy the preservation needs of the entire country. This meant that only relatively small amounts of money were available to each state requesting such funds every year. Thus, whereas NRI needed millions of dollars to achieve its grandiose plans, the State of Illinois was only capable of awarding grants of approximately $20,000 at this time,[125] an amount that would have covered only a fourth of the estimated cost of restoring a single structure at Nauvoo. Even if NRI had had the opportunity to receive federal aid under the NHPA, it is highly unlikely such funds would have been available in sufficient amounts to contribute significantly to the planned development of the restoration program.

The trustees experienced similar frustrations in their plans to attract financial contributions from various foundations. In reality, there is no evidence that this component of their fundraising campaign ever got off the ground. President McKay enthusiastically supported the idea of seeking outside contributions from foundations when Kennedy and the rest of the board first presented the notion in 1965.[126] In fact, following their meeting the LDS First Presidency issued a letter approving Kennedy's recommendation "[t]hat arrangements be made for a proper approach to financial foundations, the Governor of Illinois and certain other individuals and corporations, for the purpose of securing financial assistance for the development and maintenance of the Nauvoo project."[127] Despite having the First Presidency's full approval, this was apparently the last time the issue was seriously discussed by the board of the trustees. Part of the reason why these efforts never got under way is because Kennedy was an extremely busy man and, frankly, did not have the time to organize a massive fundraising campaign. In this light, Kennedy told his fellow trustees, "The general manager will be helpful in carrying this work forward. He should be a man of experience in meeting and negotiating with the effective people whose contributions are sought."[128]

Yet a general manager for the restoration was never hired, leaving the responsibility of fundraising in limbo.

Another possible factor in why these efforts disintegrated may relate to concerns over the interpretation of the restored site. Kennedy knew foundations would donate to the project, but only if it was presented as an authentic historical restoration. Thus, it is possible that NRI was ultimately unsuccessful in convincing foundations, corporations, and other potential donors that the restoration project was a legitimate venture. After all, the NPS had earlier refused to donate funds directly to NRI on grounds that it was too closely affiliated with the LDS Church. Regardless of the reasons why, however, it is clear the trustees' plans to attract financial contributions from foundations and similar sources of funding were never fulfilled, leaving the majority of the financial burden for the restoration with the LDS Church itself.

For the most part, plans to secure donations from descendant groups and LDS congregations went equally unfulfilled. Despite representatives approaching a number of families whose ancestors lived in Nauvoo, actual donations resulting from these efforts were relatively minimal. Apostle and trustee Delbert L. Stapley optimistically reported in 1970 that "representatives of the Browning and Pratt families, and the Driggs brothers in Arizona have been approached," but the reality was that only one substantial donation, a contribution of nearly $5,000, had been given to NRI prior to this time.[129] The only other documented donation came from descendants of Jonathon Browning, the Nauvoo gun maker, whose son, John Moses Browning, took over his father's gunsmithing business and established himself as one of the world's greatest inventors of firearms. In response to NRI's request, John V. Browning, John Moses's grandson and president of the Browning Arms Company, authorized a donation of more than $30,000 in cash, stock certificates, and vintage firearms on behalf of the Browning family in 1973. Although generous, the donation was not nearly enough to finance the restoration of the Jonathon Browning Home and Gun Shop in Nauvoo. Therefore, the donated funds were used to landscape the historic Browning property, while the firearms became part of a gun exhibit on display inside the restored home.[130] With the exception of these two donations, there is no record of other descendant groups contributing additional financial support to the restoration project. Furthermore, there is no evidence that Stapley's proposal that LDS congregations sponsor the restoration of particular Nauvoo structures was ever realized. This is most likely because, as Stapley recognized, "Doing this will be dependent upon approval of the First Presidency," which apparently was never given.[131]

The final way in which the trustees planned to offset some of the restoration project's expenses was to use revenues generated by the restoration itself. The project never produced the substantial revenues envisioned by the trustees because the facilities they hoped would produce profits were never constructed. The plan was for NRI to build the proposed visitor facilities and then lease these to companies like the Marriott organization and the Fred Harvey Company, both of which expressed interest in managing visitor accommodations at Nauvoo. This would allow NRI to retain ownership and control over the physical facilities themselves and at the same time encourage the involvement of interested parties by removing the otherwise forbidding obstacle of having to invest large sums of money in the construction of new facilities. Yet the proposed motel, golf course, and marina were never developed, primarily because NRI did not have the financial resources with which to construct such amenities.

Without financial aid in the form of federal funds or contributions from foundations and descendants, NRI's budget was restricted to whatever funds the LDS First Presidency was willing to allocate. In this sense, the restoration of Nauvoo was predominantly a Church-sponsored project, even though it was not necessarily intended to be such. Nonetheless, the LDS Church ultimately invested millions of dollars in the project, a fact that brought criticisms from some within the Church. T. Edgar Lyon, NRI's historian for many years, noted that the magnitude of the Church's investment in Nauvoo "makes people who are paying tithing and are poor feel, 'If they can throw money around like this, they don't need my tithing, they don't need my offerings.'"[132] A. Hamer Reiser also observed that some people thought the Church had invested too much in Nauvoo. Although sympathetic to this concern, Reiser understood that "if you develop a project like that, it's going to cost money." Besides, he argued, "I think the Brethren at the beginning knew it was going to cost money."[133]

Secular Support

Even if NRI was unsuccessful in garnering financial assistance from outside sources, it benefited greatly from positive relations with several local and national groups that otherwise supported the restoration project. As was the case with Kendrew and Colonial Williamsburg, many of those supporting

NRI and its plans were introduced to the restoration project through their associations with one or more of NRI's trustees. For example, it was through a relationship with Harold Fabian, NRI's vice president, that Conrad L. Wirth, director of the NPS from 1951 to 1964, and his successor George B. Hartzog Jr., director until 1972, became involved with the restoration of Nauvoo. It helped too that both men served under Stewart L. Udall, secretary of the interior from 1961 to 1969 and a member of the LDS Church. Thus, there were reasons from both above and below for the NPS to take interest in and express support for the restoration project.

Both Wirth and Hartzog actively participated in the restoration project during its early years, visiting Nauvoo on a number of occasions and attending meetings of the board of trustees when possible. Consequently, NRI benefited from the cooperation and support of the NPS throughout the restoration project's first decade. In addition to helping the project get started by awarding NRI's historian a $15,000 grant for historical research in 1962, the NPS was instrumental in working with other federal officials to plan the route of a major scenic parkway in a way that would serve the restoration project's interests. As planned by the NPS, the "Great River Road" was to run along both sides of the Mississippi River from the Gulf of Mexico to Canada, with each state constructing the section of the road that passed through its boundaries. Although the Illinois section of the road (Route 96 today) was not completed for many years, NRI officials were pleased that the NPS helped plan its route so that it passed through Nauvoo. "When the Great River Road is opened," exclaimed Kimball in 1964, "it will bring hundreds of thousands of tourists into the area, and the Nauvoo project will be one of the [parkway's] important attractions."[134] By assisting with the restoration of Nauvoo, the NPS was supporting what it believed was a worthwhile effort designed to interpret to the American public an important chapter in the nation's history. The involvement of the NPS bolstered NRI's confidence and national reputation and was influential in shaping the interpretive course of the project.

NRI found similar support at the state level with the help of trustee Kennedy. As chairman of the board of Chicago's most successful bank, Kennedy regularly interacted with powerful and influential people in the state of Illinois, including Governor Otto Kerner Jr. Recognizing the influence Kerner had on affairs in the state, Kennedy and the other trustees went out of their way to court the governor's favor. Indeed, as the restoration project got under way, NRI officials hosted the governor at a special luncheon in Nauvoo, during which they introduced him and other state officials to their plans to restore the city. Overall Kerner was receptive to the planned restoration, especially because he believed it would increase tourism in the state. "This is a great work you are doing here," he declared. "Tourism is going to grow in Illinois, and restored Nauvoo has a rightful place in the tourism picture."[135] To encourage the tourism potential of Nauvoo, Governor Kerner worked with different state agencies to promote the city to the public. In the fall of 1962, for example, he was in Nauvoo to dedicate a new historical marker, the first in a statewide series of highway signs designated "Highways to History in Illinois."[136] Kerner also offered NRI the assistance of the Illinois State Tourist Council to help advertise the restoration project. One result of this cooperative effort was the creation of a new color brochure promoting Nauvoo and its historical contributions to the nation. The Illinois State Tourist Council financed the printing of 50,000 copies of the new brochure at a cost of more than $6,500.[137] The governor also volunteered the services of the State Engineering Department and the State Bureau of Waterways to assist with the proposed, yet ultimately unfulfilled, development of a Nauvoo marina on the Mississippi River.[138] Beyond actual financial or logistical assistance, however, Governor Kerner's greatest contribution may have been the added credibility and publicity bestowed on the restoration project as a result of his involvement. Even though his support and assistance hinged primarily on his perception of Nauvoo's potential tourism benefits to the state of Illinois, his association with NRI, like that of the NPS, helped solidify the restoration project's reputation as a legitimate affair.

Having secured the backing of the NPS and the governor of Illinois, it is not surprising that NRI also had the support of the local government. Both the mayor and the City Council of Nauvoo willingly cooperated with the restoration project. At NRI's suggestion, the City Planning Commission hired the firm of Harland Bartholomew and Associates, the same group that laid out plans for Colonial Williamsburg, to conduct a study of Nauvoo's traffic, utilities, and zoning, the results of which greatly accommodated NRI's restoration plans and needs. Similarly, in accord with NRI's requests, the City Council enacted zoning ordinances in Nauvoo that protected the restoration project's interests. Overall, the city government willfully cooperated with NRI's plans to restore Nauvoo, even though not all residents were eager to have their town converted into a major tourist attraction. This is largely attributable to the personable and diplomatic skills of J. LeRoy Kimball and other employees of NRI, who won the confidence and support of the local citizenry. It also reflects, however, that NRI's relative wealth and power, combined with the encouragement and support of both the federal and state governments, left city officials with little choice but to align themselves with the restoration project.[139]

With cooperation from all levels of government, the restoration project progressed relatively undeterred throughout its first decade. Much of the work during the first several years was devoted to planning and conducting preliminary studies of the various historic structures. However, by 1970 NRI had either completed or nearly completed the restoration or reconstruction of nine Nauvoo buildings, and there was serious discussion about beginning a partial reconstruction of the Nauvoo Temple in the near future.[140] The number of visitors to Nauvoo increased proportionately with the number of structures completed during these early years.

A Visitors' Center for Nauvoo

The capstone of this early work was the 1969 announcement that a new visitors' center would be constructed in Nauvoo to help accommodate the ever-growing number of tourists to the restored city. Although not the first visitors' center to be constructed at an LDS historic site, the new center was seen as "one of the major steps in making historic Nauvoo a noted tourist mecca."[141] Given its ties to the NPS, NRI's plans were also undoubtedly influenced by the successful Mission 66 campaign, completed only three years earlier, in which the NPS constructed a number of new visitors' centers throughout the country's national parks.[142] The two-story center in Nauvoo, 155 feet square, was to be built on a sixteen-acre parcel of land north of the major restoration area but still within the historic flats. At an estimated cost approaching $1 million, the visitors' center was to be constructed in red brick reminiscent of the other historic structures in the city and was designed to house two theaters, a large library, a lecture hall, lounges, and administrative offices.[143]

Revealing of the associations they maintained with officials from all levels of government were the prominent men who participated in the groundbreaking ceremony on May 24, 1969. In addition to members of the LDS Church hierarchy, the speakers included two LDS members of President Richard M. Nixon's cabinet—NRI trustee David M. Kennedy, secretary of the treasury, and George Romney, secretary of housing and urban development. Also in attendance was R. C. Yager, mayor of Nauvoo, and George B. Hartzog Jr., director of the NPS. The latter, in his remarks to the nearly 2,000 people gathered for the ceremony, indicated that "no strand of American history was more colorful than the westward movement of the Mormon people of Nauvoo," and petitioned the crowd to "become part of preserving and developing America." Trustee Fabian echoed these comments with remarks of his own. "This saga of American history," he declared, "must be restored because it is an important part of the westward movement." "What we are doing here," he promised, "will put a spark of life back into Nauvoo."[144]

Seeds of Conflict

With nearly a decade of successful work behind them and grandiose plans laid for the future, NRI's trustees were enthusiastically optimistic at the dawn of the 1970s. Not only did they have the financial and moral support of LDS Church president McKay and others in the Church hierarchy, they also enjoyed the encouragement and advice of prominent national figures and organizations. Even if the latter could not assist financially in the project, their endorsements of Nauvoo and their recognition of its national historical significance lent NRI the credence and reputation it needed to successfully carry out its restoration mission. Indeed, Nauvoo's designation as a National Historic Landmark in 1961 was a major impetus not only in securing the financial and ideological commitment of the LDS Church but also in garnering the support of other secular institutions and organizations at the federal, state, and local levels.

By defining Nauvoo's significance in terms of its role in the westward expansion of the United States, the National Historic Landmark designation was also instrumental in shaping the way the restored city was interpreted to visitors. The only problem, however, was that for many Latter-day Saints, Nauvoo was more than just an important place in American history; it was also a place of great spiritual significance—sacred ground on which the prophet Joseph Smith and others lived, worked, worshipped, and died.

Thus, although the 1960s were a time of great success and progress for NRI's restoration of Nauvoo, seeds of interpretive conflict had been sown and were about to sprout as a new decade began. One LDS author, writing in 1970, unknowingly captured the looming interpretive dichotomy, the resolution of which would significantly alter the course of the restoration project. After reviewing NRI's accomplishments over the last decade, the author closed his article with the following observations.

In a country famous for its Jamestown and Williamsburg . . . the city of Nauvoo, Illinois, is acclaimed by scholars and historians as another "monumental effort to recreate the lessons of the past." Why? In the words of the National . . . Park Service: "Among the forces which aided in the winning of the great West, the Mormon migration and settlement in the Great Basin stood out as one of the most positive factors in carrying American civilization to the intermountain and Pacific coastal areas. . . . Nauvoo will be commemorated as a point from which this great westward migration commenced." The site is a "place of exceptional value in our national history."

Then, foreshadowing the interpretive conflict that would soon grip NRI, he concluded: "Add to this the value to the Latter-day Saint of deeply imbedding within his mind and spirit the fabric of the life and times of Joseph Smith and one quickly sees why tourists and visitors are again turning their eyes toward Nauvoo."[145]

Chapter 3

Interpretive Conflict at Nauvoo

It is highly unlikely that the restoration project would have enjoyed broad support at federal, state, and local levels had NRI not promoted Nauvoo as a place of significance to American history. The decision to interpret Nauvoo in this way, however, was not universally self-evident to those involved in the restoration project. In fact, from the beginning there existed two interpretive poles that anchored either end of an interpretive spectrum, which was constantly being negotiated by those interested in Nauvoo's interpretation. On the one hand, there was an effort to place Nauvoo in a strictly secular context, emphasizing its historical significance to America's past. On the other, there was a desire to interpret the story of Nauvoo in terms of its religious significance to the LDS Church. Although both the secular and the religious interpretations were present to some degree in all of NRI's deliberations, each was emphasized over the other during different periods of the corporation's history. Understanding the ways in which the interpretation of Nauvoo changed during this time is key to understanding major events in NRI's later years.

Nauvoo: A Base of Westward Expansion

The chief proponent of the secular approach to Nauvoo's interpretation was the National Park Service. The NPS had been interested in Nauvoo since at least the late 1930s. Although Nauvoo's role in the westward expansion of America was recognized at this time, it was not until the late 1950s that this interpretation of the city gained momentum as a result of contemporary developments within the NPS. Particularly significant was the Mission 66 program, which sought to renovate the outdated and overtaxed facilities of the national parks in the wake of increased tourism following the Second World War. Among the national parks that benefited from this surge of activity was the Jefferson National Expansion Memorial in St. Louis, where NPS officials revived their plans to commemorate and interpret America's westward expansion during the first half of the nineteenth century. Central to these plans was the construction of the Gateway Arch—conceived as a monument to westward expansion—and a modern interpretive facility where this chapter of the nation's history could be explained to the public.[1]

It was a logical extension of this renewed emphasis on national parks and the concurrent resurgence of interest in the nation's westward expansion for the NPS to support and encourage the restoration of Nauvoo. From this perspective Nauvoo, like St. Louis, possessed exceptional value in commemorating and illustrating this episode of American history.

Indeed, Nauvoo was the origin of the Mormon Trail, which, together with the Oregon, Santa Fe, and Overland trails, represented what the NPS proclaimed to be the major contributing factors in the country's westward expansion. Furthermore, as Conrad Wirth, director of the NPS, remarked in 1962, Nauvoo was unique because "The old historic beginning of the migration from St. Louis . . . is gone but here you have left actually many of the old buildings that existed at the time of the starting West."[2] For all of these reasons, the NPS designated Nauvoo a National Historic Landmark in January 1961. In so doing, NPS sanctioned and helped cement the secular interpretation of Nauvoo's significance in the public mind.

Nauvoo: A Monument to Mormon History

Although some leaders of the LDS Church advanced this kind of secular interpretation of Nauvoo in the late 1930s,[3] there was strong precedent within the Church to provide a religious interpretation of Nauvoo by the time NRI was organized some twenty years later. Beginning in the early twentieth century, the LDS Church stationed missionaries at some of its historic sites, with the assignment to interpret the significance of these places in light of the Church's history and doctrine. In this interpretive framework, the historic sites became monuments to important religious figures and events. Nauvoo was no exception. In fact, in the years preceding and immediately following the organization of NRI, the Church operated an information bureau on a portion of the Nauvoo Temple lot, where missionaries interpreted the religious significance of the city, its people, and its structures to visitors. In this perspective, Nauvoo was a testament to the prophet Joseph Smith and his followers, a grand monument to "a glorious era in Church history."[4]

Shared Attributes

Although seemingly at odds, the religious and secular interpretations of Nauvoo shared some similarities. Both approaches, for example, emphasized the inspirational character of the Nauvoo pioneers. In explaining Nauvoo's contribution to American history, the secular interpretation idealized the exemplary attributes and qualities of the men and women who made the overland migrations, just as the religious interpretation romanticized these same attributes in light of the pioneers' contributions to the history of the LDS Church. Even though the interpretive message regarding the lasting contributions of these men and women differed, both interpretations touted the exemplary and inspirational character of the men and women of Nauvoo. For the one, these attributes and qualities were exemplary of American character and identity—what all true Americans should possess—while for the other, the same characteristics were held up as exemplary of Mormon identity—what every good Latter-day Saint should seek to obtain.

Embedded in this celebration of pioneer character is a Romantic sense of manifest destiny that functioned to solidify group identity, both American and LDS.[5] Still comfortably within the glow of victory in the Second World War, it was all too easy for patriots in the 1950s and 1960s to boast of America's greatness as a nation while uncritically imposing self-aggrandizing interpretations on the country's past. In this celebratory framework, the westward expansion of the nation, of which Nauvoo was a key part, was viewed as yet another example of American supremacy. That is, just as America had triumphed over the Axis powers, so too it had conquered the western reaches of its continent nearly a century earlier. Further, the ideals, values, and principles forged in that process—the courage, determination, hard work, and endurance needed to confront and subdue the western frontier—were believed to be the very same qualities that led the country to victory in the Second World War and what would ensure the success and continued greatness of the nation in the future. National Park Service director Conrad Wirth represented this perspective well when speaking at Nauvoo in 1962: "We think that to tell our children something of the hardship of our forebearers in developing this great land for them is worthwhile and they should know it, and they must know it if this nation is going to be a better nation tomorrow."[6]

The celebration of the Nauvoo pioneers in a religious interpretative framework also reflected a Romantic sense of history that served to strengthen LDS identity in a similar way. In this light, the pioneers' accomplishments were viewed as evidence of the veracity and divinely sanctioned greatness of the LDS Church. Thus, just as the Church overcame repeated persecutions, trials, and setbacks in the nineteenth century, so it would continue to progress undaunted toward its destined glory, blessed by the faith, sacrifice, and unwavering commitment of its members.

Both the secular and the religious interpretations of Nauvoo were also motivated by efforts to proselytize. The objective in both cases was to "convert" visitors to the Romantic versions of American and Church history put forward by these interpretations and, in the process, inspire them to emulate the exemplary character of the Nauvoo pioneers in their own lives. Not surprisingly, there were compelling reasons both within and without the LDS Church to engage in this kind of proselytizing in the 1960s.

For example, the LDS Church was experiencing unprecedented success in its missionary efforts at this time, drawing tens of thousands of converts annually to the Mormon faith worldwide.[7] The desire to use Nauvoo as a missionary tool was a natural outgrowth of this expanding effort. One LDS member involved in the restoration of Nauvoo believed he and his colleagues were "helping break down prejudices," noting that "people have a different concept of the Church and its members once they have been here."[8] NRI's president, J. LeRoy Kimball, also reported with satisfaction, "There is an ever increasing number of converts who inform us that their interest in the Church was kindled through a visit here."[9] As the LDS Church's missionary effort in Nauvoo and elsewhere continued to grow, the desire to interpret the city in terms of its religious significance and use this interpretation as a platform for proselytizing grew stronger.

Outside the LDS Church, different institutions and figures had other compelling reasons to proselytize, using a secular interpretation of Nauvoo that elevated the city to national significance. The popular conception that American character and democracy were formed in the process of taming the western wilderness was not unique to postwar America. Similar beliefs were held by Thomas Jefferson and partly motivated the Louisiana Purchase. The idea was also at the root of historian Frederick Jackson Turner's "frontier thesis," which dominated the interpretation of western history throughout the first half of the twentieth century.[10] Although some scholars began to question these ideas in the years following the Second World War, they continued to be promoted by government and other patriotic institutions, especially in the context of the cold war struggle against communism and during the Korean and Vietnam Wars.

Take, for example, the sentiments articulated by the governor of Illinois, Otto Kerner, at a special Nauvoo luncheon in 1964. Speaking of a need to "convert" America's younger generation to the nation's fundamental principles, the governor expressed a concern that "so many of your young people have become so super-sophisticated that, frankly, I think they have lost the old ideas, the old philosophies on which our nation was built." "This is why," he continued, "I like to see Williamsburgs, New Salems and Nauvoos restored, so that many of these young people . . . will learn that our freedoms and our nation was built with sweat and blood, that our freedom was not just handed to us." In this perspective, Nauvoo was a place where individuals could be indoctrinated with this particular interpretation of American history at a time when such ideas were perceived to be under threat.

Officials from Colonial Williamsburg were also supportive of this approach to historic site interpretation.[11] Indeed, Colonial Williamsburg's sponsor, John D. Rockefeller Jr., was explicit in his belief that, in addition to interpreting Williamsburg's historical significance, the great value of the restored city was "the lesson that it teaches of the patriotism, high purpose, and unselfish devotion of our forefathers to the common good."[12] A. Edwin Kendrew, senior vice president of Colonial Williamsburg and official trustee of NRI, not only openly sanctioned this approach at Colonial Williamsburg but carried it with him to Nauvoo as well. On one occasion in 1965, reflecting the cold war suspicions held by many Americans at this time, Kendrew expressed his point of view regarding the proselytizing potential of both Colonial Williamsburg and Nauvoo. "We feel," he said, "that Williamsburg can contribute a good deal to combat the isms creeping into our world by reminding people of the principles of the spirit of self government and the respect for man and the right to vote. We think in Nauvoo we have another great opportunity. We have an opportunity to portray an epic in American history more and more important as time goes on."[13]

Six years later, amid the backlash of sentiments over America's involvement in Vietnam, he elaborated on this perspective:

> *[M]y heart is in this project of the restoration of Nauvoo largely because I am so interested in preserving many segments and worthy examples of our American heritage. I think it is important to the future of America that we do have places where people can go away from the distractions of the Twentieth Century and hear about early America and its past and gain inspiration from the lives and culture of the people of the eras represented and especially away from the dissenters and revolutionaries, whether peaceful or violent, who try to tear down our principles. That is why I have been so interested in having Nauvoo become a national shrine.*[14]

Thus, both the religious and secular interpretations of Nauvoo used the city and its history as a tool for proselytizing. Whereas the religious interpretation was aimed at promoting

Mormon beliefs, values, and doctrines, the secular approach focused on advancing patriotic values and principles. In both cases, the objective was twofold: to reaffirm the beliefs and sentiments of those visitors who already subscribed to the ideas being promoted while educating and convincing those not already "of the faith" of the goodness and correctness of these ideas. In this way, regardless of which interpretative approach was in use, Nauvoo was at once conceived as a shrine, either to America or the LDS Church, and a stage from which the ideals being enshrined could be disseminated.

Walking an Interpretive Tightrope

Although not mutually exclusive or diametrically opposed, the religious and secular interpretations of Nauvoo's significance were being negotiated even before NRI was officially organized. As early as 1961, when J. LeRoy Kimball and Harold P. Fabian combined efforts to create their proposed "Outline for the Restoration of Nauvoo," aspects of both interpretations were evident. According to these men, the principal purpose of restoring Nauvoo was

> *(1) To restore the Mormon Temple at Nauvoo as a shrine to those whose perseverance and faith built it, and to establish and re-dedicate it as a present day place of religious worship; (2) to provide an historically authentic physical environment for awakening a public interest in, and an understanding and appreciation of, the story of Nauvoo and the mass migration of its people to the valley of the Great Salt Lake; and (3) to dramatize the interpretation of that story, not only as a great example of pioneering courage and religious zeal, but also as one of the vital forces in the expansion of America westward from the Mississippi River.*[15]

The desire to interpret the story of Nauvoo to promote both religious and secular ideals is clearly illustrated in this initial mission statement. On the one hand, there is the specific intention to restore the Nauvoo Temple as a religious shrine to the faithful and diligent Nauvoo pioneers. On the other hand, there is the emphasis on the pioneering courage and religious zeal as reflected in the westward migration of these individuals. Tying these together is the desire to promote Nauvoo's story so the public will understand and appreciate the city's significance.

In many ways, this statement can be seen as an interpretive compromise between its two authors. Kimball, like most Latter-day Saints, was inclined to view Nauvoo's significance primarily in religious terms and in light of its place in the Church's history. The explicit call to restore the Nauvoo Temple no doubt originated in this perspective. Fabian, on the other hand, championed the secular interpretation, in which Nauvoo's role in the westward expansion of America was emphasized. Significantly, Fabian was a member of the NPS Advisory Board on National Parks, Historic Sites, Buildings, and Monuments when he helped draft the "Outline for the Restoration of Nauvoo." As a member of the advisory board, he directly interacted with high-level officials of the NPS for a number of years and learned of the agency's larger goals and plans to interpret the westward expansion of America at this time. This privileged knowledge both shaped Fabian's personal views of Nauvoo's historical significance and allowed him to promote the restoration project in a way that agreed with the preexisting interests and objectives of the NPS. Indeed, in subsequent years he repeatedly reaffirmed what NPS historians had written about Nauvoo—that it was the launching point of "one of the most dramatic events in the history of American westward expansion."[16] Significantly, it was this interpretation of Nauvoo's significance that ultimately inspired much of NRI's work throughout the 1960s and became the basis on which the restoration project was sold to influential supporters both within and outside the LDS Church.

In the beginning, perhaps no person was more important to persuade than LDS Church president David O. McKay. Given their preexisting positive relationship and McKay's knowledge of Fabian's experience and expertise in historic preservation, it was logical for the president to solicit and respect Fabian's opinion of Nauvoo. However, as head of the LDS Church, McKay was also alert to the longstanding tradition of proselytizing at the Church's historic sites, not to mention the pressures coming from those who believed Nauvoo had to be used as a missionary proselytizing tool in order to justify the vast amounts of the Church's money being expended on the restoration project.[17] Consequently, Fabian repeatedly affirmed to President McKay the necessity of maintaining a secular historical interpretation in Nauvoo. As early as 1961, when McKay asked him to visit Nauvoo and assess its potential, Fabian returned to Salt Lake City and reported:

President McKay, I think not only that you should restore Nauvoo, but I think it is an obligation on the part of your people to themselves and to their forebearers and to the people of America that Nauvoo be restored and that its cultural contribution and its history to the development of the United States and to the development of the American character be perpetually made of record in its restoration. But . . . If you undertake to restore it as a religious restoration, as a proselyting institution to get members to your church, it will not be received generally and will not have the approval of the nation. But if you will restore it as an historic restoration it must be based on all of the best things that your church has to offer and has had to offer in history and must give you all of the benefits and standing which you would not get if you tried to restore it as a religious restoration.[18]

Coupled with the formal designation of Nauvoo as a National Historical Landmark, Fabian's rousing endorsement was apparently enough to convince President McKay to move forward as Fabian proposed. After all, it must have been satisfying to know that expert non-Mormons thought so highly of a place that held great significance for the Church. Thus, in the months that followed, McKay and his counselors sanctioned the official organization of NRI and endorsed its explicit secular interpretive agenda. Indeed, at the press conference in which NRI's organization was announced, McKay was quoted as saying, "the full purpose of restoring Nauvoo is to perpetuate in history the part played by the Mormon Pioneers in the building of the west."[19]

The approval of the Church's president, together with the support of the NPS, gave Fabian, Kimball, and the rest of NRI's board of trustees confidence to move forward with the secular approach to Nauvoo's interpretation. Revealingly, the statement of purpose officially recorded in NRI's articles of incorporation was stripped of any reference to the earlier proposed restoration of the Nauvoo Temple.[20] Furthermore, by May 1964, NRI's board of trustees had adopted a new statement of purpose, one that fully reflected the secular interpretive agenda. According to the new statement, Nauvoo's significance lay in its potential to illustrate two related themes: (1) the westward expansion of America in the last half of the nineteenth century and (2) the exemplary character of those individuals who made the overland migrations. Thus, the corporation's purpose was limned as the following:

> *To restore the historically important part of the old town of Nauvoo as it was when it flourished under Mormon leadership, during the period 1839–1846, as an authentic physical environment for interpreting the story of Nauvoo and the mass migration of its people to the Valley of the Great Salt Lake, as one of the vibrant forces in the westward expansion of America; and to give an understanding of the character of those people as shown by the homes they built and the way they lived, and an understanding of the depth of their emotions and the strength of their faith that made them abandon their temple, their homes, and their city, and start on their long trek westward.*[21]

Although this interpretive approach included no formal religious component, there was still an expectation among the LDS Church hierarchy that Nauvoo would be used as a missionary tool. Given the longstanding practice of proselytizing at the Church's historic sites and the fact that Church funds were being expended on the restoration project, there remained a strong desire to seek out converts among the visitors to Nauvoo. To respond to this undercurrent of missionary zeal and otherwise promote the restoration project, NRI's trustees hosted a special dinner meeting in 1965, to which they invited most of the General Authorities of the LDS Church and during which the trustees shared their vision of the role Nauvoo would play in the Church's proselytizing efforts.

Kimball offered the opening remarks and addressed the question, why restore Nauvoo? In addition to its religious significance as "a monument to the Prophet [Joseph Smith]" and the location of so many LDS "ancestral homes," Kimball suggested the restoration project was justified because of "the tremendous historical importance of Nauvoo." Echoing the secular interpretation espoused by Fabian and drawing on the clout of the NPS, Kimball established Nauvoo's significance to the westward expansion of America as another reason for the restoration project. "I don't think," he asserted, "that there is a place in the United States . . . which exemplifies the westward development as does Nauvoo, and it was only a short time ago that the National Parks System designated Nauvoo as one of the most important points in relation to westward expansion, and thought that it should be restored."[22]

The "missionary possibility" of Nauvoo was a final consideration in undertaking the restoration project, and Kimball was "sure that that comes to the mind of the brethren." In addressing this sensitive topic, Kimball referred to a statement of Fabian's that "Nauvoo, if restored as it should . . . will do what a thousand missionaries will do in bringing people there." Confident that this was the reality of the situation, Kimball assured the LDS Church authorities that Nauvoo would be a "great instrument of missionary work."[23]

Later in the meeting, trustee David M. Kennedy was invited to speak about the possibility of attracting funding for the project from sources outside of the Church. In this context, he further clarified NRI's position on Nauvoo's role in the Church's missionary effort, noting that it would be difficult, if not impossible, to convince foundations and other donors to contribute to a project that was not historical in nature. Contrasting the Church's traditional method of proselytizing at historic sites with what he thought must be done at Nauvoo to ensure successful fundraising, he said,

I do not think we could have it [Nauvoo] just as a Mormon Church operation and do it in our way of having the Information Center there and the missionary function right on the premises. I think that the story speaks for itself . . . and I think that it would get the interest and the enthusiasm that would generate enough . . . interest on the part of a person, to answer the golden question if they would like to know more. And I think the missionary work would then have to be done, as it probably should be done, by the full-time missionaries or stake missionaries through the referral system which would come from that. And I think there would be no problem in that.[24]

Although Kennedy was speaking strictly in terms of fundraising, his point that the missionary effort could still proceed, but only as a separate function independent of the historic restoration, was a message the trustees repeated frequently to members of the LDS Church hierarchy. In fact, because President McKay was unable to attend the special dinner meeting in which these comments were made, the trustees met with him and his counselors the following morning and delivered the same message. With respect to this meeting, Kimball said that each of the trustees individually explained "that this could not be a proselyting operation but should be handled as a historical restoration in order to retain its national stature, but that through the referral system it could result in real missionary work." The distinction was apparently satisfactory to McKay and his counselors, for after the meeting they appropriated an additional $500,000 to NRI's account and authorized the trustees to investigate obtaining funds from outside sources.[25]

The idea that Nauvoo could be interpreted in terms of its national significance yet still be a part of the LDS Church's missionary program resulted in a situation in which NRI's trustees were trying to serve two masters. Recognizing the challenge involved in this dualistic interpretive approach, one NRI employee said, "It will take the wisdom of Solomon to walk the tight-rope of historic interpretation proselyting you people back there have confronting you."[26] To facilitate the successful navigation of this interpretive tightrope, NRI implemented a new guide service in Nauvoo.

Beginning in the summer of 1964, NRI arranged for a number of married couples to come to Nauvoo and serve as interpretive tour guides for visitors. The following summer the guide program was supplemented with a number of young college students to handle the swelling number of visitors to Nauvoo. The students were mainly history majors, and most had previously completed proselytizing missions for the LDS Church. In addition to a small honorarium, the student guides received college credit for a course they were required to attend in the early mornings before their guided tours began. Dr. T. Edgar Lyon, professor of history at the University of Utah and NRI's official historian, taught the course, which was an in-depth review of the history of Nauvoo. In this course, the student guides and their married couple counterparts not only learned a great deal of historical information about the city, its people, and its structures, they were also taught about Nauvoo's significance to American history.[27]

At first, the general structure and content of the interpretive tours were left to the guides' discretion. However, as time passed it became clear that more direction was needed. For example, during the summer of 1969 one individual complained that the guides were frustrated because of the lack of structure and instruction concerning the goals and content of their tours.[28] To remedy the situation, specific "Guidelines for Interpreting Nauvoo" were created. Not surprisingly, the guidelines continued to emphasize a secular interpretation of Nauvoo, stating that the interpreter's objective was "to help the visitor feel appreciation for the people of old Nauvoo who helped build America."[29] One way in which to accomplish this, as indicated by the guidelines, was for the guide to "Radiate a spiritual quality . . . not by preaching or proselyting but rather by your appreciation of America and of the Mormons who helped build it."[30] Accompanying the guidelines was a scripted sample tour that further stressed the secular framework in which Nauvoo's significance was to be interpreted. According to the script, the guides were to introduce the restoration project to visitors with the following statement: "This is the restoration of the old Mormon Nauvoo, to show its importance in American history. The Mormon migration from Nauvoo and settlement in the Great Basin of the Rockies was one of the most important factors in carrying American culture into the Western United States."[31]

The detailed historical tour that was to follow included explicit mention of Nauvoo's designation as a National Historic Landmark and posed the rhetorical question, "Why was Nauvoo chosen as a [National] Historic Site?" The answer was reserved for the conclusion of the tour, when, after repeating the question, the script proclaimed: "The Mormons helped in the expansion of the United States into the West by settling in the Great Basin of the Rockies. The aim of Nauvoo Restoration is to help us appreciate America and the kind of people who helped build it."[32]

By thus providing concrete guidelines and scripts on which the guides could base their interpretive tours, a secular interpretation of Nauvoo became an institutionalized component of NRI's guide service. Moreover, although it remained a challenging task, the guidelines and scripts helped tour guides walk the interpretive tightrope that NRI's trustees had stretched between the religious and secular poles of interpretation. Again, the hope and assumption underlying this interpretive approach was that visitors would be inspired by the accomplishments of the Nauvoo pioneers and their historic contribution to American history. Officials of both NRI and the Church believed LDS visitors would experience renewed conviction and pride in their faith and in America as a result of visiting Nauvoo. Similarly, it was anticipated that proselytizing opportunities would emerge as non-LDS visitors, stimulated by the Nauvoo story, desired to know more about the religion that motivated the Mormon pioneers.

Not all visitors, however, appreciated the interpretive message the guides offered. In fact, some LDS visitors apparently thought the secular interpretation was either confusing or inappropriate for a Church-sponsored project. Lyon recorded that LDS visitors repeatedly asked the guides questions such as "Do you have any connection with the Church?" and "Why doesn't the Church call you on missions if the Church is sponsoring this?" Others, he reported, bluntly asked, "What is this, a sort of 'bootlegging' of the gospel?"[33] Lyon and the guides felt that increased publicity was a solution to this problem. Accordingly, Kimball and the other trustees actively solicited opportunities to promote and explain the restoration project in the various periodicals produced by the LDS Church. In an interview with an LDS Church reporter that was later published in the Church's *Improvement Era* magazine, Kimball took advantage of an opportunity to explain NRI's proselytizing philosophy. In reply to the question, "To what extent will Nauvoo be a missionary tool?" Kimball explained, "The role of the Church in restoring Nauvoo envisions a different approach to missionary work." He continued,

> *Our guide service is one that tourists will find informative, educational, and inspiring, but also one that those who do not desire a proselyting approach will find acceptable. Nauvoo will first be a historical place where people will first look and then possibly listen to the gospel message. The Church will have a center located in the city where visitors will be able to talk to missionaries, discuss doctrinal questions, and receive other information. The guides in Nauvoo are fine, educated college students, most of whom have missionary experience. They tell the historical story of Nauvoo—of the people who lived there, their beliefs, and what they did—in a fashion that is attractive to tourists. We have a referral service for those who wish to learn more about the Church. We know from past experience that a good percentage of tourists want to learn more, and many have been converted. Numerous visitors have come back again and again.*[34]

As members of the LDS Church, most of NRI's trustees tolerated this "different approach to missionary work." Vice president Fabian, however, had "no patience with the proselyting interests" of the Church in Nauvoo. In fact, A. Hamer Reiser later said that "on several occasions he [Fabian] mentioned the fact that the less we had to say about Joseph Smith the better it would be." Instead, "He felt we ought to play up Brigham Young," Reiser continued, as it was Young, not Joseph Smith, who led the trek westward.[35] Fabian's outlook is not surprising considering he was the strongest proponent of a secular interpretation of Nauvoo, not to mention he was one of only two non-LDS on NRI's board of trustees. Although he understood the religious significance of Nauvoo to the LDS Church and its members, in his opinion this was of secondary importance when contrasted with Nauvoo's value on a national scale. For Fabian, Nauvoo's significance to American history was as much a credit to the Church as were the city's religious contributions—if not more so. More than once he communicated this belief to President McKay and other LDS Church officials. On one occasion he told them, "if you are restoring Nauvoo not as a religious restoration or as a proselyting medium but as a contribution to American history, you will place before the people of America in a way that they will finally understand, the story of what your people have done and the character that the Church has developed in the people and their faith in their destiny."[36]

A. Edwin Kendrew, the only other non-LDS trustee, shared Fabian's "hope that the significance of Nauvoo as a monument to Mormon Church can be adequately presented in the history of Western America."[37] Kendrew also believed, however, that the actual restoration was significant to both the nation and the LDS Church. Contrasting the restoration of nineteenth-century Nauvoo with that of eighteenth-century Williamsburg, he expressed his view that in Nauvoo, "We think we are going to be pioneers in a new phase of American history." "We think," he continued, "if we do a faithful, honest, and careful job . . . we will have a public acceptance which will redound not only to the benefit of all Americans but something that the Mormons can be proud of." Indeed, he believed the restoration of Nauvoo, if done properly, would be "one of the greatest restoration projects of all time." This, Kendrew affirmed, together with Nauvoo's story, "will reflect great credit upon the Mormon Church."[38]

Changing of the Guard

Despite such positive and enthusiastic support from professionals like Fabian and Kendrew, the secular approach to Nauvoo's interpretation came to an abrupt end in 1971, when the First Presidency of the LDS Church drastically restructured NRI's organization. Although a secular interpretation was the primary force behind NRI's endeavors since its inception nearly a decade earlier, it was permanently replaced by a religious interpretation bent on proselytizing at this time. With the loss of a secular approach, previously supportive institutions, such as the NPS and Colonial Williamsburg, withdrew their assistance from the Nauvoo project. At the same time, whatever hope there was of attracting outside funding for the restoration project was eliminated by this major shift in interpretation. If Nauvoo's significance to American westward expansion was the highlight of the project's first decade, the city's importance to the rise and development of the LDS Church was now the primary focus of the restoration. Similarly, the project, which was previously managed by experienced professionals, was now in the hands of members of the LDS Church bureaucracy, who did not necessarily have any professional training in historic preservation or restoration.

Precipitating this significant change was the death of ninety-six-year-old President David O. McKay on January 18, 1970. Succeeding him in the presidency was Joseph Fielding Smith, age ninety-three, the most tenured member of the Quorum of the Twelve Apostles. Although Smith died two and a half years later, it was during his leadership that the restoration project in Nauvoo was drastically altered. Ironically, it was the unilateral support of McKay and his counselors that contributed to these significant changes during his successor's tenure.

As president of the LDS Church, McKay periodically exhibited an independent leadership style that had the effect of estranging some of his colleagues in the Church hierarchy. Convinced of the importance of certain Church-funded projects, there were occasions when McKay exercised his authority and made important decisions either without consulting members of the Quorum of the Twelve Apostles or in complete disregard of their dissenting opinions. In the early 1960s, for example, McKay unilaterally approved the construction of what is now the Church-owned Polynesian Cultural Center in Laie, Oahu, even though the apostles had previously rejected the proposal. In fact, it was not until some months later, when Harold B. Lee, a senior member of the Twelve Apostles, was in Hawaii and saw the construction under way that the apostles became aware of McKay's private authorization of the project.[39] At about this same time, McKay also independently approved the purchase of fifty-seven acres of land near Washington DC, on which an LDS temple was later built. When asked by his counselor, Henry D. Moyle, if the prospective purchase, which totaled more than $700,000, should be approved by those members of the Quorum of Twelve Apostles who composed the Expenditures Committee of the Church, McKay simply replied, "No, I think we had better not." Six years later, McKay authorized construction of a temple on this property, much to the disapproval of some of the apostles. Significantly, it was apostle Harold B. Lee who again particularly opposed the president's decision. Although he knew "there wasn't much that could be done about it, since it had been approved by the Presidency," Lee remarked on the similarity of the situation to that surrounding the construction of the Ogden and Provo, Utah, temples. In both cases, "the Quorum of the Twelve were merely informed that such were to be built."[40]

McKay's unilateral decision to support plans to restore Nauvoo was made at this same time and with the same effect. Indeed, one observer recalled, "President McKay set this whole thing up without consulting them. He didn't consult the president of the Council of the Twelve [Joseph Fielding Smith]. He didn't consult any of the Brethren. The first thing they knew about it was when they read the announcement in the paper. So Nauvoo Restoration has had the enmity or the antagonism of Joseph Fielding Smith to begin with and most of the men in the quorum [of the Twelve Apostles] as a result of it."[41]

Beyond the frustration engendered by McKay's failure to include him and the other apostles in decisions relating to the creation of Nauvoo Restoration, Inc., Joseph Fielding Smith disagreed with the overall purpose of the project. Between 1921 and the time he became the president of the LDS Church, Smith served as the Church's official historian, in which capacity he was well known for his "notable defense of the teachings and the doctrines of the Prophet Joseph Smith and the message of the restoration."[42] Accordingly, it is not surprising he did not subscribe to the secular interpretive approach in Nauvoo or believe it could result in positive proselytizing opportunities for the Church. In fact, one participant later said Smith's attitude was, "This isn't missionary work. This is just entertaining the gentiles."[43]

Sharing this sentiment was apostle Harold B. Lee, whom Smith asked to serve as first counselor in the First Presidency following McKay's death. Second in tenure only to Smith, Lee himself became president of the LDS Church when Smith died on July 2, 1972. In addition to his express frustrations over McKay's unilateral decision making, Lee was apparently quite upset with Fabian, who was the driving force behind the secular interpretive approach in Nauvoo. David M. Kennedy observed how Lee's dissatisfaction was especially aroused during the groundbreaking ceremony for the Nauvoo Visitors Center. Although he was asked to give the invocation, Lee was allegedly very upset with the ceremony's program, which was dominated by non-LDS individuals, who failed to recognize the religious significance of Nauvoo to the LDS Church.[44] Overall, Lee believed the Church could get more proselytizing punch for its money by investing in places other than Nauvoo. According to one observer, "When Lee came into the office [of president] he said, in essence, 'The money that's going in back there can better be spent for helping the Church in lands where they need schools and where we can make more converts as a result of it. We can do greater missionary work there than we can back there [in Nauvoo].'"[45]

Harboring such feelings, it is little surprise that Smith and Lee took measures to rein in the restoration project following McKay's death. Uncomfortable with the seemingly autonomous nature of NRI, the new First Presidency took action to resituate the corporation within the bureaucracy of the LDS Church, thereby placing it under their direct control. In a letter dated March 30, 1971, President Smith and his counselors notified J. LeRoy Kimball of the move to place NRI under the direction of the Church Information and Historic Arts Committee, headed by apostle Mark E. Petersen. "[W]ithout in any way wishing to deprecate that which you and your associates have done," the First Presidency stated, "and with a view to bringing about a closer correlation of this undertaking and other related projects," the letter went on to inform Kimball of certain procedures he was to observe. First, he was to become a member of the Church Information and Historic Arts Committee, while the other members of the board of trustees were to serve as advisers to this committee on matters relating to Nauvoo. Second, the budget of NRI was to become part of the total budget of the Church Information and Historic Arts Committee. This meant the preparation of NRI's annual budgets and the expenditure of funds would now be under the supervision and direction of this committee. It also meant NRI's accounts would now be handled through the Church's Financial Department, instead of independently, as they had been previously. Finally, the letter instructed that although projects in Nauvoo on which construction had begun should be completed, "no future projects [should] be undertaken without the endorsement of the above named committee who will bring their recommendations to the First Presidency for final approval." In this way, the new First Presidency asserted control over what its members perceived to be a precariously autonomous program.[46]

In reality, however, although NRI did enjoy a certain measure of institutional independence as a nonprofit corporation in the state of Illinois, the organization was never outside the control of the First Presidency of the LDS Church. In fact, the corporation's by-laws specifically granted the First Presidency the sole nominating power for NRI trustees. Over the course of several years, McKay and his counselors exercised this power to appoint non-LDS professionals such as Fabian and Kendrew as trustees of the corporation, but they also nominated members of the Church hierarchy, including Thorpe B. Isaacson (a third counselor in the First Presidency and a member of the Church's Historic Sites Committee) and apostle Delbert L. Stapley, to serve in this capacity. With an apostle and one of McKay's counselors on the board of trustees, the First Presidency had considerable influence and direct supervision over NRI's affairs. Given that funding for the restoration project came predominantly from LDS Church resources, they also largely controlled NRI's budget. As a result, Kimball and the other trustees had to meet repeatedly with the First Presidency to present their plans for Nauvoo and request the funds needed to execute the restoration project. Ironically, Joseph Fielding Smith was made an additional counselor in the First Presidency in late 1965, and therefore was in a position to be personally involved in decisions concerning NRI. The trouble was that McKay did not communicate much of this information to other members of the Church hierarchy, including Smith, even when the latter was officially a member of the First Presidency. Thus, although in 1970 NRI may have seemed dangerously independent to President Smith and the new First Presidency, in reality the corporation had always been within the jurisdiction of McKay and at least some of his counselors. Nevertheless, by placing NRI under the direction of the Church Information and Historic Arts Committee, Smith and his counselors established their control over the corporation and set the stage to make further changes to its operation.

This relocation of NRI to within an official LDS Church committee was consistent with the emphasis on the correlation and consolidation of Church programs that characterized the 1960s and early 1970s. At this time, "Church leaders became increasingly convinced that the varied organizations had to work harmoniously together under the direction of the priesthood . . . and that administration needed to be streamlined in order to more adequately meet the complex needs of the Saints."[47] This effort had actually begun under David O. McKay's leadership but was in large part the work of then-apostle Harold B. Lee, who, as head of the General Priesthood Committee, directed what came to be known as priesthood correlation. A major part of this effort was the formation of a churchwide coordinating council whose purpose was "to formulate policies governing the planning and operation of all Church programs."[48] Significantly, although this correlation effort was well under way before President McKay's death in 1970, he did not see fit to formally correlate NRI's work in Nauvoo with the work at other historic sites owned by the LDS Church. There were specific reasons why McKay supported the establishment of NRI as a nonprofit corporation in the state of Illinois, not the least of which was to facilitate funding from sources outside the Church. Thus, under his leadership NRI remained its own entity, separate but not totally independent from the priesthood leadership of the LDS Church. Yet when Joseph Fielding Smith came to the helm, with apostle Lee as his first counselor, NRI's work in Nauvoo was resituated within the committee responsible for the other Church-owned historic sites. This was done, as the letter from the First Presidency declared, "with a view to bringing about a closer correlation of this undertaking and other related projects."[49]

Beyond making NRI an official part of the LDS Church bureaucracy and therefore subject to their control, the new First Presidency sought to resolve the concern, expressed by both Smith and Lee, that Nauvoo was failing to meet its proselytizing potential. Unsupportive of the secular interpretive approach that had guided the restoration for nearly a decade, President Smith and his counselors moved to align the project with the proselytizing goals of the Church. The first change came in June 1970, six months into Smith's presidency, when a new mission of the LDS Church was created in Nauvoo.[50] Prior to this time, J. LeRoy Kimball was authorized to invite couples and young college students to serve as interpretive guides in Nauvoo. By creating a formal mission of the Church in Nauvoo, however, the guide system became an official function of the Church's larger missionary effort. Although Kimball was asked to serve as president of the new mission from April 1971 until April 1974, he was no longer solely in charge of selecting interpreters.[51] Instead, officials of the LDS Church now formally called full-time missionaries to serve as guides in the restored city. These missionaries were usually older LDS couples, but young missionaries who were transferred to Nauvoo from other missions in the region supplemented the work of the senior couples during the busy summer months.[52] Finally, although NRI was formerly responsible for the message and materials distributed by their guides, the interpretive materials to be disseminated by the new missionary guides were to be prepared by the Missionary Committee of the LDS Church, in collaboration with NRI's Interpretive Section.[53]

These actions were informed by the recommendations of a "Nauvoo Committee" that, at the request of President Smith and his counselors, put together a report in March 1971 outlining suggestions for future work in Nauvoo. Significantly, the three-man committee was comprised of three of the twelve apostles of the LDS Church—Mark E. Petersen, Delbert L. Stapley, and Spencer W. Kimball. Although they expressed approval of the restoration project, calling it "splendid" and "a credit to the church," and recommended that "it continue with such additional projects as shall be approved by the Brethren and financed by them," the committee suggested the project be more fully integrated with the proselytizing program of the Church. Aware of the fact that "[t]he original [restoration] program did not provide for missionary work," the three Apostles recommended "a combination of effort that will guarantee a maximum of preaching the Gospel." To achieve this blending of historic site interpretation and religious proselytizing, it was suggested that "Both [missionary] couples and younger missionaries will use the restored buildings and other historical media to introduce and teach the gospel in its principles and ordinances as they would do in other missions except the historical facts would be woven in their presentations."[54]

By creating the Nauvoo Mission and populating it with full-time missionaries who were instructed to use the historic site as a platform for proselytizing visitors, the new First Presidency took control of the interpretive program at Nauvoo, placing it squarely within the established missionary system of the LDS Church. However, conscious of the opposition of some board members to the Church's missionary efforts in Nauvoo, President Smith and his counselors decided it was necessary to reorganize NRI's personnel to fulfill their desire to "expand the purposes of this kind of enterprise [NRI], and bring into it additional activities not previously undertaken." Thus, in a letter dated May 13, 1971, the First Presidency released all the trustees from their positions as board members of Nauvoo Restoration, Inc.[55]

The following week, at the annual meeting of the board of trustees in Nauvoo, J. LeRoy Kimball broke the news. After reading the letter of March 30, in which NRI was officially incorporated into the LDS Church bureaucracy, Kimball announced the members of the new three-man board of trustees, as nominated by the First Presidency. Kimball himself retained his position as president of NRI, while apostle Delbert L. Stapley also remained in his post as a trustee. The third and final member of the new board, however, was a newcomer to the corporation—apostle Mark E. Petersen, chair of the Church Information and Historic Arts Committee, which now had stewardship over NRI. Highly symbolic of the change thus enacted, the new trustees were officially elected on the motion and second of the only two non-LDS members of the outgoing Board, A. Edwin Kendrew and Harold P. Fabian. Then, on the motion and second of apostles Stapley and Petersen, the newly released trustees—Fabian, Kendrew, Reiser, Kennedy, and Marriott—were named as Advisory Group to the corporation.[56]

Although on paper the retiring trustees maintained an advisory role and, therefore, potentially some measure of influence with NRI, the true meaning of the reorganization was evident to everyone involved. The former champions of a secular approach to the interpretation of Nauvoo had been replaced with men whose task was to interpret the city in terms of its religious significance to the LDS Church. Instead of being explained as a place of national importance, Nauvoo would now be interpreted in the same fashion as the rest of the historic sites owned by the Church. Petersen reflected this new interpretive vision when, on being elected a trustee, he explained that each of the Church's historic sites "was localized and interpreted [in] its relation to the history of the Church and that the Nauvoo Visitors Center and historic area would tell the story of the Nauvoo period."[57]

Sensing the impact this change would have on the interpretation and management of Nauvoo as a historic site, Kendrew assumed his new role as adviser and delivered some final advice to the new board. First, he stressed the importance of authenticity in historic site restoration, outlining the "essential laws for preservation that must be carefully followed in order to be accurate and right." At the same time, he admitted that "At Nauvoo we are now showing buildings which fall far below the desirable standards, and I do hope that steps will be taken soon to bring up their quality." In light of this, he expressed his additional hope "that whatever is done here [in Nauvoo] will not be undertaken lightly and that a most competent staff will be maintained to do it correctly on the basis of sound research." It was Kendrew's belief, however, that such a staff could not be found among members of the LDS Church alone. On the contrary, he thought public reaction would be tempered and improved, and a better balance would be achieved, "if you had others of different beliefs from your own Church members" involved in the restoration.[58]

In a similar vein, Kendrew expressed his opinions about NRI's program of interpretation to the new board. "I believe," he stated, "you should tell all sides of the story," meaning "the physical environment, the life of the people, and the principles of those men and what they stood for and believed, also the conditions of the times in which they lived." All of this, Kendrew contended, would provide the appropriate background for the great events that took place in Nauvoo during the 1840s. In this light, he argued, "It would be as wrong to pass over the names of Joseph Smith and his principal followers as it would be for Catholics to leave out mentioning the Pope to visitors at the Vatican."[59]

In spite of this, however, Kendrew counseled the new board "to be very careful about [a] missionary emphasis which may offend more people than you attract." Although he understood religion was an essential part of Nauvoo's history, he unequivocally shared his opinion that NRI would make "a great mistake if it lured people here on the basis of a historic site and then took the opportunity for excessive proselyting." The more appropriate and desirable alternative, as far as Kendrew was concerned, was to have "flexibility in adapting any interpretation to the varying desires of the visitors." To emphasize this point, Kendrew shared a personal story about the time he and his family were offended when visiting Salt Lake City for the first time. "We had a tight time schedule," he related, "and when we tried to leave politely, the guide said to us, 'You can't leave until I am finished telling my story to you.'" Such intransigence, Kendrew believed, would be similarly offensive to visitors in Nauvoo by failing to recognize and respect the varying desires of individuals visiting the restoration. A more effective approach, he argued, would seek to adapt the interpretation to the desires and needs of the visitor. Thus, "For those people who are largely interested in the religious side [of Nauvoo], an in depth interpretation should be available." But, he added, "I think there may be those who . . . will find an explanation of the places and culture of the period enriching to their lives and religious experience."[60]

Among the last to speak at this meeting in which the reorganization of NRI's board was announced was Fabian, the corporation's former vice president. Like Kendrew, he too sensed the reorganization involved certain changes in NRI's interpretive program. Although undoubtedly aware that he no longer retained the influence he enjoyed with President McKay, Fabian appealed to McKay's support of the restoration project in a final attempt to persuade the new board of Nauvoo's national historical significance. As he had done many times before, Fabian also reiterated his belief that "Nauvoo was a great story, a great American story, that of an historic movement with its origins in the religious."[61] In spite of such efforts to combine the secular and religious interpretations of Nauvoo, however, the reorganization of NRI's board ensured that a religious interpretive paradigm, one that emphasized Nauvoo's significance to the LDS Church and viewed the restoration in terms of its proselytizing potential, would guide the work of the corporation in the future.

Proselytizing Takes Over

Leading the way in this effort was apostle Mark E. Petersen. Although a newcomer to NRI's board of trustees, Petersen, as chairman of the Church Information and Historic Arts Committee, had been involved with the corporation since at least 1967, primarily in relation to the discussions surrounding the development of the Nauvoo Visitors Center. During that time "He expressed approval of the guide system and the historical approach, and the project in general."[62] Yet he was also intimately aware of the longstanding tradition of using the Church's historic sites as platforms for proselytizing and was sensitive to the desires of his colleagues in the LDS Church hierarchy to employ this practice in Nauvoo. As a result, Petersen continually attempted to mix the historical with the religious when dealing with the interpretation of Nauvoo. In 1968, for example, when President McKay was still alive, he expressed enthusiasm for Nauvoo and the proposed visitors' center, citing both historical and religious reasons for supporting the project. To NRI's trustees and the First Presidency, he declared, "Nauvoo should attract hundreds of thousands of people because of its historical importance in the State of Illinois and to the development of the West. If a suitable Visitors Center is erected the story of the rise of Nauvoo and its influence can be told to many visitors. A film can show the place of Nauvoo in American history." Yet Petersen was quick to add that, in addition to its national historical importance, "Nauvoo should compare historically with places like Gettysburg because of the number of important things which happened there," citing Joseph Smith's "King Follet" sermon, in which the Latter-day prophet outlined some of Mormonism's most elaborate doctrines, as a prime example. Moreover, he added, "At the Temple site information can be given as to why we build temples."[63] In this way, Petersen suggested that Nauvoo's interpretive message could blend American and Church history and, in the process, proselytize the LDS faith to visitors.

Petersen outlined a similar blended approach to the interpretation of Nauvoo following McKay's death and the creation of the Nauvoo Mission, but prior to his election as a trustee of NRI. Following a meeting of the three men who would soon become NRI's new board of trustees, Petersen outlined his ideas for an interpretive program in a July 1970 letter to apostle Stapley, a copy of which was forwarded to J. LeRoy Kimball. By focusing on the LDS pioneers whose Nauvoo homes had been restored and discussing with visitors what made these pioneers "tick," Petersen believed NRI "will be able to preserve the historical significance of the entire Nauvoo project and at the same time preach the gospel to the people in a way like the following."[64]

Using a tour of the Wilford Woodruff Home as an example, Petersen suggested the guides first deliver a bit of history to the visitors. "We would explain the house all that we wanted to and then say: 'We are very sure that you would like to know something about Wilford Woodruff as a man and what his beliefs were, etc.'" "Then," Petersen explained, "I would tell them a little bit about where he was raised, how he joined the Church, his admiration for the Prophet Joseph Smith and what his conversion meant." Finally, Petersen stated he would then "explain that he [Woodruff] was one of the great missionaries of the Church and that he was instrumental in bringing about 3,000 people into the Church in Great Britain alone."[65]

Having established some historical background for the man and his relationship to the LDS Church, Petersen then suggested the tour focus on Woodruff's doctrinal beliefs.

And then I would explain that he [Woodruff] was so convinced of the truthfulness of the mission of the Prophet Joseph Smith that he devoted his entire life to this mission. After that, I would explain what the mission was and how he met Joseph Smith and how he received the story of Joseph Smith and explain that he fully believed that there had been a falling away from the truth and that now a restoration is made through the Prophet. And then I would mention something about his belief in the Book of Mormon and how he sustained the Prophet.[66]

By recounting the beliefs of the Nauvoo pioneers as part of their tours, guides could place contemporary religious doctrines in a historical setting, allowing them to passively, yet effectively share LDS theology with visitors. As Petersen himself recognized, "you are still telling the story in terms of history, but at the same time you are satisfying the desire of the brethren [in the LDS Church hierarchy] to preach the gospel." Pragmatically, he concluded, "It seems to me that this is the only way you can do it."[67]

Petersen recommended the same interpretive approach be taken in each of the restored homes and at other important sites like that of the Nauvoo Temple. His outline for the interpretive message at the soon-to-be-completed visitors' center also followed this pattern. Here, Petersen suggested, visitors could be taken into a "Joseph Smith room," where a guide would "tell the story of how there came to be a Nauvoo—that it all originated with Joseph Smith as a fourteen-year-old boy who read his Bible and had the first vision, brought forth the Book of Mormon, established the Church, suffered persecution and eventually, because of persecution, the saints came to Nauvoo as a place of refuge." "In this way," Petersen concluded, "we can get over the Joseph Smith story and the coming forth of the Book of Mormon." This interpretive technique, in which key LDS doctrines were communicated in the context of the larger Nauvoo story, was central to Petersen's plan for proselytizing at the historic site. "It can be done emphatically," he declared, "and yet in the guise of history."[68]

Conspicuously missing from Petersen's interpretive program, however, was any mention of Nauvoo's national historical significance for which he had previously voiced support. Indeed, references to Nauvoo's role in American westward expansion were replaced with statements about the city's significance to the LDS Church and biographical histories of major LDS figures, creating opportunities in which LDS doctrines and beliefs could be communicated. This is clearly seen in his proposed program of interpretation for the Nauvoo Visitors Center, where instead of introducing visitors to the story of Nauvoo in an American historical context and highlighting its role in the westward expansion of America, Petersen recommended contextualizing Nauvoo's story strictly in terms of its relation to the history of Joseph Smith and the LDS Church. The same is true for Petersen's discussion of the Brigham Young Home, where Nauvoo's role in American westward expansion could have been perhaps best interpreted. Although he acknowledged that "Brigham Young was probably America's greatest colonizer," Petersen suggested the tour instead focus on the fact that "it was Joseph Smith's idea in the first place to come West." Thus, as far as Petersen was concerned, the interpretive message was that "although Brigham Young was the great colonizer, he did it in fulfillment of what Joseph Smith had said." In this way, the tour's emphasis was diverted away from Nauvoo's national historical significance as one of the principal starting points of American westward migration in the nineteenth century, highlighting instead Joseph Smith and his prophetic role in the Mormon migration. This shift of emphasis in turn created an opportunity in which fundamental LDS doctrines and beliefs (such as Joseph Smith's role as a prophet of God) were reaffirmed to visitors.[69]

Beyond pure proselytizing, however, Petersen described secondary motives for incorporating LDS religious beliefs into the guided tours. For him, this was an opportunity not only to make converts but also to validate fundamental truth claims in light of competing interpretations. This is seen again in the proposed tour of the Brigham Young Home, where Petersen stressed, "I think it is very important that we emphasize the Prophet's prediction that the saints would go to the Rocky Mountains in view of the fact that the Reorganites [members of the RLDS Church] make the claims that they do." "This," he concluded, "pins the label of authenticity upon the Utah Church [LDS], and lets them [the visitors] know that Joseph Smith intended the saints to go there." Similarly, Petersen believed it was especially important to tell visitors "that Joseph Smith was the original temple builder and that Brigham Young and his associates merely carried on the program that Joseph Smith started as a temple builder and that it was the intention of Joseph Smith that the Latter-day Saints be temple builders continuously." "And then," he concluded, "I would call attention to the fact that the Utah Church has continued this program."[70] Given the doctrinal differences between the LDS and RLDS Churches, most of which centered on Brigham Young, Petersen thought it imperative to authenticate LDS beliefs during tours of the restored homes in Nauvoo. By rooting contested LDS doctrines in history and in the teachings of Joseph Smith, he sought to validate LDS identity and simultaneously discredit the competing claims made by the RLDS Church. This is another reason why he believed it was more important to address LDS religious beliefs in a tour of the Brigham Young Home, rather than discuss the part Young and the rest of the Nauvoo pioneers had played in the history of the American West.

Although Petersen's ideas about the proper blend of religious and secular interpretation in Nauvoo came before he was elected to NRI's board, this move away from interpreting Nauvoo's national historical significance became more pronounced once the new board of trustees was in place. This was especially evident during the dedication of the Nauvoo Visitors Center on September 4, 1971. Although this was the first major act of NRI's new board of trustees, a few of the former trustees, released just over three months earlier, participated in the dedicatory services. David M. Kennedy and A. Edwin Kendrew, for example, each gave brief remarks, while J. Willard Marriott offered one of the prayers. Even George B. Hartzog Jr., director of the NPS, was present and made a small speech. These were the men who had espoused and actively promoted a secular interpretation of Nauvoo for nearly a decade. Their involvement in the dedication of the visitors' center, however, was more due to the fact that plans for the ceremony had been made months in advance than it was an endorsement of the secular interpretation they represented. In fact, outside of their participation, the proceedings of the ceremony made it clear that a new interpretive schema was now in place for Nauvoo.

In many ways, the dedication of the visitors' center contrasted sharply with the groundbreaking ceremony of the same structure two years earlier. Apostle Harold B. Lee had complained about the latter, objecting to what he believed was an overly secular lineup of speakers, who failed to represent Nauvoo's religious significance to the LDS Church.[71] The same complaint could not have been leveled at the program for the visitors' center dedication. Indeed, as if to compensate for the lack of religious representation at the groundbreaking ceremony, the key figures in the dedication of the visitors' center were important members of the LDS Church hierarchy, who explicitly put forward a religious interpretation of Nauvoo. Consider, for example, the remarks of N. Eldon Tanner, then second counselor to President Smith in the First Presidency, who offered the dedicatory prayer for the structure. Taking advantage of the opportunity to speak to the approximately 4,000 people in attendance, Tanner addressed the audience before offering the prayer. Instead of relating the story of Nauvoo and its role in the westward expansion of America, he told the story of Joseph Smith and the organization of the LDS Church. Whatever comments could have been made about the Mormons' contribution to the development of the American West were replaced by Tanner's declarations of religious belief.[72]

Apostle (and NRI trustee) Delbert L. Stapley also emphasized LDS Church history and Nauvoo's religious significance in his remarks at the dedication ceremony. As the event's main speaker, Stapley had the greatest opportunity to convey Nauvoo's significance to the large crowd. Although a former proponent of a secular interpretation of Nauvoo, Stapley, like Tanner, focused his comments on the history of the LDS Church and Nauvoo's significance to that history. For example, he told the assemblage "We should care about what happens here [in Nauvoo] because it is all so meaningful to the building up of the kingdom of God." Rather than being a "dark and shameful part in the history of the Church," Stapley said Nauvoo "was the revolutionary, newly organized Church of Christ struggling for its existence and ultimate success." By framing the Church's history as a divinely directed drama, Stapley represented Nauvoo as an important chapter in the overall development and eventual triumph of the LDS Church. The same is true for the way he spoke of Nauvoo's relationship to the Mormon migration to the American West. "Nauvoo was not a failure even when the [Latter-day] saints were forced out," he declared, "They took all that was learned here [in Nauvoo] and incorporated it in the building of Salt Lake City and the Intermountain West." Thus, whereas the secular interpretation that dominated the groundbreaking ceremony emphasized Nauvoo's role in the westward expansion of the United States, the religious interpretation espoused by Stapley and Tanner at the visitors' center dedication two years later highlighted Nauvoo's place in the westward expansion of the LDS Church.[73]

Although President Joseph Fielding Smith died ten months

after the visitors' center dedication at the age of ninety-five, his successor and former first counselor, apostle Harold B. Lee, continued to endorse a religious interpretation of Nauvoo. As the two most senior apostles, Smith and Lee had both felt marginalized by David O. McKay's unilateral decisions with respect to NRI. Both men had also worked closely during Smith's presidency to rein in the restoration project, bringing it within the official bureaucracy of the LDS Church and significantly reorganizing NRI's board of trustees. Thus, when Lee became president of the LDS Church on July 7, 1972, the institutional changes underlying the renewed religious interpretation of Nauvoo had already been implemented. Even though President Lee died only eighteen months after assuming the presidency, he and his counselors took measures that solidified NRI's organizational and interpretive changes during the brief time they led the LDS Church.

Although there was some question as to whether or not President Lee would dissolve NRI as a corporation, over time it became clear that he intended to stay the course set by his predecessor with respect to the management of NRI.[74] In September 1972, President Lee and his counselors appointed John H. Vandenberg trustee of NRI.[75] Vandenberg had recently been called as an assistant to the Quorum of the Twelve Apostles and had served as the LDS Church's presiding bishop since 1961. As presiding bishop, Vandenberg was intimately involved with the allocation of the temporal resources of the LDS Church and directly responsible for maintaining the budgets of its various departments. His appointment to NRI's board of trustees solidified the transition from a corporation run by non-LDS professionals to an organization managed by individuals from within the Church hierarchy. Given his knowledge of and experience with LDS Church finances, Vandenberg's appointment was also a way for President Lee and his counselors to ensure that NRI's budget, which under McKay's leadership had been seemingly boundless, would now be carefully monitored and managed.[76]

With additional members of the LDS Church hierarchy involved in the restoration project, it is not surprising that the emphasis on interpreting Nauvoo in a solidly religious framework continued during President Lee's tenure. This was perhaps most clearly evident at the dedication of five historic Nauvoo structures in May 1973—the only major event of the restoration project during the eighteen months of President Lee's leadership. Noticeably absent from this dedicatory ceremony were former trustees Kendrew, Kennedy, and Marriott, all of whom had had at least a small role in the dedication of the visitors' center a year and a half earlier. Their absence was particularly peculiar given that the bulk of work on four of the five structures being dedicated was completed during their tenure as trustees of NRI.[77] In their place were representatives of the LDS Church hierarchy, including apostle Marion G. Romney, second counselor to President Lee, and apostles Spencer W. Kimball and Gordon B. Hinckley, both future presidents of the LDS Church. Unsurprisingly, these men continued to highlight Nauvoo's religious significance in their remarks to the some 1,500 persons gathered for the dedication service.

At a press conference held prior to the dedicatory rites, for example, Romney affirmed the LDS Church's proselytizing interests in Nauvoo when he told a group of reporters, "The restored buildings should attract visitors by the tens of thousands to Nauvoo, and thus further the missionary work of the church." Later, during his remarks at the actual ceremony, Romney situated the Nauvoo pioneers and the Nauvoo story within a faith-promoting history of the LDS Church, just as his fellow apostle, Stapley, had done a year and a half earlier at the dedication of the Nauvoo Visitors' Center. The early Mormons of Nauvoo, Romney affirmed, "had been literally charged by the Almighty to build up the Kingdom of God in the earth. They were, here in Nauvoo—as they had been before and have ever since continued to be—about their Father's business." By focusing on the ideal attributes and characteristics of the Nauvoo pioneers, Romney recast the story of Nauvoo and of the Mormon westward migration as exemplary history. Speaking of the "superb courage, faith, fortitude and self discipline" of the Nauvoo pioneers, Romney declared, "These are the things we hope these restored edifices will help to impress upon the minds and hearts of all of our Father's children who visit this sacred place, hallowed by the accomplishments and sacrifices of the builders of Nauvoo."[78]

Seven months to the day following Romney's remarks at this dedication ceremony, President Harold B. Lee died at the age of seventy-four. Thus, in the four short years between President McKay's death in early January 1970 and the passing of Harold B. Lee in late December 1973, the secular interpretation of Nauvoo had been almost entirely eclipsed by a religiously driven interpretive program bent on proselytizing. With the reorganization of NRI's board of trustees and the creation of the Nauvoo Mission, this religious interpretive approach had become solidly institutionalized within the LDS Church. Moreover, the Church hierarchy had consistently reinforced this interpretation in both public and private settings, emphasizing Nauvoo's significance in the history of the LDS Church over the city's central role in the westward expansion of the United States.

Finally, in an effort to legitimize these changes, the proselytizing interpretive approach was artificially read into the founding philosophies of NRI. Early in 1974, just days into Spencer W. Kimball's presidency, J. LeRoy Kimball wrote the new LDS Church president with recommendations on how to "preserve the historic-proselyting approach envisioned in the Articles of Incorporation." NRI's articles of incorporation, of course, stated that the corporation existed to interpret the story of Nauvoo. They also expressed that Nauvoo's story is about pioneering determination and courage, and the westward expansion of the United States. The articles, however, said nothing about proselytizing. Nonetheless, by reading a religious interpretive approach into NRI's articles of incorporation, Kimball sought to justify and legitimize the proselytizing activities introduced by Presidents Smith and Lee.[79]

Therefore, by the time Spencer W. Kimball became president of the LDS Church on December 30, 1973, the religious interpretation of Nauvoo had become fully routine. J. LeRoy Kimball revealed how marked this shift in interpretation had been in his letter to President Kimball. In stark contrast to the original secular historical purpose of the restoration project, he affirmed, "We keep foremost in mind that the basic purpose of the restoration is to proselyte, and therefore the Church and its doctrines are woven into the historic story, which brought the visitors to Nauvoo."[80]

Although Spencer W. Kimball had been only marginally

involved with the restoration project prior to his ascension to the presidency, he had not developed the negative sentiments that his predecessors, Smith and Lee, had acquired toward NRI. It helped that President Kimball and Dr. J. LeRoy Kimball were second cousins, both connected to Heber C. Kimball, the early Mormon apostle.[81] Their relationship reached back more than thirty years, during most of which Spencer W. Kimball was a patient of his doctor-cousin. Given their close and intimate affiliation, it is not surprising that the restoration project underwent somewhat of a renaissance during the twelve years (1974–85) President Kimball led the LDS Church.

As early as June 1974, only six months after he became Church president, Kimball authorized $600,000 for additional restoration projects in Nauvoo. Although this was $250,000 less than what NRI's trustees had requested, this was the first major appropriation for the restoration project since the passing of President McKay.[82] Nearly $600,000 in additional funds was also made available in early 1978.[83] With the financial support of the LDS Church again sustaining the project, NRI went to work restoring and reconstructing more than double as many structures as had been completed prior to this time. The climax of this flood of activity came on August 14, 1982, when Gordon B. Hinckley, first counselor to eighty-seven-year-old President Kimball, dedicated the newly renovated and landscaped Nauvoo Temple block and sixteen historic buildings that NRI had either restored or reconstructed over the past decade.[84] Including the Sarah Granger Kimball Home, which had been restored with funds from the LDS Church's Women's Relief Society and dedicated earlier in the year, the total number of restored or reconstructed structures in Nauvoo now reached more than twenty-five. Sixteen of these buildings were open for public tours, while the remainder served as residences for the missionary guides.[85]

Although President Kimball actively supported the restoration project, he still firmly subscribed to a missionary approach in Nauvoo. Indeed, in 1971 he was one of the three-man "Nauvoo Committee" that explicitly recommended that a proselytizing element be incorporated into the interpretive program of NRI.[86] Thus, although the physical restoration of Nauvoo expanded under President Kimball's leadership, the interpretation of the city and its history remained solidly entrenched in a religious framework. This overall interpretive philosophy was represented well by Hinckley, who, during his remarks at the large dedication ceremony in August 1982, continued to emphasize Nauvoo's significance to the rise of the LDS Church. In speaking of Nauvoo and its restoration, he said, "Nauvoo the beautiful. Nauvoo, City of Joseph. Nauvoo, the crucible of Mormonism where Joseph [Smith] was buried and the church began an exodus to greatness. Through the restoration that has occurred here and which we commemorate this day, I pray that we shall remember those who came here to build and grow and who left here for conscience sake."[87]

Consistent with the sustained religious interpretation of Nauvoo, the historic site continued to be used as a proselytizing venue under President Kimball's leadership. During this period, full-time missionaries continued to serve as interpretive guides for the thousands of visitors coming to view the restored city each year. Cognizant of the desires of his superiors in the LDS Church hierarchy, J. LeRoy Kimball continued to emphasize the proselytizing potential of the site. Speaking soon after the Nauvoo Temple block had been newly landscaped, Kimball told a reporter from the LDS Church that "Every move in the restoration has been done with proselyting in mind, but the temple site is the most effective missionary tool here." "A number of people," he continued, "come to the site and hear the story of the temple and those who built it. This opens the door for missionaries to visit in their homes at a later time." Although Kimball professed that the Temple site was "the most important part of the [restoration] project," he also justified the restoration and reconstruction of Nauvoo's more secular structures in terms of their missionary potential for the Church. In response to the question of why a blacksmith shop, a gun shop, or a printing press was needed to proselytize, Kimball replied, "These things give the visitor a glimpse of the people who lived here and what their ideals were," adding that "[t]he main objective is to make friends for the Church." In this way, Kimball concluded, "When the missionaries go to the doors of people who have visited Nauvoo, they're better received."[88]

This explicit missionary emphasis did not go unnoticed by visitors to Nauvoo. One writer for the *Chicago Tribune* wrote about his visit to the restored city and made specific mention of his experience in the LDS Visitors Center. "Subject matter," he wrote, "is about 50 per cent history and 50 per cent religion." "The Mormons," he continued, "are active recruiters, as most Chicago householders know from the periodic visits of the polite, well-dressed young men from Utah." Reflecting on the obvious proselytizing element in the visitors' center tour, the author congenially concluded, "There is no pressure of any kind in the center tour, but you will come out knowing a lot about Joseph Smith and the principles of the religion he founded."[89]

In addition to the restored and reconstructed buildings, the visitors' center, and other sites, there were additional LDS-sponsored activities in Nauvoo that were likewise driven by a desire to proselytize visitors. One such event was the annual production of the theatrical pageant, "City of Joseph." Although performed at a smaller scale since the early 1970s, the pageant was staged for the first time on a grassy hill near the Nauvoo Visitors Center in 1976, where it was produced annually for almost thirty years (weather permitting). With "a heavy emphasis upon the positive, happier experiences of the Nauvoo saints," the show depicts life in Nauvoo during the six and a half years the Mormon pioneers occupied the city. Akin to J. LeRoy Kimball's comments concerning the purpose of the restoration project, R. Don Oscarson, the pageant's author, fundamentally viewed his production as a missionary tool. "The show," he said, "is designed for the non-member. It is low key; it doesn't preach . . . yet it shows Joseph [Smith] going into the grove to pray and presents all the principles of the gospel." Like the restored and reconstructed buildings, the visitors' center, and other Nauvoo sites, the "City of Joseph" pageant was used as a platform for proselytizing the Mormon faith and reflected the religious interpretation that continued to dominate the restored city during President Spencer W. Kimball's tenure.[90]

The RLDS's Response

Coinciding with the continued emphasis of the LDS Church on a religiously driven and proselytizing-minded interpretation was the rise of a more explicit missionary approach to the

RLDS interpretive services in Nauvoo. Prior to this time, RLDS interpreters distanced themselves from the original secular interpretation espoused by NRI, choosing instead to focus on their church's continuous history in Nauvoo. Kenneth Stobaugh, director of RLDS sites in Nauvoo, stressed this point to a newspaper reporter in 1974. "Here," he stated, "we're not so much emphasizing that this was the Mormon jumping-off place to the West. . . . Our own history continued to be in this area and so we talk here of the continuing relationship we've had with the town dating all the way from the 1840s."[91]

Whereas the LDS Church had added an unequivocal missionary campaign to its interpretive program starting in 1970, RLDS interpreters at this time continued to concentrate their energies on effectively communicating the details that supported their historical claims. Their stated mission was "to explain the Nauvoo story against the background of Hancock County, the state of Illinois, and the nation."[92] The historical interpretive program that evolved from this situation was acknowledged beyond the borders of Nauvoo. In recognition of what they identified as an "effective internship in historic site interpretation," which involved students from the RLDS Church–sponsored Graceland College (in Lamoni, Iowa), the American Association for State and Local History awarded the Joseph Smith Historic Center (the organization responsible for RLDS sites in Nauvoo) and Graceland College a Certificate of Commendation in 1978.[93]

Although the RLDS interpretive program emphasized the historical, it did so for religious reasons. By telling their version of the Nauvoo story, replete with historical details concerning the split with their Utah counterparts and the subsequent history of the Latter-day Saints that remained in the Nauvoo area, the RLDS Church was seeking to legitimize its identity and validate its beliefs in the face of the seemingly competing claims made by the LDS Church. Thus, the historical interpretation of Nauvoo was a missionary tool for RLDS members just as it was for their LDS cousins. Here was a way to communicate to themselves and to others what their religion and faith were all about.

Although interpreters at the RLDS sites had always used the properties to tell their version of Nauvoo's history, their efforts became consciously more missionary motivated beginning in 1980. Responding to the rise of non-RLDS visitors in Nauvoo, RLDS president Wallace B. Smith wrote to Kenneth Stobaugh on March 3 of that year, asking him to implement a stronger missionary emphasis in the historic sites program in Nauvoo. He also requested that interpreters no longer detain visitors in hopes of arguing them into joining the Church.[94] At about that same time, Stobaugh made explicit the religious and proselytizing motivations underlying the RLDS Church's restoration work in Nauvoo. "Our main thrust," he explained, "is to help people understand who Joseph Smith was, and what kind of life he lived." Of course, the RLDS conception of Joseph Smith differed in significant ways from the LDS understanding of the prophet and his life. Thus, although on the surface, the goals of their interpretive program were purely historical in nature (that is, to understand Joseph Smith), there was an unambiguous missionary motive driving the RLDS interpretation. For all their missionary zeal, however, the RLDS guides were not to try to convert visitors on the spot. "We low-key our proselyting," Stobaugh explained, because "We don't want to get into arguments." Besides, as Stobaugh clarified, "in a forty-minute period, we probably couldn't change anyone's mind anyway."[95] In this and other ways, the RLDS interpretation of Nauvoo closely paralleled the historic-proselytizing program of their LDS counterparts. Although it came a decade after the LDS Church markedly shifted its interpretive program toward proselytizing, this renewed missionary emphasis by the RLDS Church ensured that visitors to Nauvoo would continue to hear different interpretations of the city's significance and history.

Assisting the RLDS guides in their interpretive work was a new visitors' center, which was dedicated on May 3, 1980. Following in the footsteps of their LDS counterparts, RLDS officials conceived the visitors' center as a place where visitors could become acquainted with RLDS doctrine and history. Its intended purpose was to provide the visitor with "a positive experience in a setting of peace and beauty, by preserving and interpreting Latter-day Saint heritage, inviting further exploration."[96]

Dedicated at the same time as the new visitors' center was a recently completed reconstruction of Joseph Smith's Red Brick Store, which was also poised to play an important role in the renewed missionary emphasis of the RLDS interpretive program in Nauvoo. Although the Red Brick Store was a hub of economic, religious, political, and social activity in the early 1840s, the RLDS Church was primarily interested in the structure because of "one towering incident" that occurred there, "the blessing of Joseph Smith III by his father as his successor to the prophetic office." Given that much of the interpretive division between the two churches centered on the question of succession, the RLDS believed its legitimacy as a religious organization rested largely on this one historical event. Thus, it was extremely important for the RLDS interpreters to have a place where they could proclaim, "Clearly, [Joseph] Smith intended that his son would succeed him in becoming president of the church." The reconstructed Red Brick Store provided the venue in which to communicate this fundamental tenet of the RLDS faith.[97]

After touring both the LDS and RLDS sites in Nauvoo, visitors easily recognized the different interpretive agendas of the two churches. One writer, after summarizing the history of the schism, declared, "The historical rift between the two is obvious even as Nauvoo is reborn today." Not only did visitors encounter two visitors' centers in Nauvoo, one for each Church, they also found that "[e]ach gives a free tour of its own turf and presents a different perspective based on its historical interpretation and distinct religious beliefs." Stobaugh, the director of RLDS sites, agreed there was "a funny paradox in town." "Both churches," he explained, "try to interpret Nauvoo from the city that was here. The problem is, the 19th century church isn't the only thing here anymore. You run into the 20th century and the fact that part of the church has reorganized and the division still exists."[98]

Improved Relations

No matter how deliberate and, therefore, obvious this interpretive rift seemed to be, the longer the two churches coexisted in Nauvoo, the more their relationship improved. As early as 1969 there were signs that individuals from both churches desired to present a more unified interpretation of Nauvoo's past. At that time, following a meeting between officials of NRI and the RLDS Church, during which they collaborated on plans for the future development of the historic site, Daniel T. Muir of the RLDS Department of History remarked to T. Edgar Lyon, historian for NRI, "[I] Hope this will be the beginning of a new era for both of our churches. There is no reason why visitors to Nauvoo should get two conflicting interpretations of the Nauvoo story, as they do at present." "There should be," he continued, "a cooperative effort to present a unified story, that the interpretation will have unity and a picture of a people with great ideas, and the differences minimized." To this Lyon replied, "There is no reason why it can't be done in that manner, if each of us will face the reality of the historic records, get rid of our pre-conceived emotional attachments, and let the record of the people, made at that time, speak for the united city of Nauvoo." "This, he concluded, "is the best field for attempting any type of reconciliation. The field of theology and that of religion are too deeply involved with emotional feelings to provide a common ground to commence understanding a common problem."[99]

Although at least two individuals were hoping for a more reconciliatory interpretive approach in 1969, their desires proved to be slightly premature. Nevertheless, over the next two decades the relationship between the two churches gradually improved. With each passing year there were additional opportunities for the two groups to cooperate. J. LeRoy Kimball himself "treasured amicable relations with other church leaders in the area" and "helped mend fences by encouraging the young [NRI] guides to meet their RLDS counterparts."[100] As the restoration projects of both churches matured, the more understanding and receptive each group became. By 1989, LDS officials could publicly express gratitude for the cooperation of RLDS leaders in the work of restoring of the city. "I'm pleased to say," announced one LDS official during the dedication of four new Nauvoo structures in 1989, "we enjoy a cordial and harmonious relationship" with the RLDS Church.[101]

One manifestation of the improved relationships was a 1991 real estate transaction in which the RLDS and the LDS swapped portions of their respective Nauvoo properties. The trade involved the land on which the RLDS church building sat, which by that time was surrounded by the restored and reconstructed buildings of NRI, and some properties owned by the LDS that bordered the major RLDS land holdings in Nauvoo. Although the deal was ten years in the making, the end result was mutually beneficial to both churches and evidence that relations had indeed improved.[102]

Another highlight of these improved relations came also in 1991, when the renovated Smith Family Cemetery was dedicated in Nauvoo. Despite the divisive doctrinal differences that existed between the two churches, their shared belief in the prophet Joseph Smith served as a catalyst for cooperation and understanding. Although the graves of the Smith family—including that of Joseph Smith himself—were on property owned by the RLDS Church, members of both churches joined forces to help repair and beautify the cemetery. A nonprofit organization, the Joseph and Hyrum Smith Family Foundation, comprised of descendants of Joseph, Hyrum, and Emma Smith, was formed and immediately set out raising funds and gathering information for the cemetery project. Speaking of the way the project brought individuals from both churches together,

Daniel M. Larsen, the foundation's executive director, said, "I feel privileged and blessed to be a part of the Joseph and Hyrum Smith Family Foundation, and to be a part of the project we have undertaken. I truly believe this can be the beginning of an extraordinary relationship between Smith Family members and the RLDS and LDS Churches, and an opportunity to once again work together in old Nauvoo."[103]

More than 1,000 people from both churches attended the August 4, 1991, dedication. RLDS president Wallace B. Smith, a great-grandson of Joseph Smith, officially dedicated the cemetery, while LDS apostle M. Russell Ballard, a great-great-grandson of Hyrum Smith, looked on. The latter, when given the opportunity to speak during the ceremony, expressed what he hoped would come of this cooperative project. His comments captured the reality of the improved relations that had developed between the two churches over the years. "I hope," he said, "that as we conclude the services here by dedicating the improved cemetery that this will be the beginning of wonderful times together as the Joseph Smith, Sr. and Lucy Mack Smith family. I for one pledge to [RLDS] President Smith that I will do all that I can do to see that we are always standing by, both as family and as the LDS Church, to be supportive and helpful and loving neighbors, friends, and relatives."[104]

Enduring Proselytizing

Having served as the president of the LDS Church since December 1973, Spencer W. Kimball witnessed the improving relations between his church and that of the RLDS firsthand. However, after nearly twelve years of leadership, President Kimball died in early November 1985, at the age of ninety. As is evident from the events following President David O. McKay's death in 1970, there is always potential for significant reorganization and sweeping reform every time there is a change in the leadership of a large bureaucratic organization like the LDS Church. Nonetheless, after operating for approximately fifteen years as an official extension of the Church bureaucracy and under the management of Church officials, NRI's restoration project had been shaped in such a way as to make it a respectable and well-liked program in which the Church and its leaders could take great satisfaction. Thus, during the eight and a half years (1985–94) that Spencer W. Kimball's successor, Ezra Taft Benson, led the LDS Church, relatively few changes were made to NRI and its restoration project in Nauvoo. In fact, what was perhaps the greatest change during President Benson's tenure resulted in the restoration project becoming even more entrenched in the bureaucracy of the LDS Church.

The event that precipitated this change was the retirement of Dr. J. LeRoy Kimball at the end of 1986. After serving as NRI's president for more than twenty-four years, Kimball, then eighty-five years old, decided it was time to step down. Since the major reorganization of NRI in 1971, Kimball remained the only member of the board of trustees who was not an official member of the LDS Church's leading hierarchy. Never again would NRI have a non-Church official as a trustee.

Replacing Kimball as president of NRI was Loren C. Dunn, a member of the LDS Church's First Quorum of the Seventy and president of the Church's North America Northeast Area. Dunn's counselors in the area presidency were called to serve as the corporation's vice president and secretary, and together the three men constituted NRI's entire board of trustees. Although at the time of their appointment, the new board expressed its commitment "to carrying on the basic ideals and goals of the organization," little restoration work was completed during the time they led the organization.[105] Even though the men inherited a historic site at which more than twenty-five structures had already been either restored or reconstructed, there was still plenty of additional work to be done in Nauvoo. Yet with Dr. Kimball no longer part of the corporation's governing body, there was little support for the original expansive and ambitious plans to restore more of the historic city. What remained in force, however, was the religious interpretation of Nauvoo that had guided the restoration project for the last sixteen years. Although Dunn and his counselors occasionally acknowledged NRI's original interpretive emphasis on the westward expansion of the United States, it was clear they felt that Nauvoo and the Church's other historic sites "help us keep intact our spiritual and cultural heritage and are visible evidences of our roots and the beginnings of the restoration of the gospel."[106]

What was accomplished during this time was completed in conjunction with the 1989 sesquicentennial celebrations of Nauvoo's founding. Although not in Nauvoo proper, the first major activity of the anniversary year was the renovation of the jail in nearby Carthage, where Joseph Smith and his brother Hyrum were killed in 1844. The $1 million project, which included an expanded visitors' center and extensive landscaping of the surrounding property, was dedicated on June 27, 1989—the 145th anniversary of the Smiths' deaths. Consistent with the religious interpretation that had become standard fare in Nauvoo, Dunn proclaimed the site's merits in terms of its significance to the LDS Church. "Carthage," he told the crowd of more than 4,000 people gathered for the dedication, "has become more than a place of martyrdom. It marks the triumph of Joseph Smith the Prophet and his brother Hyrum as servants of the Lord in bringing forward this great latter-day work."[107]

Another aspect of the sesquicentennial celebration was the renovation of the Nauvoo Visitors Center's interior. Replacing the old displays were new exhibits focused entirely on the history of the LDS Church. As Dunn explained, "The west wing will depict where the Latter-day Saints come from; the center wing will deal with the Latter-day Saints in Nauvoo; and the east wing will speak of where the Latter-day Saints went after they left Nauvoo and what became of them."[108] This explicit emphasis on the westward movement of the LDS Church was a distortion of NRI's original focus on the westward expansion of the United States. Yet it was consistent with the missionary-minded religious interpretation that had been stressed in Nauvoo since the passing of President McKay. Commenting proudly on the fact that the number of missionary referrals in Nauvoo had dramatically increased since the installation of the new exhibits, Dunn reported, "The missionary couples working at the visitors' center tell us that it is easier to get referrals with the new interior exhibits." "The emphasis, of course," he continued, "is to bring people in through the door of history. The history of the Church, properly told, can create great interest. And when you tell the story of Nauvoo, you tell the story of the Church."[109] Thus, the renovation of the visitors' center was simply the latest example of the ways in which the LDS Church purposefully used Nauvoo as a platform for proselytizing the Mormon faith.

Finally, in addition to the Carthage complex and the exhibits in the visitors' center, the sesquicentennial activities included the refurbishing of a historic Nauvoo cemetery, the construction of a period barn to house public restroom facilities in Nauvoo, and the reconstruction of two historic Nauvoo shops, the Riser Boot and Shoemaker Shop and the Stoddard Tinsmith Shop. The dedication of these places on October 7, 1989, brought the total number of LDS sites open to the public to twenty-three. Moreover, it marked what Dunn and other Church leaders identified as "the completion of restoration projects as presently planned." Citing the accomplishments of the previous twenty-seven years, Dunn declared the restoration of Nauvoo officially complete. "With the homes and shops the Church has restored over the years," he affirmed, "plus the visitors' centers at Nauvoo and Carthage, there is enough of a flavor of the old city there now to give people a good idea of how it was."[110]

Dunn's declaration proved to be somewhat premature, for work in Nauvoo has continued, albeit sporadically, up to the present. Not only have the interiors of some of the buildings been refurbished, either for historical reasons or more contemporary needs, but additional structures have also been reconstructed. In particular, a number of log cabins have been replicated in an attempt to portray a more historically accurate architectural picture of 1840s Nauvoo.[111] Contradicting this worthwhile goal, however, and significantly undermining the historical integrity of the restored city was the construction of more than twenty modern brick-faced missionary residences throughout the historic district in 2002.[112]

The most significant project, however, since Dunn's 1989 declaration was the reconstruction of the Nauvoo Temple (figure 7). Although interested parties, including the Illinois House of Representatives, had talked of rebuilding the Nauvoo Temple since the 1930s, it was not until the close of the century that the project became a reality. Coincidentally, it was LDS Church president Gordon B. Hinckley, son of Bryant S. Hinckley—another early proponent of rebuilding the Temple—that made the announcement during one of the semiannual General Conferences of the Church. "In closing now," he stated, "I feel impressed to announce that among all of the temples we are constructing, we plan to rebuild the Nauvoo Temple. A member of the Church and his family have provided a very substantial contribution to make this possible. . . . [T]he new building will stand as a memorial to those who built the first structure there on the banks of the Mississippi."[113]

Following an open house that lasted several weeks, during which time any and all visitors could tour the rebuilt structure, the new Temple was dedicated on June 27, 2002—the 158th anniversary of Joseph Smith's death. Although the Temple's exterior was reconstructed as historically accurately as possible, its interior reflects the spatial needs of modern LDS temple rituals. Because it was constructed to be a modern, functioning temple and not necessarily a historic site, only members of the LDS Church possessing recommends based on their worthiness may enter the building today. In harmony with the religious interpretative approach that highlights Nauvoo's significance to the LDS Church, President Hinckley said the

7. The reconstructed Nauvoo Temple. Courtesy of the Archives of the Church of Jesus Christ of Latter-day Saints.

following concerning the reconstruction and dedication of the new Temple: "We not only dedicated a magnificent building, a house of the Lord, but we also dedicated a beautiful memorial to the Prophet Joseph Smith."[114]

All of this recent work in Nauvoo has been carried out under the direction of members of the LDS Church hierarchy, who concomitantly serve as officers of NRI. The pattern of priesthood officials managing the restoration project, first established in 1971 with the reorganization of the original board of trustees, continues to the present. This has ensured the continuation of the religious interpretation of Nauvoo, in which the historic city's importance to the LDS Church is emphasized over any other significance it may hold. It has also guaranteed the persistence of proselytizing in Nauvoo. At present there are more LDS missionaries than ever interpreting Nauvoo to the public. In contrast to NRI's original interpretive scope, wherein Nauvoo's significance to American history was highlighted, the missionaries' message continues to focus on the history of the LDS Church and the fundamental doctrines of their religion. This is perhaps best reflected in the words of a Nauvoo missionary himself, who said, "As we tell about the history, we include gospel principles. . . . This is a mild, sincere way of bearing testimony and generating questions and interest. If people are interested only in the history, at least they leave with a little more knowledge of us."[115]

Chapter 4

Historical Archaeology at Nauvoo

An important element of the restoration of Nauvoo was the archaeological investigation of the houses and sites selected for restoration or reconstruction. Significantly, these investigations occurred at the same time that historical archaeology as a discipline was emerging as a professional scholarly endeavor. Consequently, the Nauvoo excavations stand as a classic example of much of the early development of historical archaeology in North America. In many ways, these excavations serve as an illuminating case study of an important period of transition in the discipline's history.

Archaeological Antecedents

Although LDS-sponsored historical archaeology began at Nauvoo in the early 1960s, Latter-day Saints' interest in archaeology began more than a century earlier and was centered on finding archaeological evidence of the Book of Mormon's antiquity among the Mayan ruins of Mesoamerica. In 1842 a copy of John Lloyd Stephens's book, *Incidents of Travel in Central America, Chiapas, and Yucatan*, was given to Joseph Smith in Nauvoo.[1] The book was the first to describe, in both words and images, the massive and elaborate ruins of complex societies on the American continent—the very subject of the ancient record Joseph Smith claimed to have translated into the Book of Mormon. Accordingly, the contents of Stephens' book were quickly appropriated as confirmation of the Book of Mormon's validity and antiquity. On June 25 of the same year, Joseph Smith recorded that "Messrs. Stephens and Catherwood have succeeded in collecting in the interior of America a large amount of relics of the Nephites, or the ancient inhabitants of America treated of in the Book of Mormon."[2] Thus began the Latter-day Saints' interest in American archaeology.[3]

It was not until the middle of the twentieth century, however, that the LDS Church became actively involved in actual archaeological research. A department of archaeology was established at the Church-sponsored Brigham Young University in December 1946, with M. Wells Jakeman at its head. The department's mission at this time was explicitly to pursue archaeological research of the scriptures, especially the Bible and Book of Mormon. Two years later Jakeman formed the University Archeology Society to assist the department in its research and the dissemination of its findings, and in matters of funding. In 1967, the UAS changed its name to the Society for Early Historic Archaeology (SEHA). Significantly, this change came at a time when the archaeological pursuit of the scriptures (especially the Book of Mormon) had fallen into disfavor with many of the LDS Church hierarchy. Removing the word "university" from the society's name was a way to disassociate BYU (and the LDS Church) from this pursuit and refocus the efforts of the department on objective, scientific archaeology. This transition was completed in 1980, when the SEHA became completely independent of BYU, a situation that contributed to the society's ultimate demise a decade later.[4]

Overlapping with these developments was the formation of the New World Archaeological Foundation (NWAF) in 1952. Although this organization was initially independent of the LDS Church and BYU, its original mission to provide archaeological confirmation of the Book of Mormon by investigating Pre-Classic Maya sites closely matched that of the university's archaeological programs. In response to requests for financial backing, however, President David O. McKay decided to subsume the NWAF in 1960, electing to monetarily sponsor the foundation by making it an official organ of BYU. At the same time, McKay and his counselors significantly altered the foundation's purpose by eliminating the scriptural component from its stated objectives. From then on, the foundation was to pursue archaeological research from a strictly secular viewpoint. Presently, the BYU-NWAF continues to function and is generally respected by its peers for the significant contributions it has made to the field of Mesoamerican archaeology for more than fifty years.[5]

The various attempts of the past half-century to generate archaeological evidence in support of the authenticity of the Book of Mormon have drawn criticism from scholars both inside and outside the LDS Church. Michael Coe, a prominent Mayanist, made one such critique in 1973, when he argued that the LDS Church's support for and interest in New World prehistory would never confirm its theological assumptions about either the peopling of Precolumbian America or the origins of Mesoamerican civilizations. At the same time he suggested that a more potentially productive relationship could be forged with the emerging field of historical archaeology. Specifically, he wrote,

I would like to be the advocate for a kind of research that has only begun: the archaeology of the Mormons themselves. In all parts of the western world, and in Latin America, scholars are discovering that there is no more important research than the study of how we ourselves came to be what we are. There is a tremendous amount of information about our Euro-American background which just does not appear in history books or in the documents on which they are based. In the Pilgrim settlements of Plymouth, in frontier forts of the French and Indian War, and the American Revolution, in industrial sites of the early nineteenth century, archaeologists are not only throwing light on the material culture of our forbears, but are adding new theoretical dimensions enabling us to interpret the social, political, and economic aspects of all ancient societies. There can hardly be any part of American history more exciting and inspiring than the story of the Latter-day Saints, from their humble beginnings in New York State, through the turbulent years in the Middle West, to the triumphs of Utah. . . . [T]hink of all the Mormon remains which simply cry out for excavation![6]

Continuing, he wrote,

I would begin with the early nineteenth century cellar holes in the hill country of Vermont, in the villages of Sharon and Whitingham which nurtured the young Joseph Smith and Brigham Young. How much do we really know of Palmyra and the "burned-over district" in which the Book of Mormon was born? What about Kirtland, its Temple, and its way of life? The great city of Nauvoo itself is only partly known from excavation, recent findings there represent only a fraction of what could be learned from the site. And how many excavations have ever been carried out in the homesteads of those unsung heroes, the Mormon pioneers? We have the numberless quilts, chests of drawers, family portraits, and so forth in room after room of the fascinating pioneer museums of Salt Lake City, but what about the day- to-day life, spatial arrangements, division of labor, and family structure that resulted in such products? Only the spade and trowel of scientific archaeology could answer such questions.[7]

Finally, Coe concluded with a charge to "Continue the praiseworthy excavations in Mexico, remembering that little or nothing pertaining to the Book of Mormon will ever result from them. And start digging into the archaeological remains of the Saints themselves."[8]

Significantly, as Coe recognized, by 1973 the LDS Church had already established a firm and primary tie with historical archaeology through the restoration project at Nauvoo. Even though as a profession the discipline was still relatively young at the time Coe made these remarks, the LDS Church had already sponsored historical archaeology in Nauvoo for more than a decade. Indeed, President McKay's decision to support the restoration project came only months after his decision to sponsor the archaeological program of the NWAF. Similarly, the mandate given to the NWAF to approach their archaeological research from a strictly secular perspective coincided with President McKay's support for the secular interpretation of Nauvoo. Consequently, in the same way that the NWAF excavations in Mesoamerica garnered the respect and admiration of noteworthy non-LDS archaeologists, the restoration of Nauvoo initially drew the attention and support of nationally prominent non-LDS historic preservationists.

As discussed earlier, Harold P. Fabian and A. Edwin Kendrew were two such individuals who, although not members of the LDS Church, greatly influenced the work of restoration in Nauvoo. Given their years of experience with similar projects, both men understood the importance of archaeology to the restoration process. As a member of the Advisory Board on National Parks, Historic Sites, Buildings, and Monuments, Fabian reviewed and consulted on dozens of restoration projects involving archaeological excavations. Similarly, with nearly forty years of experience at Colonial Williamsburg, where archaeology had been employed since 1929, Kendrew was intimately familiar with the vital role of archaeological excavations in a restoration project.[9] Thus, it is no surprise that archaeological investigation was, from the beginning, an integral part of the overall plans for the restoration of Nauvoo. Not only was archaeology highlighted in the original plans for the project, as set forth in Fabian and Kimball's "Outline for the Restoration of Nauvoo,"[10] it was also specifically mentioned in Kendrew's "General Principles for the Restoration of Nauvoo." This latter document in particular was explicit in stating that, among other things, "The basis of all reconstruction and restoration work shall center on careful and skilled examination of existing remains and archaeological findings, all available historical records and other evidence of this nature."[11]

Early Excavation of the Nauvoo Temple

Given this emphasis on the importance and necessity of archaeological investigation, it is not surprising that some of the first work performed for the restoration project was the excavation of the Nauvoo Temple site. From the beginning, NRI's board of trustees and the LDS Church hierarchy saw the Nauvoo Temple as the centerpiece of the restoration project, and there was substantial enthusiasm early on with respect to its possible reconstruction.[12] Consequently, even before the official formation of NRI, the LDS Church, with the help of Kimball and Fabian, hired Dr. Melvin L. Fowler, curator of North American archaeology and assistant professor of anthropology at Southern Illinois University in nearby Carbondale, to conduct preliminary excavations at the Nauvoo Temple site. Interestingly, Kimball and Fabian had originally approached Dr. Jesse D. Jennings, noted archaeologist at the University of Utah, to direct the excavation. Jennings declined the offer but recommended his colleague, Fowler, at SIU. Although Fowler was a prehistoric archaeologist with little experience excavating historic sites, he was more geographically proximate to Nauvoo and was also a member of the RLDS Church.[13] Thus, in the middle of December 1961, Fowler directed the placement of several exploratory backhoe trenches across the frozen Temple lot in what was the first historical archaeology investigation ever conducted at a Mormon-occupied site.

The purpose of this preliminary investigation was "to locate through the application of archaeological techniques, the exact location of the temple foundations." After carefully excavating three test pits by hand and placing six additional test holes throughout the site using a small well auger, Fowler had a good idea of the site's dimensions and general stratigraphy, which included layers of ashy soil, charcoal, and rubble. He then employed "a more rapid technique of testing" in the form

8. Standing on an excavated pier of the Nauvoo Temple, 1961, J. LeRoy Kimball (second from left) and Harold P. Fabian (far right). Courtesy of the Archives of the Church of Jesus Christ of Latter-day Saints.

of a backhoe, which soon thereafter encountered the large blocks of limestone with which the Temple's foundation was constructed (figure 8).[14]

In all, Fowler located four masonry piers, which he interpreted as part of the Temple's south foundation wall, and the ghost impression of what he believed was a segment of the structure's east wall.[15] In the process, he also discovered a skeleton in a recent grave, a large number of artifacts, and an area highly disturbed by bulldozing a few years prior to his digging that had badly disturbed a significant portion of the site.[16] In addition to reporting his findings, Fowler recommended that a thorough archaeological excavation of the Temple basement be undertaken, as "it represents an important historical 'archive' not only for the building of the temple itself and the reconstruction of old Nauvoo, but also for the interpretation of the life and times of the western frontier of the 1840s." He estimated that such an excavation could be completed at a cost of $15,000, and dutifully promoted the use of the university to accomplish the proposed project.[17]

When the positive results of this preliminary investigation were reported to the LDS Church hierarchy, a full season of archaeological investigation was authorized for the following summer. Interestingly, the contract for archaeological work was arranged through Dr. John O. Anderson, associate dean of the Graduate School and coordinator of Research and Projects at SIU, who also happened to be the president of a small congregation of the LDS Church. Although Fowler was interested in continuing the excavation of the Temple basement, his other commitments required that he participate only in a supervisory role as general director of the project.

9. Dee F. Green at the Nauvoo Temple site, summer 1962. Courtesy of the Archives of the Church of Jesus Christ of Latter-day Saints.

However, he recommended one of SIU's graduate students in anthropology, Dee F. Green (1934–2002), as the project's field supervisor (figure 9). Green had no more experience excavating historic sites than did Fowler, but as a member of the LDS Church from Salt Lake City he enthusiastically accepted the opportunity to direct the excavations at the Temple site during the summer of 1962.[18]

Work began on June 15, 1962, and lasted for three months. Working with Green was a twelve-person crew comprised of students from SIU and BYU, as well as other experienced individuals from Utah and Illinois. The first several weeks of excavation were productive, but the work progressed slower than anticipated, primarily because of confusion created by the misidentification of the architectural features discovered by Fowler the previous December. For a long time Green and his crew worked under the assumption that the masonry piers uncovered by Fowler constituted the south wall of the Temple's basement. It was not until excavation extended beyond these piers, however, that Green and others realized the piers were not part of the Temple's south wall but supports within the basement's interior. Once this discovery was made, the true southern limits of the Temple's basement were located and the excavation of the foundation walls proceeded more smoothly.

Although this early confusion slowed the project considerably and resulted in some areas of the site being excavated at levels deeper than expected, it did lead to one of the major discoveries of the season, namely, that the Temple's basement floor was not level. That is, because the crew was unintentionally excavating in the interior of the Temple's foundation, they uncovered sections of the sand floor that sloped downward to the center of the basement. This was at first puzzling to Green and others, but once the true location of the southern foundation wall was revealed, the nuances of the basement's floor plan began to be understood. It was realized, for example, that a series of rooms, indicated by the remains of masonry partitions, were situated along the basement's north and south foundation walls. These rooms had floors that were clearly level, but just beyond their limits the sand floor began to gradually slope toward the basement's center, where, according to historical documents, the Temple's large baptismal font once sat. Confirming the font's existence, fragments of the carved stone oxen on which the font originally rested were discovered in some of the deeper excavations.

In addition to creating some early confusion, the sloping nature of the Temple's basement floor created other unanticipated difficulties. At the time the contract outlining the parameters of the Temple excavation was drafted, Fowler, Kimball, Fabian, and others believed the Temple's basement floor was uniformly level. Indeed, the language of the contract reflects this assumption, requiring that "The depth of the excavation shall be on a horizontal level with the bottom of the old Temple foundation walls."[19] Given that a large portion of the actual basement floor sloped to a depth well below the bottom of the Temple's foundation walls, this particular clause in the archaeology contract prevented Green and his crew from excavating the central portion of the Temple's basement. Although the contract could have been modified, Kimball, Fabian, and others decided instead to enforce the original language of the agreement. Green regretted this decision and recorded his feelings in his journal.

Today has been rather traumatic to say the least. Dr. [John O.] Anderson, Brother [A. Hamer] Reiser, Mr. [Harold P.] Fabian, + Dr. [J. LeRoy] Kimball held their meeting. The result is a literal interpretation of the contract that calls for the exposure of the walls, and the uncovery of the floor, nothing below. This is unfortunate in many ways, since it will mean re-staking + excavation another year if negotiations can be worked out. It also means a highly increased tempo of work. . . . We'll be moving a lot of dirt the next few weeks, and the crew will have to be kept at top strength.[20]

A short while later, after he had reviewed the contract and

confirmed the stipulation that limited the depth of the excavation to the bottom of the Temple's foundation walls, Green again expressed his disapproval in his journal:

This means that on the inside [of the Temple's basement] we'll only have to drop squares to about 5 ft. deep. This is well above the floor level + the font or the remains thereof. It will therefore mean another season if things are to be done right + completed. The interpretation being put on the contract, at least at present, is very literal. Although I do not agree with this as the best way to do the job archaeologically, I'm afraid that at this point I have no other choice. I'll have to do the very best job that I can within the bounds set for me + hope that something is done soon or at least next year to clear up these problems, so that we can go about our work in a more scientific manner.[21]

Undoubtedly, part of the reason for the literal interpretation of the contract's language was the desire to have the excavation completed—at least to some degree—before the season ended. Fowler had assured representatives of both NRI and the LDS Church that the entire project could be completed in a single season. However, when the excavation did not progress as quickly as anticipated, Kimball, Fabian, and others began to worry the project would be left unfinished. Realizing that full excavation of the Temple basement would not be possible, the men resorted to a literal reading of the contract's clause, hoping not to have to extend what was supposed to be a single summer's work into a multiyear undertaking. Enforcing the limitation on the excavation's depth, therefore, was a way to minimize their losses and guarantee some sort of closure for the project.

With this mandate, and with a determination to resume

his graduate studies in the fall, Green resolved to fulfill the contract by September 15. The task was ambitious, as there were still large portions of the site that had to be excavated to the desired depth. Nonetheless, by supplementing his crew with ten additional diggers, and by having them work six days a week instead of five, Green set out to rapidly complete the excavation. The quickened pace of work not only tested the stamina of the crew, it also strained Green's ability to adequately supervise and interpret the site. He wrote, "The thing I dislike most about having to move the dirt so fast, is that I don't get enough time to study the profiles, and find it hard to keep up with what is going on all over the site." "I need more time," he continued, "to let the information sink in, and to mull it over + meditate. The speed with which we are working not only makes this impossible, but sometimes a profile is out before I even get a chance to see it. I hope that next year we can slow things down a bit."[22]

In spite of such challenges, Green and his crew expeditiously removed the remaining five feet of overburden from much of the site and successfully completed the excavation by September 14. Although hurried, the excavation was productive in that it revealed a number of the Temple basement's important features (figure 10). For example, in addition to discovering the sloping basement floor and a number of smaller partition walls, the north, south, and east foundation walls were located and uncovered. Furthermore, although most of the west foundation wall was on property not then owned by the LDS Church, portions of the basement's northwest and southwest corners were excavated, making it possible to know the general dimensions of the Temple's basement. The excavation in these corner

10. Excavation of the Nauvoo Temple site, summer 1962. Courtesy of the Archives of the Church of Jesus Christ of Latter-day Saints.

areas also revealed sections of the circular impressions left by the Temple's northwest and southwest stairwells. Equally important was the discovery of a large interior wall near the west end of the basement, thought to have been constructed to provide additional support to the Temple's tower. Finally, the "most intriguing and unexpected find of the season" was a long stone tunnel, believed to be the drain for the baptismal font that once sat in the Temple's basement.[23]

In sum, although rushed to complete the excavation on time, Green and his crew uncovered the remains of most of the major elements of the Temple's basement floor plan. These included the central font room with the sloping floor, a number of side rooms along the north and south walls, the circular stairwells in the northwest and southwest corners, and a large interior support wall at the west end of the basement. Equally significant is what they did not find, namely, rooms along the east wall of the Temple basement, which some historians believed existed. Moreover, even though the central font area was not dug to the basement floor, leaving a good portion of the site unexcavated, the 1962 excavation generated more than 1,200 bags of artifacts and approximately 150 cardboard boxes of dressed Temple stone, including some pieces of the carved stone oxen on which the Temple's baptismal font once rested.[24]

By December 1, 1962, Green had completed a detailed report of the excavation's findings, copies of which were forwarded to NRI officials and the LDS Church hierarchy in Salt Lake City. Although the deepest levels of the site remained unexcavated, the men seemed generally pleased with the results of the archaeological work. Upon receipt of the report, Kimball wrote to Anderson at SIU to tell him, "The over-all response has been very good and we feel that we can commend you upon the work that has been accomplished."[25] This initial positive response was encouraging to Anderson, Fowler, and Green, who were hoping SIU would be asked to return to Nauvoo to excavate the rest of the Temple site. For a number of reasons, however, their contract was never renewed.

First, there was confusion over which entity of the LDS Church had responsibility for the Nauvoo Temple site. Since the 1930s, when the Church had first purchased portions of the Temple lot, the site was under the stewardship of the Church's Northern States Mission. Thus, when Richard W. Maycock, then president of the Northern States Mission, received word in late December 1961 that Kimball and Fabian were having the Temple lot excavated, he sent a telegram to Howard W. Hunter, one of the Church's twelve apostles, asking him, "Are they authorized [?] If so under whose direction are they working [?] What if any is my responsibility [?]"[26] A reply telegram from the Church's First Presidency arrived the following day, informing the mission president that "Fabian et al [are] making a preliminary survey only," and assuring him that the Church hierarchy "will advise you as to future operations."[27]

Complicating this situation was the formation of Nauvoo Restoration, Inc., in June 1962, days after Green and his crew began their full season of excavation. In addition to the Northern States Mission, NRI constituted a second Church-sponsored organization with a vital interest in the Nauvoo Temple site. Therefore, the LDS Church hierarchy had to decide which of the two entities would ultimately have responsibility for the site. Writing to Green in late December 1962, Kimball expressed his hope for the situation. "There has not been much progress made as to who is assuming authority for next year's work on the Temple Block," he wrote. "We hope we [NRI] may receive the assignment, but we are not sure as at present."[28] Kimball communicated similar sentiments to Anderson at SIU a short while later. "We are not sure just yet," he wrote, "as to what procedure will be followed this summer, though I feel that Nauvoo Restoration will have control of the area."[29] Unfortunately, a second excavation season during the summer of 1963 was put off because a decision concerning the Temple site had not been reached. In fact, it was not until later that year the LDS Church hierarchy granted NRI control of the Temple site and all other Church-owned properties in Nauvoo. By this time, however, another problem had surfaced that further stalled additional archaeological work at the site.

In the middle of July 1963, Kimball called Anderson at SIU and "indicated that it was the feeling in Salt Lake that the University had not fulfilled its portion of the agreement and that it should undertake a very thorough analysis of all of the artifacts which were taken out of the Nauvoo [Temple] excavation."[30] This took Anderson completely by surprise, as it was his understanding, and that of Fowler, that the university had fully complied with its part of the contract. At issue was a phrase in the contract that called for the university "to complete the project of excavation, archaeological survey and report *including a cultural analysis of the findings in the area*."[31] On the one hand, because Green's archaeological report did not include an analysis of the artifacts found in the course of the excavation, officials of the LDS Church believed the university had not adequately met the terms of the contract. On the other hand, Anderson and Fowler argued that the language of the contract did not indicate such a complete analysis. Given that more than 1,200 bags of artifacts had been recovered from the excavation and that the university had already incurred more than $5,000 in additional expenses on the project, it is not surprising that Anderson and Fowler were concerned with this new demand. Adding to their frustration was the fact that the request came more than six months after they had submitted the original archaeological report. Commenting on what he perceived to be unrealistic expectations, Anderson wrote, "I cannot help but feel that the Church misunderstands what can be accomplished in a research program of this nature in such a limited period of time."[32]

In spite of such frustrations, however, and partly because of their continued interest in future work at the site, Anderson and Fowler agreed to provide the LDS Church with an analysis of the artifacts from the Temple site. Given their time and financial limits, Fowler told Kimball "it would be physically impossible to give you a complete catalog of all the specimens recovered." He also noted that because the excavation stopped at the bottom of the foundation walls, "most of the artifacts we have are from the time after the Mormon occupation of Nauvoo."[33] Thus, as a compromise, Fowler provided a short report that analyzed only a sample of the total artifacts recovered at the site. Focusing on the artifacts from only two of the site's excavation squares, Fowler demonstrated that "nearly all of the artifacts from the site are to be found in the ash zone," below the level of the foundation walls where the majority of the excavation stopped. He also reiterated his belief that "[u]nless it is desired to learn about the details of the post-Mormon occupation of the site those materials above the ash zone can be largely disregarded."[34]

Beyond these general conclusions, Fowler's report also attempted to interpret some of the artifacts uncovered at the site. For example, he argued that "[t]he large number of square nails from the ash zone are indicative of the extensive amount of wood construction inside the temple walls." He also suggested the appearance of lead fragments in the ash zone reflected their use as cushions in the joints between large masonry pieces, as indicated in contemporary historical accounts. Moreover, he proposed "that by carefully plotting the fragments of glass from the different squares . . . one might be able to suggest the actual locations of the windows in the building." Finally, Fowler observed that the numerous pieces of worked limestone recovered from excavations provide many details about the Temple. In particular, he described how particular fragments of the stone oxen that once supported the Temple's baptismal font upheld documentary evidence that "the oxen were buried up to their knees in a brick foundation." In closing, Fowler affirmed, "There is no doubt in my mind that a detailed analysis of these artifacts can add greatly to the knowledge of the architectural detail of the building," and "There is no doubt that there is significant data yet to be gained from the site."[35]

The artifact report was completed by late June 1964 and sent off to Salt Lake City. Although it analyzed only a sample of the total artifact assemblage, the report was enough to appease officials of both the LDS Church and NRI. Upon receiving the report, Kimball remarked, "Their interpretation and our interpretation, according to the contract signed, are not in agreement, but I suppose the best has been done and we will have to be satisfied."[36] Accordingly, the contract with SIU was finally closed. Even though Fowler and others remained convinced that a more detailed study of the Temple artifacts could provide important insights into the nature of the building, it does not appear the rest of the artifacts from the 1962 excavation were ever analyzed.[37]

Wanted: Historical Archaeologist for Nauvoo

Although NRI's first experience with historical archaeology had not been entirely pleasant, it did prove that archaeological investigation could reveal important information about the structures in Nauvoo. Convinced that such work was necessary for the success of the restoration project, and eager not to miss another excavation season, the trustees began making plans to resume archaeological work in the summer of 1964. Despite their frustrations with the earlier excavation of the Temple lot, they considered the possibility of once again engaging the services of archaeologists at SIU to conduct additional excavations in Nauvoo. However, Fowler himself expressed the belief that "N.R.I. would be better off to hire its own archaeologist . . . rather than have S.I.U. or any other institution undertake further excavation." Fowler recommended Green as a capable and conscientious candidate for the job, but cautioned that Green would need direction, "as he is self-willed and quite unwilling to take suggestions after being placed in control."[38] The trustees were not interested in hiring Green, however, partly because they felt the 1962 excavation, although valuable, "was not of sufficiently high caliber."[39] Instead, they continued searching in earnest for a qualified archaeologist who could finish the excavations at the Temple site and direct additional archaeological work in Nauvoo.

As early as September 1962, the very month Green and his crew completed the Temple excavation, the trustees had established contact with LDS apostle Howard W. Hunter concerning the possibility of having an archaeologist from BYU participate in the Nauvoo restoration project.[40] Hunter was the chairman of the advisory board for the BYU-New World Archaeological Foundation and as such was intimately involved with the Church-sponsored archaeology being conducted in Mesoamerica.[41] Unfortunately, Hunter reported there was nobody from BYU available at the time, so the search continued.[42] Several months later, Kimball contacted Jesse Jennings at the University of Utah, hoping Jennings could again recommend an archaeologist for the job. He also recruited the help of A. Edwin Kendrew of Colonial Williamsburg in the search. Although a number of prospective archaeologists had been interviewed by late May 1964, none was available to work for NRI.[43] After more than a year and a half of searching, it became rather obvious to the trustees that it was exceedingly difficult in the early to mid-1960s to find a willing and adequately trained archaeologist with experience excavating historic sites. "It looks like the best thing to do," wrote Kimball early in the summer of 1964, "is to start looking for a competent archaeologist who can begin work in the spring of 1965." "It is too late," he declared, "to get one this year."[44]

Although the search was slow-moving, the trustees were unwilling to put their restoration plans on hold any longer. Thus, at the beginning of June 1964 they authorized NRI's historian, T. Edgar Lyon (1903–78), to "supervise the completion of the excavation on the temple block and such other archaeological investigation as is authorized by the management."[45] Lyon was an accomplished LDS historian, but he was also somewhat of an amateur archaeologist, having developed an interest in the discipline and its potential contributions to the study of history while completing courses in archaeology at the University of Chicago during his graduate studies in the early 1930s.[46] Aware of his interest and background in the discipline, the trustees temporarily gave Lyon responsibility for the archaeological component of the restoration project and authorized him to employ an assistant to help with this work. Within weeks, no fewer than four graduate students had responded to his advertisements for a part-time archaeologist, demonstrating that it was evidently much easier to find students who were willing to spend their summer in Nauvoo than it was to locate a qualified full-time archaeologist for NRI.[47] Despite the positive response, however, a student assistant was not hired. Instead, Lyon teamed up with NRI's resident architect, Kevin R. Watts, to carry out his archaeological responsibilities. Although Watts's archaeological qualifications are unknown, he understood the importance of archaeology to his primary assignment, which was to make architectural drawings and reports for six of the historic Nauvoo homes, preparatory to their restoration.

Together, Lyon and Watts supervised archaeological explorations around some of the old Nauvoo homes during the summer of 1964. These small-scale excavations were geared at locating buried architectural features, such as foundations, walks, cisterns, wells, areaways, and the like, in the vicinity of the standing historic structures so that these too could be restored.[48] Although limited archaeological work around some of the historic homes proceeded in this fashion, additional excavations at the Temple site were not undertaken at this time. In fact, as the summer progressed Lyon was told, "it would be best to leave the temple lot investigation alone," and that NRI would "prepare to start the real archaeological investigation in the spring."[49]

In preparation for the start of the real archaeology the following spring, Lyon spent the month of October 1964 visiting several successful restoration projects, including Salem, North Carolina; New Salem, Illinois; and Colonial Williamsburg,

Virginia. At the latter, Kendrew arranged for Lyon "to visit the various departments and spend between one and three hours with each of the various department officials." "From them," Lyon reported, "much was learned concerning the magnitude of restoration work and the need for careful planning, careful record keeping, and honesty in dealing with historical facts." Included in his itinerary was a visit to Colonial Williamsburg's archaeological laboratory, where Lyon observed the "cleaning and preservation of artifacts—leather, fabrics, wood, china, glass, etc." He also observed some of the ongoing site work and learned something about "dating items and periods" and "recording data" on archaeological sites. In this way, even the archaeological program at Nauvoo was subject to the influence and guidance of Colonial Williamsburg.[50]

These experiences proved useful as Lyon made plans for the 1965 archaeological season. His proposed budget for the upcoming year outlined what he hoped would be accomplished in terms of archaeology in Nauvoo. First, he suggested making another trip to Colonial Williamsburg to, among other things, "learn the best workable techniques in historic archaeology." Then, in addition to completing the excavation at the Temple site, Lyon budgeted for additional excavations in the vicinity of Nauvoo's standing historic structures. As before, these excavations were focused on locating buried architectural features, such as "wells . . . barns and carriage houses . . . the original log houses and fireplaces . . . summer or outdoor kitchens . . . 'necessary houses' . . . [and] original brick or stone cisterns." Lyon also proposed excavating one or two of Nauvoo's streets to determine if there were any sidewalks, brick pavements, or graveled surfaces and to better understand the nature and age of the stone curbs that still lined the roads. Finally, he planned a number of excavations designed either to investigate the visible foundations of known historic buildings or to pinpoint the location of certain buried foundations.[51]

Although he was prepared to supervise the proposed archaeological work, Lyon did not intend to actually perform the excavations himself. On the contrary, he and NRI's trustees continued to diligently search for a qualified archaeologist to direct the archaeological program in Nauvoo. Indeed, Lyon alone had written letters to eleven universities in search of a competent and experienced archaeologist, but as late as February 1965 had not received a single favorable response.[52] As the summer drew near and their desperation increased, the trustees' expectations shrank. At one point, it appeared they were prepared to hire a graduate student from BYU, but even he declined, believing the financial compensation ($3.00 an hour) was not sufficient for his needs.[53] Thus, with less than three months before the 1965 archaeological season was to begin, NRI was still without an archaeologist.

J. C. Harrington

Fortunately for the trustees, A. Edwin Kendrew was also actively working on locating an archaeologist for the Nauvoo project at this time. As senior vice president of the nation's preeminent historic restoration, Kendrew was well acquainted with the top professionals in the field of historic preservation. These connections proved valuable in his search for an available and qualified archaeologist. By the end of March 1965, Kendrew

11. J. C. ("Pinky") Harrington, "the father of historical archaeology." Courtesy of the Archives of the Church of Jesus Christ of Latter-day Saints.

had located such an archaeologist among his associates in the National Park Service—Jean Carl Harrington (1901–98), commonly known as "Pinky" (figure 11).[54]

Whereas Fowler, Green, and many of the other archaeologists with whom NRI had contact were principally prehistoric archaeologists, Pinky Harrington was a bona fide historical archaeologist with nearly thirty years of experience excavating historic sites for the NPS. Indeed, he is widely regarded as "the father of historical archaeology" because of his early work at Jamestown, Virginia, where he pioneered many of the methods and techniques still used in the discipline today. Given his years of experience, there truly was no archaeologist better qualified for the work at Nauvoo than Pinky Harrington at this time.[55]

Ironically, when Harrington entered graduate school to study archaeology at the University of Chicago in 1932, he had no intention of pursuing a career excavating historic sites. No archaeologist at that time recognized the recent past as a subject suitable for archaeology. Harrington later recalled how unsympathetic his colleagues were toward such work. They said, "This is not our business; this is the business of historians. We are here to deal with pre-history."[56] It is not surprising, then, that Harrington had no desire to work at Jamestown when the NPS first approached him about the job in 1936. He later wrote, "I had no interest in working for the Federal government, preferring an academic association, nor did I see any future in digging a site only 300 years old."[57] So, when the NPS asked him to name his minimum salary, Harrington purposefully put it high ($3,200), thinking this "would get [him] off the hook."[58] Yet, much to his surprise, his offer was accepted. "Oh, that was a lot of money," Harrington later said, "So I had to take the job."[59]

The NPS was chiefly interested in Harrington because of his background in both archaeology and architecture, both of which they believed were essential in excavating a historic site like Jamestown. Harrington later described how the archaeological procedures at Jamestown were "patterned, in part, after those already developed at Colonial Williamsburg, which meant that the project was architecturally oriented." This led to the belief among NPS employees that, "everything else being equal, an architect was best qualified to uncover and interpret structural remains."[60] Thus, in the eyes of the NPS, Harrington was an ideal candidate for the Jamestown position, given his experience in both archaeology and architecture.

Harrington's background in architecture stemmed from his days as an undergraduate at the University of Michigan, where he completed his bachelor's degree in architectural engineering in 1924. For his senior thesis project he joined the School for American Research in Santa Fe and made measured drawings of Spanish missions in New Mexico during the summer of 1923. While there, Harrington developed an interest in archaeology and a love for New Mexico, leading him to return to the area following graduation. Although he worked first for the New Mexico Highway Department, and later for a mining company designing mining buildings, he spent some of his free time pursuing his newfound interest in archaeology. On more than one weekend he and his friends visited the well-known archaeologist A. V. Kidder, who was excavating at Pecos during this time. Ultimately, however, Harrington returned to the Midwest and took a position with an architect in South Bend, Indiana, where he remained until 1932, when, in the midst of the Great Depression, the architectural office closed down. It was then that Harrington, faced with unemployment, decided to pursue a graduate degree in archaeology. "[I]t was a matter of three choices," he later said, "either working for the Government, selling apples, or going back to school and doing graduate work. So I chose the latter."[61]

Harrington's experiences in New Mexico had engendered a genuine interest in prehistoric archaeology and prompted him to pursue a Ph.D. at the University of Chicago, where he "had every intention of becoming a straightforward anthropologist."[62] Little did he know, however, that his background in architecture would launch his career excavating historic sites. Nonetheless, in 1936, having learned of his experience in both archaeology and architecture, the NPS offered Harrington the job at Jamestown. His active career with the NPS prevented him from ever completing his Ph.D.

In the spring of 1965, when Kendrew approached him concerning the project in Nauvoo, Harrington was preparing to retire after nearly thirty years with the NPS. His excavations in Jamestown, in which the institutional origins of historical archaeology took shape, began in 1936 and continued until the Second World War, when Harrington was made acting superintendent for Colonial National Historic Park. After the war, in 1946, he was promoted to Eastern Regional archaeologist for the NPS, at which time he undertook excavations of significant historic sites such as Fort Raleigh, North Carolina, Fort Necessity, Pennsylvania, and the Glasshouse at Jamestown. Finally, in 1954, he was promoted to regional chief of interpretation and became involved in developing interpretive services for the new visitors' centers being built in connection with the Mission 66 program, which was just getting under way. All in all, in his nearly thirty years with the NPS, Harrington personally excavated or supervised more than forty archaeological projects at both historic and prehistoric sites.[63] His contributions to the NPS and to the field of historical archaeology were duly recognized in 1952, when the secretary of the interior awarded him the Department of the Interior's highest honor, its Distinguished Service Award. Among other things, the award recognized Harrington's contributions to the young field. The commendation read, in part,

As archeologist in charge of the Jamestown project, he has pioneered in the field of historic site archeology and today is recognized as the outstanding authority in his field in the United States. In the course of his work, he has developed new methods and techniques of research which are accepted as standards in his profession. By papers presented at meetings of professional societies, in lectures to conservation groups, and in his publications, Mr. Harrington has done much to further a high standard of research in historic site archeology, resulting in a better understanding and appreciation of American history.[64]

In accordance with NPS policy, all of Harrington's excavations at historic sites "were only done if the [archaeological] information was essential for some kind of development."[65] In other words, the primary purpose of the excavations was to secure information for reconstruction.[66] This is the main reason why the NPS tended to emphasize architecture in its excavations, and why NPS leadership believed Harrington, with his architectural background, was perfect for such work. It was his extensive experience with such reconstruction-driven historical archaeology that made Harrington an ideal candidate for the restoration project in Nauvoo. Indeed, during the five years he excavated at Nauvoo, Harrington continued to do what he had done from the time he started digging Jamestown in 1936: "restoration-related archaeology."[67]

When Harrington agreed to participate in the Nauvoo restoration project, NRI acquired an invaluable resource. J. LeRoy Kimball recognized the caliber of the man he was dealing with on first meeting Harrington in Nauvoo in May 1965. Concerning that occasion, he wrote to Kendrew,

I had the very great pleasure of visiting with Mr. Harrington in Nau-

*voo. . . . I do not know just what I expected, but Mr. Harrington was a pleasant surprise. I enjoyed his wit and was impressed by his evident understanding of archaeological work. He and Mr. Hepburn [restoration architect] seemed to correlate their ideas very well and with Ed Lyon [*NRI *historian] and our historical department cooperating, we have the makings of an efficient team. As I met Mr. Harrington that morning riding around the project with Andy Hepburn, he said, "last night I decided I was going to be very reserved but you got me so stirred up I couldn't help saying a lot of things I had not planned to say." All these things were very interesting and gave me a better idea of the type of man whose services we are procuring.*[68]

As Kimball alluded to, Harrington himself was equally excited about his first visit to Nauvoo. On returning from the trip, Harrington wrote Kimball to express his support and enthusiasm for the project.

There is no need, I am sure, to tell you that I was greatly impressed with Nauvoo, and with the restoration program. . . . [I]f we can make a sound and productive start this season, we should be in a good position to plan a long-range archaeological program, in which I hope I will be able to participate. I am pleased, of course, that I can have a part in organizing and launching the archaeological work, which will constitute an important phase of the overall program. . . . [N]eedless to say, I am looking forward to this summer's project with keen anticipation. . . .the Nauvoo restoration should develop into one of our country's truly significant landmarks.[69]

From the beginning, Harrington sensed the importance of the Nauvoo project and emphasized the role of archaeology in the successful restoration of Nauvoo. "In meetings all over the country," he said, "archaeologists, historians, preservationists, and national trust groups are starting to say, 'What is going on in Nauvoo?' Everybody is watching Nauvoo. What is done will be respected only if the archaeology and the total project is done right." Harrington also understood that the Nauvoo project stood to benefit greatly from the work preceding it. "Ours is a big project," he told the trustees, "getting under way with all the knowledge available today." "We have all the warnings and benefits of previous experience," he continued. "We do not have to go through these struggles and do these things the wrong way, but we ought to be able to do everything right . . . from the beginning. This is a great benefit and this is the reason people are going to be watching critically."[70]

In this sense, Harrington was conscious of the Nauvoo project's place in the history of the field. "In 1929–30," he said, "there were no historical archaeologists. They had to feel their way at Williamsburg. Today we are fortunately in the position where we are going to do it right."[71] Indeed, Harrington considered it both "a privilege and a challenge to be in on the ground floor of what promises to be a milestone in historical archeology."[72]

Harrington's contributions to NRI went beyond mere field excavation. He was also instrumental in planning and implementing a coordinated and long-term archaeological program in Nauvoo. Given his desire to not "become too involved in a particular job after retirement, but still . . . have sufficient work to keep him interested," Harrington and the trustees originally conceived of his role as that of archaeological adviser and supervisor, in much the same way that

Kendrew was NRI's architectural adviser.[73] In this capacity, the trustees looked to Harrington to guide them in their archaeological pursuits.

Restoration Archaeology and Public Interpretation of the Nauvoo Excavations

Harrington's vision for the archaeological program in Nauvoo was clearly outlined in his "Prospectus for Archaeological Investigations" for the summer of 1965. In this document he elucidated a number of general principles to guide the historical archaeology in Nauvoo, all of which were consistently adhered to throughout Harrington's tenure with NRI. First, he succinctly stated the overall purpose of the archaeology program in Nauvoo. "The objective of the archaeological program," he wrote, "is to furnish information and objects which will contribute to the authentic restoration and effective interpretation of Nauvoo."[74] This emphasis on restoration was continually repeated throughout Harrington's career with NRI and plainly reveals his expertise in "restoration archaeology," born of nearly thirty years of previous experience with the NPS. Indeed, in a later proposal for archaeological work in Nauvoo, he wrote, "The primary aim [of the Nauvoo archaeological program] will be to determine the date, identification, and construction details of standing portions of the structures, or of missing elements, such as outside cellar entrances, porches, terraces, walks, and other architectural features which have a functional relation to the buildings and a bearing on their restoration."[75]

Harrington's conception of historic site restoration, however, was by no means simplistic. He understood the larger goals of this kind of work and designed his archaeology to help meet these objectives. "Restoration," he later wrote, "in the broad sense, involves more than the rebuilding and refurbishing of a structure to its former condition. It means the re-creation of the total scene, or some unit of that scene, in so far as practical, in order that visitors may figuratively step back into the past."[76]

Significantly, artifacts not related to architectural or other restoration-related features did not figure prominently in Harrington's archaeological plans for Nauvoo. On the contrary, although Harrington anticipated discovering a large number of such artifacts during excavations in Nauvoo, his "Prospectus" was explicit in stating, "It is highly important that discretion and good judgment be used in uncovering and retaining such material." The procedure he outlined for processing artifacts was decidedly selective. "All excavated material that is not discarded in the field," he explained, "will be placed in marked paper sacks and taken to the field headquarters, where it will be washed, sorted, and numbered." "At this time," he continued, "a second 'screening' will eliminate further irrelevant material, which will be discarded as soon as feasible."[77]

Although highly selective, this practice of retaining only "relevant" artifacts was solidly in line with NRI's larger restoration agenda. From this perspective, artifacts were useful insofar as they contributed to the larger goals of restoration, either by helping date certain structures or architectural features or by becoming part of the permanent furnishings or exhibit collections in the restored buildings. As a trained archaeologist, Harrington knew the scientific value of the thousands of pottery fragments he inevitably encountered during excavation. But as an archaeologist with years of experience with development projects and as an employee of a large-scale restoration program, he also understood that such information was secondary to the overall goals of restoring the historic structures in Nauvoo. The ways in which Harrington dealt with the excavated artifacts in Nauvoo clearly reflects this understanding. Artifacts not suitable for display or dating purposes were frequently discarded, while archaeological reports, although greatly detailed, limited the discussion of artifacts to matters of dating.[78]

Finally, although the Nauvoo archaeological program was heavily oriented toward the restoration of structures and buildings, Harrington understood the broader implications of historical archaeology's role in the restoration project. As he wrote, and firmly believed, "Any excavation project at Nauvoo serves other purposes than just furnishing information for site development and interpretation." In his opinion, there were at least three such extra-restoration purposes of historical archaeology in Nauvoo:

First of all, archaeology in progress is of great interest to visitors. It can fill an interpretive deficiency in the early stage of the development program when there are relatively few things for visitors to see and do. Secondly, it is good for the general "image" of the overall project, and for the cause of historic preservation generally, in demonstrating the scholarly and meticulous manner in which restorations are carried out. In this connection, it provides a point of reference for leaders of guided tours to tell about the restoration program and the various kinds of research that are involved. This is much easier to do, and far more effective, at an excavation than by just driving past an old house. Thirdly, archaeology furnishes subject matter and facts for use in other phases of interpretation, such as audio-visual presentations in the information center, guide leaflets, and other interpretive media.[79]

As with other aspects of the Nauvoo archaeological program Harrington implemented, this explicit public interpretation component of the Nauvoo excavations was rooted in his long career with the NPS. Indeed, Harrington and his wife, Virginia, were pioneers in public archaeology during their excavations at Jamestown in the late 1930s. In addition to tearing down a fence built by their predecessors that encircled the excavation area, they instituted guided interpretive tours of the archaeological excavations for visitors.[80] This strong commitment to the public interpretation of archaeology forged at Jamestown was incorporated into the archaeological program in Nauvoo.[81] One of the general guidelines outlined in the 1965 "Prospectus" for the Nauvoo excavations stated, "In so far as practicable, and when not detrimental to archaeology, visitors will be permitted to observe work in progress. The archaeologists will cooperate in explaining the project to visitors and will assist in training programs for guides, if desired."[82] In some cases, the student excavators themselves, mainly recruited from BYU and other Utah schools, were directly involved in the interpretive process, serving as tour guides during the summer evenings and weekends when the excavations were idle.

The policies Harrington outlined for the Nauvoo archaeological program—namely, the emphasis on restoration, the selective use of artifacts, and the public interpretation of excavations—actively guided the historical archaeology conducted in Nauvoo during his tenure with NRI. They also significantly influenced the archaeological work of others in the restored city. Based on Harrington's years of experience running archaeological projects for the NPS, these policies helped shape a successful and active historical archaeology program in Nauvoo that played an integral role in the larger restoration project.

With general archaeological policies in place, Harrington proposed a modest program of excavation for the 1965 season. The main focus of the proposed work was excavation of the lot on which Brigham Young's house stood. NRI had selected the Brigham Young site for early restoration not only because Brigham Young was "one of the best known personalities of Nauvoo" but because "the house was in serious need of stabilization if it was to be kept standing."[83] Moreover, the site was of interpretive interest to both NRI and the LDS Church because of Young's role in leading the westward Mormon migration of 1846–47.

Not surprisingly, the primary goals of the excavation were directly related to the planned restoration of the Brigham Young House. "We have set the following goals for this summer's work at the Brigham Young Lot," he explained.

1. *Locate fence lines on four sides of Lot.*
2. *Establish fence construction details (spacing of posts; size and depth of post holes).*
3. *Determine soil conditions and other controls.*
4. *Uncover and explore immediate vicinity of small stone foundation partially excavated last year.*
5. *Explore likely areas in search of barn, outhouse, walks and paths.*[84]

Reflecting his own restoration bias, Kendrew expressed

approval of these goals, but also articulated his hope that the excavation would reveal additional information necessary for the structure's authentic restoration. "I think that the goals you have set up for the Brigham Young lot are fine," he declared, "except for the fact that I hope it will be possible to undertake more work around the house itself to establish slope, bulkheads, original topography, walks, etc." "Such evidence," he affirmed, "should be helpful toward determining the period to which the house should be restored and will be vital to the preparation of working drawings for the restoration of the house."[85]

Clyde D. Dollar

Once the board of trustees had approved the approach outlined in Harrington's "Prospectus" for the 1965 season, excavation of the Brigham Young site was ready to begin. As he was still six months from official retirement from the NPS, Harrington was not able to devote his services full-time to the archaeological project. Instead, it was understood that he would find a competent archaeologist to carry out the excavation under his general supervision. To facilitate this situation, the NPS allowed Harrington to schedule three one-week field trips to Nauvoo over the course of the summer, during which he would oversee the Brigham Young site excavation.

Fortunately, Harrington knew a young, self-trained archaeologist named Clyde D. Dollar (1932–83) (figure 12), who in 1965 was completing a series of short-term contracts with the NPS for research on the first Fort Smith (Arkansas).[86] Dollar's academic training was in history, not archaeology, and he approached the field of historical archaeology from this viewpoint. Indeed, he did not hide his belief that the singular goal of historical archaeology was to recover "information

12. Clyde D. Dollar (top row, second from right) and staff of Fort Smith National Historic Site, ca. 1965. Courtesy of Fort Smith National Historic Site.

from America's historic past for use in re-creating this past for America's present and future."[87] In this, his philosophy paralleled that of Kimball, Fabian, Kendrew, and others, who similarly viewed the Nauvoo restoration project in terms of its significance to the nation's history and its benefits to the American people.

Although he was not a professionally trained archaeologist, Dollar had developed a specialized knowledge of nineteenth-century artifacts from his work at Fort Smith. Aware of this, and conscious of the flexible and temporary nature of his contract work with the NPS, Harrington invited him to participate on the Nauvoo project. Flattered by the offer, and believing the job would supply him material for a master's degree thesis, Dollar accepted the invitation. In a letter written shortly before the summer's excavation began, Harrington wrote to Dollar to confirm their agreement and stress the importance of the upcoming season. "I am very pleased," he wrote, "that you are interested in participating in the Nauvoo restoration project, and am confident you will find it both challenging and professionally rewarding. As I have explained to you, this summer's work will be a proving ground for the contribution that archaeology can make to the Nauvoo program."[88]

As agreed upon, Dollar reported at Nauvoo for ten weeks of fieldwork on June 14, 1965, and began the excavation of the Brigham Young lot in earnest. When judged in terms of the five restoration-oriented goals outlined by Harrington, Dollar's excavation was a great success. Indeed, by the close of the archaeological season in September, Dollar had (1) located fence lines on all but the south side of the lot, (2) established important details concerning fence construction, (3) determined historical grade levels and other soil conditions at the site, (4) further excavated the small stone foundation that had been partially uncovered by Lyon and Watts the previous year, and (5) explored the standing barn and located walks on the north and west sides of the lot. Additionally, Dollar investigated the structure's rear basement entrance, discovered what he interpreted to be Brigham Young's original well and cistern, and uncovered a section of brick pavement at the rear of the house.[89] All things considered, the trustees seemed generally pleased with the results of Dollar's excavation. "Although the archaeological work has been painfully slow," wrote Kendrew, "it is being well done and illustrates the benefits of such careful research."[90]

As is common for many archaeological projects, it took Dollar several months to write up the results of the 1965 excavation. Nonetheless, in March of the following year, Dollar submitted a detailed report of his findings to the trustees of NRI. As there was still a great deal of excavation that remained, this was necessarily an interim report. Consequently, most of Dollar's conclusions were explicitly tentative, qualified by statements that "final solutions to many problems inherent in the Brigham Young site must await the close of the next season's work."[91]

Significantly, an entire section of the report was dedicated to the artifacts uncovered during the summer's excavation. Although Dollar's training was in history, not archaeology, his experience with the excavated materials from Fort Smith made him one of the few experts in nineteenth-century artifacts at the time. Reflecting this interest, his interim report included a lengthy treatise on the value of artifacts to archaeological research and an explanation of the relative dearth of information related to artifacts of the early nineteenth century. In light of this situation, Dollar confidently expressed his hope that "as the restoration work at Nauvoo becomes known and recognized, it will serve as both a focal point and a center for the assimilation and dissemination of pertinent early nineteenth century archaeological information."[92]

Dollar's confidence was somewhat bolstered by the large number of artifacts discovered during the 1965 excavation, which he classified into three general categories: (1) construction material, consisting of nails, bricks, and window glass; (2) personal effects, including marbles, porcelain doll parts, toothbrush and comb fragments, straight pins, cloth, buttons, and slate pencil leads; and (3) household items, which included oil lamp chimneys, drinking glasses, bone-handled knives and forks, chamber pots, and large quantities of bottles and dishes. The historic ceramics seemed especially to excite Dollar. Indeed, to highlight how truly impressive this assemblage was, he exuberantly declared, "not even the Smithsonian Institution can claim to have the quantity, quality, or style spectrum of early nineteenth century ceramics as the ceramic artifacts discovered at the Brigham Young site this past summer!"[93]

Of all the artifacts, those discovered during Dollar's excavation of the small stone foundation uncovered by Lyon and Watts the previous summer were of particular interest. What was originally thought to be a shallow stone foundation turned out to be a large stone-lined shaft (later interpreted as a privy vault), more than seven feet deep, filled with "building debris, junk, and household garbage of all types."[94] In the lower levels of this vault Dollar discovered a number of pottery fragments of a previously unknown pattern of blue transfer ware, some of which revealed a distinctive sunburst stamp that enclosed the words "Poonah/J." Although Dollar was enthusiastic that these ceramic fragments "added what might be an original and very interesting ceramic pattern to our knowledge of early nineteenth century ceramics," later research proved unfruitful in identifying the precise age or origin of this pottery.[95] To this day the "Poonah" wares from Nauvoo remain a mystery.

Notwithstanding their uniqueness, and despite Dollar's recognition of their potential utility in dating the site and determining "cultural affinity," the artifacts from the 1965 Brigham Young excavation were never subjected to thorough archaeological analysis.[96] On the contrary, consistent with the general nature of historical archaeology in Nauvoo at the time, the artifacts were only selectively utilized in the restoration project. Thus, despite their known scholarly potential, the artifacts unearthed at the Brigham Young lot rarely served a purpose other than to date specific sites and features or illustrate the kinds of objects found at the site. Their function was simply to illustrate the kinds of objects Brigham Young might have used, and not necessarily to interpret the material culture of the Nauvoo period. As Harrington observed, "This collection will make possible a far more convincing and exciting presentation to visitors when used in connection with the furnishings in the restored home."[97] After all, as is common for sites associated with famous individuals, most visitors were interested in seeing something either built or used by Brigham Young.[98]

In addition to revealing information useful for the authentic restoration of the Brigham Young House and yielding large numbers of artifacts, the 1965 excavation was successful in demonstrating the popularity of interpreting archaeology to the public. At the close of the season, Harrington remarked how the summer's excavation confirmed what he had seen in dozens of projects for the NPS, "that digging in archaeology is most exciting to the people. They really like to get excited about it. It's wonderful. It takes the time of archaeologists but it pays off a hundred times over."[99]

By all accounts, then, the 1965 excavation of the Brigham Young site was a great success. Dollar successfully achieved the modest goals for the excavation, with the advantage of the policies, guidelines, and supervision provided by Harrington. Although in many ways the 1965 season was a trial run for historical archaeology in Nauvoo, the successful outcome ensured the continuation of the archaeological program in future years.

Conflict with Harrington

When NRI's trustees began discussing the future of the archaeological program in July 1965, the excavation of the Brigham Young site was well under way. As far as they were concerned, the excavation was proving a success, confirming the value of historical archaeology to the restoration project and solidifying their positive opinions of Harrington and Dollar. Accordingly, plans were made to continue the archaeological program.

As Harrington's retirement was only months away, he agreed to take a much more active role than previously possible. Specifically, he committed to devoting "approximately four months a year to the Nauvoo project, primarily in planning and directing the archaeological program." About ten weeks of this time would be spent in Nauvoo, leaving him an additional six or seven weeks "for preparation of reports, long-range planning, consultation with the restoration architects and others in the organization, and possibly some special research at points away from Nauvoo." All in all, Harrington was delighted to continue his association with NRI. He wrote to Kimball,

> *After learning more of your overall plans for Nauvoo during my last visit, I am more interested than ever in having a part in the program. I was especially pleased with the frank talks I had with you and Ed Kendrew, and flattered that you both seemed anxious for me to join the "team." I can say without qualification that both Virginia and I are looking forward to my retirement with greater enthusiasm than we ever had before—not just for the professional challenge that the Nauvoo project offers, but even more to the personal association with a friendly and stimulating group of people.*[100]

At the time Harrington's plans were being solidified, Dollar's future with the restoration project looked equally bright. In fact, Harrington openly expressed complete approval of Dollar's work and genuinely advocated on his behalf. "In my opinion," he declared, "Clyde Dollar has shown a very fine spirit of cooperation and interest, as well as demonstrating superior professional competence. I believe he will be a definite asset to the organization and I hope we can work out a satisfactory arrangement to work him into our future plans."[101] Remarkably, however, less than two months after Harrington expressed these sentiments, he and Dollar were at seemingly irreconcilable odds.

Although the seeds of this conflict can be traced to discussions held several weeks earlier, during which Harrington, Kimball, and Kendrew had worked out plans for future archaeological work, the dispute with Dollar reached a rapid climax during Harrington's third and final one-week visit to Nauvoo in mid-September 1965. The trip had been scheduled to coincide with the annual meeting of the board of trustees on Saturday, September 18, during which Harrington was to report on the results of the excavation at the Brigham Young site. Earlier that week, he and Dollar had a number of opportunities to discuss future plans for the site and the archaeological program at large. It was during these conversations that the conflict between the two men ultimately emerged.

Over the course of the summer, Dollar had developed a number of ideas for expanding the archaeological program in Nauvoo, and he took advantage of the opportunity to share these with Harrington during the week prior to the September meeting of the board of trustees. In essence, Dollar proposed an expanded archaeological program in which excavations would be conducted eight months of the year, instead of just the three months during the summer. In addition, Dollar suggested the archaeological program expand to encompass a number of research projects, which he believed would greatly facilitate the correlation of archaeological findings with the actual restoration work of NRI. These included, among other things, developing chronologies for historic ceramics, nails, and bricks, as well as developing better methods for locating historic areas and improving excavation techniques.

Dollar's proposed expansion of the Nauvoo archaeological program was based on his experiences excavating the Brigham Young site. Nonetheless, according to Dollar, Harrington "completely and categorically vetoed all of the research projects" on the basis that "this was not the time to do anything but be concerned with a future no further away from tomorrow."[102] In reality, however, although Harrington did not support the immediate implementation of the research proposals, he did express sympathy for Dollar's ideas. "I can understand your motives," he wrote, "in 'thinking big' and developing plans for a research center and a broad scientific program." "But," he added, "we are just not ready for it yet. . . . It just is not in the cards right now to develop the broad program you had hoped for, although I can see the day when this will be done, and hope it is not too distant."[103]

Making matters worse was Dollar's perception that Harrington was trying to eclipse his future role in the archaeological program. It was Dollar's understanding "that the archaeological end of the business, with the exception of general guidelines and overall policy, would be left up to [him] to carry out." But when Dollar learned that Harrington would "call the shots" in future archaeological work, he accused Harrington of trying "to easily capitalize on any reputation which I have made here at Nauvoo and take control of an already constructed organization."[104] It was clear from Harrington's point of view, however, that Dollar had severely misunderstood the nature of his assignment. "First of all," he wrote to Dollar, "my indication that you were to be directly in charge of the dig this summer [1965], subject to general supervision by me, should never have been taken to mean that you were to be the 'archaeologist-in-charge' in the long-range program." Although Harrington was "deeply grateful to [him] for jumping in on short notice and assuming responsibility in a demanding and uncertain situation," and praised his many contributions to the summer's dig, he was frank about Dollar's future involvement in the project. "I am sure you realize," he wrote, "that I must direct the archaeological work as my experience and judgment indicate, and as Mr. Kendrew and Dr. Kimball expect of me. If you do not think that the kind of position you would have to accept is one you can happily fill, now is the time to make the decision."[105]

Even before he received Harrington's letter, however, Dollar had taken steps that ultimately resulted in his termination from the archaeological program at Nauvoo. At the center of the ensuing controversy was a nine-page report Dollar wrote entitled "Long Range Plans for Nauvoo Historic Archaeology Research Program."[106] In this report, Dollar committed to writing the ideas he had earlier discussed with Harrington about extending the program's excavation season and implementing a number of ancillary research projects. The report was seen as an incredible act of disloyalty.[107] Not only was it sent to the president of NRI without Harrington's knowledge, but its structure and contents suggested that Dollar was, in effect, taking upon himself the task that Harrington was hired to accomplish—the long-range planning of the archaeological program. Perhaps the clearest indication of Dollar's defiance, however, was the way in which he directly usurped Harrington's supervisory responsibilities with respect to the archaeological work. "In making recommendations concerning the Management and Personnel requirements for the long range Historic Archaeology Program," the report stated, "Harrington, as Consulting Archaeologist, would continue to exercise the same prerogatives which he has for the past season, i.e., general archaeological planning and direction, and the Resident Archaeologist [Dollar] would continue to have direct supervision of all archaeological work in the field and laboratory, including the [proposed] research programs." Dollar's report continued, "This would be a practical matter, of course, as direct supervision cannot be exercised by one individual for eight months and then assumed by another for the remaining four."[108]

Dollar's insistence on having direct supervision of all archaeological work in Nauvoo, and the way in which he chose to publicize a report that was never his responsibility to write, clearly reveal his aversion to be supervised by others. "I must," he later wrote, "be able to work in my own manner and not run the risk of being 'smothered' by Pinky."[109] Exacerbating this situation was Dollar's lack of academic credentials, which fueled insecurities concerning his place among more academically qualified peers. In fact, the prospect of having to work under Harrington's supervision must have been especially difficult because, although Harrington had an esteemed reputation built on nearly thirty years of experience excavating historic sites, he, like Dollar, never finished his Ph.D.

Nonetheless, Harrington had the full confidence of Kimball, Kendrew, and NRI's other trustees. In reference to Dollar's report, Kimball wrote to Harrington and expressed approval and support. "We [the trustees] could see here that the archaeological work could be carried out in no other way than through you, even though some effort had been made to funnel information direct to some of us." Moreover, Kimball made it clear the trustees were leaving the situation with Dollar in Harrington's hands. "As indicated in my last letter," wrote Kimball, "there is no purpose in spending money on Clyde . . . until it is determined what his tenure is to be, and this we will leave up to you."[110] Accordingly, Harrington informed Dollar in late October 1965 that his services with the archaeological program at Nauvoo were terminated.[111]

Although he was dismissed at this time, Dollar was told he would be reconsidered for a place on the project if he were willing to come back on the terms and conditions defined by Harrington.[112] The door was left open in this way primarily because of concerns that important information about the Brigham Young site would be lost if Dollar did not complete the excavation. After all, Dollar still had not submitted his interim report on the Brigham Young site excavation, and there was already some indication that he had taken certain excavation records with him following the close of the dig.[113] Nevertheless, Harrington maintained, "I do not believe it will be at all serious if he does not complete the Brigham Young project himself." "Assuming the records are available," he continued, "there is no reason why someone else cannot finish the work there and write up the [final] report."[114]

Unfortunately, Dollar continued to manifest a cantankerous disposition toward Harrington following his initial termination. Thus, once he was certain Dollar would indeed complete his interim report on the Brigham Young site, Harrington notified him of his final decision. Referencing the occasion of Dollar's original dismissal, Harrington wrote, "Events since that [time] have demonstrated very clearly that you are unwilling to work under me in a secondary position. Your personal attitude toward me and your professional manners have deteriorated to the point that it would be unwise, if not impossible, for you to have a part in the Nauvoo program. The action taken in my letter of October 26, therefore, must stand; namely, that your services with Nauvoo Restoration, Incorporated will not be renewed."[115]

From his perspective, Dollar thought Harrington had swindled him into coming to Nauvoo. He accused Harrington of withholding information about the future of the project and believed Harrington only wanted him involved to tide things over until he could retire from the NPS and assume command.[116] In reality, however, Harrington and his superiors had every intention of making Dollar a permanent part of the organization. Conscious of his age and expressed desires to enjoy his retirement, restoration officials agreed that Harrington would help get an archaeological program up and running only to later turn it over to a much younger archaeologist, who would direct it for years to come. Ironically, Dollar was in position to fill that role until his "failure and expressed unwillingness to work through [Harrington] on any and all Nauvoo matters" became apparent.[117] In short, although Dollar had much to offer the Nauvoo project, and although he stood to benefit greatly from being involved with such a program, his demand to work independently, coupled with his overzealous and premature desires for the archaeological program, in the end ruined his relationship with Harrington and resulted in his termination from NRI.

With Dollar's termination, there arose a need to quickly locate another qualified person to assist Harrington with the archaeological work during the summer of 1966 and beyond. As before, this proved to be a difficult task. "I am working diligently toward securing a qualified archaeologist to assist me," reported Harrington, "but this is not easy." Although he knew of individuals in museums and universities who were qualified for the job, none was able to work under the given circumstances. As Harrington put it, "the type of man we want just isn't available on a seasonal basis."[118] In fact, after searching fruitlessly for several months, Harrington became acutely aware that "until we are working on a more permanent basis, it will not be feasible to secure the services of a competent, experienced archaeologist."[119] Unfortunately, as the restoration project was still in the early stages of development, and because its future funding was far from certain, a permanent, year-round archaeological program, with a second full-time archaeologist, was not immediately forthcoming.

Virginia Harrington: Archaeological Helpmeet

In spite of all this, as Harrington prepared for his first full summer of excavation in Nauvoo, he could take comfort knowing that his wife, Virginia, an archaeologist in her own right, would be available to assist in the archaeological program. Virginia Harrington (1913–2003) came to archaeology by way of history, which she studied as an undergraduate at Swarthmore College in Pennsylvania. Desiring to pursue her interest in archaeology, she enrolled in the graduate program in anthropology at the University of Chicago, where she completed a master's degree in the 1930s. During this time, she worked as a seasonal ranger at Mesa Verde National Park, one of the earliest women rangers ever employed by the NPS. It was also during her graduate studies that she first met her future husband, who was pursuing his Ph.D. in the Department of Anthropology at the University of Chicago at this same time. Although they knew of each other in the Anthropology Department, their relationship did not blossom until after Virginia took a job as a ranger at Colonial National Historical Park in the summer of 1937, the year after her soon-to-be husband took over the archaeological program there. At Jamestown, Virginia helped convert her husband to the practice of interpreting archaeology to the public by initiating a program called "This Week at the Excavations," which involved a weekly archaeological exhibit and daily guided tours of the excavations. This innovative outreach program had a profound impact on her husband. "It taught me something," he remarked. "I'd never had that experience before dealing with the public. But what a pleasure it was to do something like this with the general public and particularly with school children that we encouraged to come."[120]

Although her work at Jamestown was extremely successful, Virginia placed her professional career on hold to raise her two children, during which time she held leadership positions with the Girl Scouts of America and the Parent-Teacher Association.[121] Nonetheless, given her husband's active career with the NPS, she was never too far removed from her interests in archaeology. By the time her husband was invited to work at Nauvoo, their children were grown, leaving Virginia the opportunity to again participate in archaeological excavation and interpretation. In fact, Harrington later recounted how "when he got the idea about coming to Nauvoo, Mrs. Harrington said he could come . . . and give a certain amount of time if she could come and help."[122]

Unsurprisingly, Virginia's conceptualization of archaeology at Nauvoo was directly in line with her husband's. In fact, in a public lecture delivered to the Nauvoo Historical Society entitled "Why Archaeology at Nauvoo," she, like her husband, argued that "the most obvious reason [for doing archaeology in Nauvoo] is that archaeology provides information that is not otherwise available in spite of all the records, books and historical research." To support this assertion, she cited specific examples from the Nauvoo excavations that illustrated how historical archaeology contributes to knowledge of the past. Predictably, the examples all dealt with architectural features—a well, a vegetable cellar, the dimensions of foundation walls—previously unknown from the historical record yet essential to the authentic restoration of the historic sites. In the context of the overarching goals of the restoration project, she concluded, "In spite of the recency of the time and the extent of the historical records, archaeology is necessary to make the data complete."[123]

In addition to contributing information essential for the authentic restoration or reconstruction of a historic site, Virginia explained that artifacts recovered in archaeological excavations also provide important information. However, consistent with her husband's view of artifacts, Virginia expressed her opinion that artifacts were useful primarily as illustrators. Indeed, she explained that artifacts "indicate what was owned and used in times past and throw light on the people who possessed them." For example, she believed artifacts could help answer questions such as "were they rich or poor, self-made or well educated, simple or sophisticated? Did they use elegant chinaware and glass on their tables or were they content with homemade pottery and utensils?" She argued that artifacts also shed light on the craftsmanship of the people and their concern for their work. Like her husband, then, Virginia viewed Nauvoo's artifacts in terms of their ability to illustrate the types of objects used in the past and the kind of people who used them.[124]

Finally, although she believed the primary rationale for historical archaeology in Nauvoo was to retrieve information necessary for the authentic restoration of historic sites, Virginia explained additional reasons for the excavations. First, she noted that archaeology gives a certain amount of prestige to historical restorations. "It is the thing to do," she said. "It makes for status in State and National organizations." Similarly, she explained that archaeology is of great interest to the visiting public. Specifically, she emphasized how archaeology "makes a good show" for visitors, who "tell you that they have heard and read about this kind of thing, but never supposed they would have an opportunity to see it going on, right here in this country." Ultimately, she argued that historical archaeology should be done at Nauvoo, because "What the visitor can see with his own eyes, touch with his fingers, and know with assurance were the actual surroundings and possessions of real people, help him to understand better than written or spoken words how their owners played their part in the Westward Expansion of the United States." Thus, consistent with her efforts at Jamestown thirty years earlier, Virginia joined her husband in promoting the public interpretation of the Nauvoo excavations.[125]

United, therefore, in their views on archaeology's role in the Nauvoo restoration project, Virginia and her husband made significant contributions to NRI's archaeology program from 1966 until 1969, when J. C. Harrington assumed a strictly supervisory role. Indeed, during the four seasons they were at Nauvoo, the Harringtons accomplished a great deal, including the successful excavation and interpretation of the Brigham Young Home, the Wilford Woodruff Home, the Webb Blacksmith and Wagon Shop, and the Times and Seasons Building (which housed the printing office and is now called the Post Office), the results of which were written up in professional reports.[126]

In line with the Harringtons' understanding of archaeology's role in the restoration of Nauvoo, these excavations continued to be oriented toward the larger development and interpretation goals of the restoration project. Consequently, the principal motivation was to provide the architects with data necessary for authentic restoration or reconstruction. For example, in his report on the 1966 season, Harrington explained the purpose of the dig at the Wilford Woodruff site. "The primary objective," he stated, "was to secure information needed in restoring the Woodruff house (porches and other entrance features, basement bulkheads and windows, and 'historic' grades adjacent to the house)." The same was

13. J. C. Harrington excavating cisterns behind the Brigham Young Home, 1966. Courtesy of the Archives of the Church of Jesus Christ of Latter-day Saints.

14. J. C. Harrington in front of the restored Brigham Young Home, 1969. Courtesy of the Archives of the Church of Jesus Christ of Latter-day Saints.

true of the continuing excavations at the Brigham Young site that year (figures 13 and 14). These, Harrington wrote, "were concentrated immediately around the house for the primary purpose of securing information needed in its restoration and to salvage significant information before the ground was disturbed during restoration work."[127]

As planned, however, this emphasis on restoration- oriented archaeology meant that excavated artifacts were primarily used for the select purposes of helping to date a site and its features, or to illustrate the kinds of objects once used at the site. The latter use of Nauvoo artifacts, in particular, resulted in a preference for complete objects, or at least those that could be reconstructed to their original complete (or near complete) form. Hence, with respect to the artifacts from the 1966 excavation of the Wilford Woodruff and Brigham Young sites, Harrington could report that "no particularly interesting artifacts were recovered, other than a nearly complete iron kettle, although artifacts aided materially in dating the numerous questionable features."[128]

The emphasis on the project's larger restoration goals also resulted in the excavations being openly interpreted to the visiting public. The Harringtons both promoted and supported the incorporation of their ongoing excavations into NRI's interpretive guide program. Again, at the end of the 1966 season, Harrington expounded on this element of the archaeological program. "Archaeological excavations in progress," he wrote, "offer a wonderful opportunity to provide a memorable and valuable experience to visitors. I am convinced that a great deal more can be done along this line than in the past, and without affecting the efficiency of the archaeological program." "But," he continued, "it will take a little more planning and more concerted effort on the part of both the archaeological and interpretive staffs. It will require better and more frequent training sessions with the guides, and possibly the use of special supplementary (mimeographed) materials."[129]

Thus, throughout the four seasons he and Virginia actively excavated in Nauvoo, NRI's archaeological program typified what Harrington called "restoration archaeology." With the benefit of their years of experience excavating and interpreting historic sites, it is little wonder the Nauvoo program exemplified this kind of historical archaeology. Indeed, in many ways the Nauvoo archaeological program was the capstone to both of their careers. Whereas from 1936 to 1942, Pinky and Virginia were formulating the practice of historical archaeology and the public interpretation thereof in Jamestown, thirty years later they were applying their accumulated expertise to the restoration of Nauvoo. Consequently, the Harringtons' historical archaeology at Nauvoo was, in essence, the epitome of the restoration archaeology that characterized the early development of the field in the United States.

Rediscovery of the Nauvoo Temple

Of all the sites the Harringtons excavated at Nauvoo, their complete investigation of the Nauvoo Temple site was perhaps their greatest achievement. By the time they became involved with the restoration project, in 1965, the Nauvoo Temple site was an "eyesore" and in disarray. Harrington described it as "an irregular vertical-sided hole in the ground some five feet deep and roughly 100 by 125 feet in size."[130] This, combined with the fact that the earlier excavation by SIU had not reached the Temple's original basement floor, led the Harringtons to propose additional archaeological work at the site.

The first proposal was to renovate and stabilize the site, putting it in a condition "that would permit regular maintenance without damage to archaeological remains, and at the same time, provide better interpretation to visitors."[131] This was readily approved, and the work was carried out in the summer of 1966. The eroding earthen walls left by the former excavation were sloped back, creating a uniform bowl-shaped

15. Excavation of the Nauvoo Temple, 1969. Courtesy of the Archives of the Church of Jesus Christ of Latter-day Saints.

depression, and the entire area was covered in grass. In addition, for interpretive purposes, a five-foot square stone pillar was placed at each of the four corners of the Temple's original foundation. Furthermore, as part of the overall renovation, Virginia excavated a ten-foot-square area around the original Temple well, during which she restored the well to its original level and appearance. The results of this small excavation were influential in planning for additional excavation at the site.[132]

What followed were three additional seasons of excavation, which ultimately revealed the original layout of the entire Temple basement, including the discovery of a number of significant yet previously unknown features (figures 15 and 16).[133] In reality, it was Virginia who directed most of the excavation at the Temple site, with Pinky assisting in the interpretation and digging as needed. Thus, it is appropriate that Virginia was the senior author of the fully illustrated hardbound re-

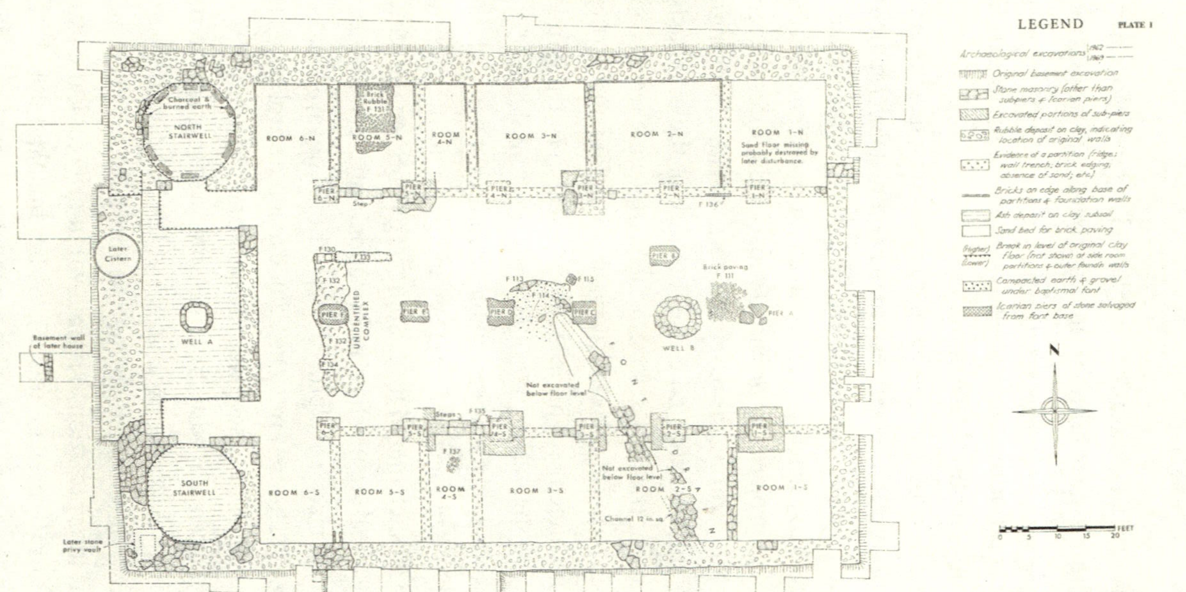

16. J. C. Harrington's drawing of the archaeologically recovered floor plan of the Nauvoo Temple. Originally published in the Harringtons' book on the Temple excavations, *Rediscovery of the Nauvoo Temple: Report on Archeological Excavations* (Salt Lake City: Nauvoo Restoration, Inc., 1971).

port of the Temple excavations published in 1971. Moreover, it is a fitting tribute to both Virginia and her husband that the archaeologically recovered floor plan of the Nauvoo Temple basement is prominently displayed on the back of the SHA's J. C. Harrington Medal (see figure 1).[134]

As would be expected, the Temple excavations, like the others, were primarily oriented toward the eventual development and interpretation of the site. Indeed, following the final season of excavation at the site, Harrington could confidently state, "The Temple project . . . provided most of the information necessary for restoring the basement portion with a fairly high degree of authenticity." Likewise, because of the emphasis on restoration, the artifacts from the Temple site were seen primarily in terms of their relative value to understanding the Temple's architecture. This is made very clear in Harrington's "Proposed Archaeological Program for the Temple Site," in which he stated, "After a reasonable sampling of nails, glass, and lead has been secured, there would be no point in trying to reclaim all such material. . . . Stone fragments, on the other hand, may reveal architectural information, and every fragment of reasonable size or sculptured shape should be saved for future study. . . . The crew must be trained to ignore broken glass and rusty nails, but to save significant stone fragments."[135]

Finally, consistent with the larger interpretive goals of the restoration project, the excavations at the Temple site were intentionally interpreted to the visiting public. Given her interest in interpretation, Virginia voluntarily took the lead in this effort (figures 17 and 18). As her husband noted, although he "was not able to give too much personal attention to visitors," Virginia "went out of her way to meet and talk with visitors, particularly to couples and families who stopped at the Temple site before joining a tour group."[136] Virginia herself reported that these visitors "seemed to welcome the opportunity to ask questions informally and hear about the archaeology, the Temple, and Nauvoo Restoration."[137] Indeed, early on it became "abundantly clear . . . that visitors not only are immensely interested in an archaeological dig, but when the dig involves the Nauvoo Temple, it is even more exciting and intriguing."[138] Building on these experiences, Virginia submitted a "Report on Interpretation at the Temple Site," in which she related the evident public interest in the site and proposed that a "trailside exhibit" be constructed for the purpose of interpreting the excavations to the public. The exhibit, she wrote, "would, primarily, be used for displaying some of the more interesting artifacts, such as melted glass, a series of nails, and some of the sculptured and moulded stone." "There should," she continued, "be brief identifying labels, and probably a simple plan of the [Temple] basement with the visible features marked" in addition to "photographs of the excavations . . . if the space permitted."[139] Beyond the on-site interpretive activities at the Temple lot, Virginia and her husband described and explained the results and significance of the excavations in language free of jargon and comprehensible to the lay public in their final published report. Their motives for writing in this fashion are clearly described in the volume's introduction. "Though this publication is a professional archaeological report," they explain, "it has been prepared with the interests of visitors and members of the Church of Jesus Christ of Latter-day Saints in mind."[140] Thus, through direct interactions with visitors, on-site exhibits, and popular writ-

17. Virginia Harrington interpreting the Nauvoo Temple well, 1966. Courtesy of the Archives of the Church of Jesus Christ of Latter-day Saints.

ings, the Harringtons endeavored to interpret the archaeology at the Nauvoo Temple site to the general public. In so doing, they believed they were providing "an impressive demonstration of the scholarly and sound approach being taken by Nauvoo Restoration, Inc., in its program to interpret the city and life of the Mormon period."[141]

New Kid on the Block: Dale L. Berge

Even though the Harringtons were a competent and efficient archaeological team, NRI's trustees remained anxious to find an "understudy" for the archaeological program. They knew Harrington's age and retired status would prevent the long-term employment of him and Virginia, and they were eager to "expedite the amount of work that needs to be accomplished."[142] Consequently, the search for a second archaeologist continued.

Following the passage of the 1966 National Historic Pres-

18. Virginia Harrington displaying part of a stone ox leg found during the excavation of the Nauvoo Temple, 1969. The original Nauvoo Temple had a baptismal font in its basement that was supported by twelve carved stone oxen. Courtesy of the Archives of the Church of Jesus Christ of Latter-day Saints.

ervation Act, the employment opportunities for individuals with experience in historical archaeology greatly increased as government agencies set out to fulfill the law's mandate to preserve and maintain the historic properties within their respective jurisdictions. Although historical archaeology was still a relatively young discipline, the demand for those with skills was on the rise. "Jobs in this field," observed Harrington in 1967, "are going begging, and a man with relatively little experience can step into one of several at $10,000 a year." In spite of the increasing demand, however, there simply were not enough established historical archaeologists in the United States at this time. Indeed, Harrington admitted, "There are not over ten such men in the country today, and they are all in permanent, secure positions . . . each making from $12,000 to $20,000 a year." Furthermore, although classes in historical archaeology began to appear in American universities as early as the 1960–61 academic year, the first generation of professionally trained historical archaeologists had yet to appear. Again, Harrington recognized the predicament of the situation:

At present, there is no school in the country that trains people for this type of work, although a few offer some of the essential courses. Men with conventional archaeological training have invariably been trained in prehistoric archaeology and lack the very important knowledge and abilities in architecture, architectural history, documentary research, and identification of cultural materials of non-Indian origin. Moreover, these people are not oriented to, nor interested in concentrating in the field of historical archaeology. As it now stands, this highly specialized field can only be learned from experience, and, conservatively, it takes at least five years to acquire the minimum background.[143]

Despite the lack of experienced historical archaeologists at this time, there were strong indications that things were beginning to change. The organization of the SHA in January 1967 was perhaps the most promising sign the discipline was professionally maturing. Given their place during this key moment in the development of the discipline, the Nauvoo excavations were poised to take part in the professionalization of the field. Sensing the historical significance of the situation, Harrington declared, "The Nauvoo archaeologist, in my opinion, has a golden opportunity to make a place for himself

19. From left, J. C. Harrington, T. Edgar Lyon, Dale L. Berge, Ray T. Matheny, J. LeRoy Kimball. Courtesy of the Archives of the Church of Jesus Christ of Latter-day Saints.

in historical archaeology."[144] Nevertheless, owing to the lack of experienced individuals, it was not until 1968 that a promising candidate was located.

In mid-February of that year, Ray T. Matheny, assistant professor of anthropology and archaeology at BYU, notified NRI of a new faculty member in his department named Dale L. Berge (figure 19). According to Matheny, Berge was "one of the few experts in historic ceramics . . . [and] about the best candidate you will be able to find to assist at Nauvoo."[145]

Berge was indeed well qualified for the Nauvoo job. He had both a bachelor's degree in geology (1961) and a master's degree in archaeology (1964) from BYU, and he was finishing a Ph.D. in anthropology at the University of Arizona. Although he went to Arizona to study Paleoindian archaeology, it was there where Berge was first exposed to historical archaeology. It was Bernard Fontana's classes on historical archaeology—among the first of such courses taught at a North American university—that initially attracted him to the emerging field. His interests in historical archaeology were solidified at the Arizona State Museum, where he worked while in graduate school. As a research assistant at the museum, Berge was assigned to identify the historic artifacts in the museum's collections, a task that led to his developing a classification system for historic artifacts of the American Southwest, which he ultimately submitted as his Ph.D. dissertation.[146] Ironically, however, in spite of his interest and experience with historic artifacts, Berge was hired by BYU in February 1968 to fill the vacancy left by two archaeologists specializing in prehistoric Mesoamerican cultures who had taken sabbatical leaves. Nevertheless, it was his background in historical archaeology that caught the attention of NRI's trustees at this time.[147]

After confirming Matheny's claim that Berge "was the best qualified man to be found,"[148] the trustees moved quickly to make arrangements for Berge to join the Nauvoo archaeological program. Berge's employment was seen as a significant step in establishing a more permanent archaeological program at Nauvoo. Since the termination of Clyde Dollar, Harrington had been serving as both general adviser for the Nauvoo program and as the immediate supervisor of a number of specific excavations. With Berge on board, Harrington could now begin to prepare to limit his activities to the advisory role for which he was originally hired. The plan was first to give Berge a small project of his own, to see if he was truly as capable and compatible as anticipated; then, if his performance was satisfactory, he would replace Harrington as NRI's head archaeologist, leaving Harrington to continue in a strictly advisory capacity. Given the amount of time and energy that had been spent searching for Harrington's replacement, the prospect posed by Berge was welcomed indeed. "If Mr. Berge works out satisfactorily," wrote Harrington, "we will really be 'in business.'"[149]

Although Berge had a solid background in historical archaeology, there were some vital differences between him and Harrington. Whereas Harrington was the father of historical archaeology, the man who had ushered in the discipline's institutional beginnings and the champion of "restoration archaeology," Berge represented the next generation of historical archaeologists, those who had received university training in the subject, and who characterized the professional development of the field. This distinction became patently visible during the 1968 season, when the two men worked together for the first time.

As in previous years, the 1968 summer excavations were focused on uncovering information needed for the restoration of particular Nauvoo sites. Harrington finished the investigations at the Brigham Young lot and the Webb Blacksmith and Wagon site, while Virginia continued excavations at the Temple site and Berge began excavations at the recently acquired property of the noted Nauvoo gunsmith, Jonathon Browning (figure 20). Consistent with the restoration objectives guiding the archaeology, Harrington reported that the Browning excavation "will be planned so as to secure information on the house itself as soon as possible, and thus be out of the way of restoration work."[150] Significantly, however, Berge had never before excavated a historic site, let alone one scheduled for restoration. Although educated in historical archaeology at the University of Arizona, his technical experience in the discipline prior to coming to Nauvoo had been limited to historic artifacts.

20. Dale L. Berge (front row, second from left), J. C. and Virginia Harrington (front row, right), and crew behind the Jonathon Browning Home and Gun Shop, 1968. Courtesy of the Archives of the Church of Jesus Christ of Latter-day Saints.

Moreover, his graduate education at Arizona exposed him to anthropological archaeology, in which artifacts are viewed not only as useful tools in dating archaeological sites but as representative of the cultural practices of those individuals who occupied the sites. Indeed, Berge's dissertation, in addition to formulating a typological classification for historic artifacts, sought to "demonstrate the relationship between artifacts and people."[151] In essence, Berge was an anthropologically trained historical archaeologist with an expertise in historic-period artifacts.

The contrast between Berge's anthropological approach to historical archaeology and Harrington's restoration archaeology was clearly manifest during the summer of 1968. Given their dissimilar backgrounds and differential experience excavating historic sites, the two approached the archaeology in Nauvoo in fundamentally different ways. As early as the first week of digging their differences were clearly evident.

Whereas Harrington and his crew of three had (1) removed the earth backfill from their site, (2) completed the excavation of the structure's interior, and (3) begun digging within the foundations of a second structure, all by the end of the first week, Berge and his two-man crew in the same period of time had only uncovered portions of a brick walk from the post-Mormon era, a few inches below the ground surface. In further contrast, Virginia and her two-person crew completely excavated four 5 x 10-foot trenches at the Temple site to a depth of five to eight feet during this same time.[152]

Although his frustrations with the situation are not detectable in the progress report he submitted to NRI at the time, Harrington was quickly losing patience with Berge's approach. NRI's historian, T. Edgar Lyon, who observed the situation, later recounted how Harrington was aggravated with Berge's work, "because he [Berge] was doing the meticulous kind of thing that you get on government jobs that just drives Pinky [Harrington] up a tree." Even though he felt the situation was enough to make him "lose what little hair I've got left," Harrington exercised constraint and resolved to let Berge continue the excavation in his own way. "I'm just not going to go in and do it," he told Lyon at the time, "I'm going to wait for him till he gets up to the point and doesn't know what to do."[153]

Apparently unaware of Harrington's irritation, Berge continued to painstakingly excavate the Browning property, which only irritated Harrington more. "Pinky was just astir," recounted Lyon. In fact, as Harrington's frustrations mounted, Lyon remembered him saying, "How long is it going to take him [Berge] to see that he can't do this? If you're digging a fort and got unlimited government funds on it, you can take every shovel full of dirt out with a trowel but there's no need for it. What he's digging there doesn't represent the Browning period. It represents a German period. He isn't deep enough yet. He'll find the Mormon site far down underneath. He ought to dig down, take a test pit here and here and see it."[154]

Despite his frustration, however, Harrington continued to refuse to interfere with Berge's excavation. In fact, even when Lyon encouraged him to approach Berge about the situation, Harrington allegedly said, "Oh, no . . . he's got to dig it and we'll have better relations after he does."[155]

Eventually, Harrington's patience paid off. According to Lyon, "when Dale Berge saw what Pinky was doing there at the temple [Lyon misremembered; it was Virginia digging at the Temple site], what he had accomplished up there, with no more men than he had down here, he went down to Pinky's one night and said, 'I guess I need some help.' And Pinky spent about two hours with him. He called me about eleven o'clock that night. He said, 'Ed, it's happened. Dale came to me tonight. He's gone home, and we're going to move a tractor in on that yard tomorrow and go to work.'"[156]

Accordingly, the next morning plans were made to use a front-loader to quickly scrape off the upper inches of earth from the Browning site.[157] Among other things, the heavy machinery uncovered the remains of several privies, barns, cisterns, and wells. "Dale [Berge]," Lyon remembered, "by the end of the summer had a whole yard torn up all the way around and the tops of foundations." In short, what would have taken Berge several weeks, if not entire summers, to complete was accomplished in a matter of days. Instead of randomly digging in search of remains, Berge could now focus his energies on identifying the features revealed by the tractor. Lyon later recalled how this was a pivotal moment in the relationship between the two archaeologists. "Well," he recounted, "the next day they worked and they've just gotten along famously ever since, mutual admiration"[158]

Several years later, Berge confirmed this observation. Speaking of his relationship with Pinky and Virginia Harrington in Nauvoo, he said,

> *Well, I'd go over to his site and he probably got tired of me asking him questions, but he was always gracious in filling in details of why he was doing this and why he was doing that, and he would ask me "What do you think of this, that we're digging up here, and that?"... And he would always congratulate me.... And he was never down or negative on a person about things. If I did it wrong, he'd say, "What about this and what about that?"... So it was a very, very good relation. We would go over to their house and have dinner.... And in the lab too, we were using electrolysis and cleaning artifacts, and that was really the first time I had seen that done and I learned how to build the apparatus and procedures in the lab. So he was really a great teacher too, really helped me along a lot in Nauvoo.*[159]

Following the completion of the 1968 season, Harrington assessed Berge's potential to continue on with the project. Although he believed Berge had "a great deal to learn beyond his academic training in anthropology" and, in general, lacked "the architectural and restoration experience that is so helpful on a project like ours," Harrington was optimistic that Berge could "pick it up," but cautioned that "it will take some time and a great deal of motivation on his part."[160]

Apparently, Berge was sufficiently motivated to remain on

the project. By the end of the following summer (1969) Berge had not only completed the Browning excavation (figure 21) but had successfully (and expeditiously) conducted the archaeological investigation on the Winslow Farr lot as well.[161] Once he caught on to the restoration archaeology espoused by Harrington, Berge's successful performance ensured him a future position with NRI. Harrington openly expressed his approval of Berge as his potential replacement. "I have had a couple of good discussions with Dale Berge," he wrote to Kendrew at the close of the 1969 season, "and I am more optimistic about his ability to carry on here than I was earlier." "Dale does, in fact, seem to be reconciled," he continued, "to the necessity for emphasis on 'restoration archaeology,' for the immediate future." However, Harrington noted, "He is still thinking in terms of his doing one comprehensive dig, with a second smaller crew working on limited projects close to certain structures high on the emergency restoration list."[162] Nonetheless, by the start of the 1970 season, Harrington resumed a strictly advisory role in the archaeology program, while Berge—having adjusted to the needs of the restoration project—took over as NRI's new head archaeologist (see figure 20).

In spite of Berge's adaptation to a restoration-oriented archaeology he never gave up his interest in historic artifacts, or his hope that the Nauvoo archaeology program could serve both his own academic interests and the restoration agenda of NRI. His concern for artifacts was clearly reflected in his excavations in Nauvoo. Whereas Harrington frequently left the remains of privy pits unexcavated, believing the discovery of their location was far more important, and far less cumbersome, than the abundance of artifacts they normally contained,

21. Excavated foundations of the Jonathon Browning Home and Gun Shop, 1968. Courtesy of the Archives of the Church of Jesus Christ of Latter-day Saints.

Berge eagerly sought out such pits because of the scholarly research potential of the many artifacts he was likely to uncover within their walls.[163] Aware of Berge's propensity for discovering artifacts, Harrington, somewhat facetiously, exclaimed at the end of the 1970 season, "I continue to be impressed with your ability to find remains of outhouses, which you have again demonstrated in your explorations at the rear of the Chauncey Webb tract!"[164] Conversely, Berge was genuinely disturbed at Harrington's selectivity in artifact conservation. As he later recalled, "It shocked me that he [Harrington] wasn't a great saver of every little artifact that was found. He kept some things that were dateable for certain features and so forth. [But] A lot of stuff he threw away."[165] In fact, Berge was so disturbed by this practice he would rummage through the dumpster in Nauvoo, retrieving artifacts Harrington had earlier discarded.[166] Given his background in anthropological archaeology and historic artifact analysis, it is not surprising Berge maintained a genuine interest in Nauvoo artifacts, while puzzling over his mentor's highly selective conservation of the same objects.

In the same way that Berge's approach was rooted in his background and training, Harrington's treatment of artifacts was a product of his many years of experience with restoration archaeology. He understood, however, that "Dale will have different standards and objectives than I had—for carrying out the digs, studying the artifacts, and writing the reports."[167] Thus, Harrington's career with restoration archaeology did not prevent him from understanding the rationale behind Berge's academic approach or the need for artifact interpretation in historical archaeology in general. On the contrary, he readily admitted that "no active archaeologist of standing or one trying to build a reputation would do what I am doing at Nauvoo—it would be professional suicide."[168] For this reason, he sympathized with Berge's desires to studiously analyze the artifacts from Nauvoo excavations. After all, Berge was fresh out of graduate school and trying to establish his archaeological career at BYU. Whatever sympathy Harrington maintained, however, was ultimately overshadowed by his pragmatic concerns for the restoration archaeology of Nauvoo. Indeed, Harrington observed that "with his specialized academic background he [Berge] may not prove to be as practical in some respects, but we just don't know until we give him a chance. I can already see the signs of disciplined academic training in his great interest in artifacts and his reluctance to get out a report until he has everything in order. This is a major problem with the majority of archaeologist[s] and historians on restoration projects."[169]

Reflecting his emphasis on artifact analysis and his affiliation with BYU, Berge proposed a collaborative project in which the artifacts from Nauvoo would be processed, analyzed, interpreted, and stored at the university. The partnership would be mutually beneficial, meeting the needs of Berge, the university, and NRI. Insofar as NRI needed Berge's archaeological site reports—so that the architects and reconstruction crews could make plans for restoration—and because to write such reports, Berge needed access to the excavated artifacts, it was agreed the Nauvoo artifacts would be brought to BYU where Berge and others would process and analyze them. This arrangement not only facilitated the writing of site reports but also assisted BYU's Department of Anthropology and Archaeology by providing students "experience with interpretation and identification of artifacts and the cultural phase of life which produced the artifacts."[170] It was believed students would be better prepared to assist in the Nauvoo excavations after having some experience processing the artifacts under Berge's supervision. Storing the Nauvoo artifacts at BYU also made them available to other historical archaeologists and for publication opportunities. Moreover, while at BYU, the Nauvoo artifacts were available for display in the university's Museum of Archaeology and Ethnology, where they could stimulate interest in the restoration project. For their part, NRI's trustees supported the partnership with BYU because it provided a virtually perpetual source of student labor, professional personnel, lab facilities, and additional resources for the archaeology program in Nauvoo. Therefore, in many ways, the joint venture between NRI and BYU fulfilled not only Berge's academic interests and desires but also the goals of the university and the needs of the restoration project.[171]

Nightfall on NRI's Historical Archaeology

At the dawn of the 1970s, the future of NRI's archaeology program looked promising. Harrington had successfully initiated a program of excavation aimed at providing information needed for the authentic restoration of the historic city, while Berge was prepared to take over the operation and carry it forward with the additional resources of BYU. Although Berge's academic emphasis on artifacts went beyond Harrington's focus on restoration archaeology, both men were optimistic about the program's future. Indeed, at the close of his final report to the trustees of NRI, Harrington enumerated the reasons why he felt the archaeology program, under Berge's direction and in partnership with BYU, would continue to benefit the restoration project. "The new organization plan," he wrote, "will eliminate the need, at least for present, of having a year-round professional staff at Nauvoo; it will carry the essential study of artifact material farther than presently possible; it should provide a better qualified excavating crew and in other ways improve the excavating program; and it would provide an outlet for publishing technical reports (possibly as a series by the University)."[172]

The 1970 season was indeed productive. With his five-man crew, Berge excavated at six different sites over the course of the summer.[173] Although not all of the six sites were ultimately restored or reconstructed, these excavations were successful in uncovering a number of architectural features and other restoration-related evidence. In his third year of Nauvoo archaeology, Berge clearly understood the goals and objectives of restoration archaeology. But this did not deter his academic interest in the study and publication of the nonarchitectural elements of the Nauvoo excavations. Reflecting his anthropological training, he asserted, "Valuable data is being unearthed in Nauvoo and all information should be published when it can be utilized by historians, archaeologists, or whatever." "In time," he continued, "the excavated information will provide a new dimension to the understanding of the people of Nauvoo in the 1840s and possibly of later periods."[174]

In spite of such anthropological optimism, however, Berge's ideals were never realized. Although his archaeological reports did eventually get written, he struggled to balance his report-writing responsibilities with his university teaching duties. More than once he asked for a reduced teaching load so he could devote more time to writing reports for NRI.[175] Furthermore, if there was little time to write site reports, there was even less to publish academic articles in professional journals. In fact, although he excavated a number of archaeological sites in Nauvoo, only the excavation of the Jonathon Browning site was published in a scholarly journal. Predictably, in this article Berge emphasized the contributions of artifacts as much as architectural remains in interpreting and restoring the Browning site in Nauvoo.[176]

Perhaps the greatest deterrent to Berge's archaeological ideals, however, was the major reorganization of NRI's board of trustees in 1971. Fortunately, by May of that year, when the new First Presidency of the LDS Church, headed by President Joseph Fielding Smith, released everyone but J. LeRoy Kimball as trustees of the corporation, the archaeological program for that summer had already been planned. Consequently, the 1971 excavation season proceeded as scheduled under Berge's supervision.[177] However, given the new First Presidency's mandate that NRI undertake no new projects without their approval, historical archaeology in Nauvoo came to a standstill following the 1971 excavations. Harrington captured the uncertainty of the situation in a letter written two months following the reorganization of the corporation. "Are you folks still there?" he wrote. "Are the Harringtons on some sort of black list? What is happening at Nauvoo? Is Dale [Berge] digging there this summer; and where? For all we know, NRI has gone into bankruptcy. We just can't put Nauvoo completely out of our thoughts and concern, even though we are no longer actively involved."[178]

Harrington had good reason to be concerned. Although President Smith and his counselors had authorized the completion of unfinished restoration projects, for the first time in seven years NRI did not sponsor archaeological excavations in 1972. Indeed, in response to his letter, Harrington was informed the archaeology program in Nauvoo was being "deferred for a time."[179]

In reality, NRI's archaeology program remained idle for the next three years. It was not until the summer of 1975, when Spencer W. Kimball, the new president of the LDS Church, lifted the moratorium on additional restoration work, that Berge returned to Nauvoo to excavate a number of additional sites.[180] The restoration project, however, had been fundamentally altered during this three-year interlude. Indeed, the replacement of NRI's original board of trustees with members of the LDS Church hierarchy precipitated changes that ultimately affected the way historical archaeology was viewed and, therefore, conducted at Nauvoo. Of particular consequence was the shift in NRI's interpretive program. The concern for authentic restoration that had characterized the efforts of the original board dwindled as the new trustees prioritized the communication of religious ideals over historical accuracy. In other words, the message became more important than, and independent of, the method. This was a complete reversal of NRI's original program, in which the methods used to authentically and accurately restore Nauvoo—the methods of historical archaeology—were inextricably linked to, and an integral part of, the message delivered to visitors. Accordingly, the role of historical archaeology in the overall restoration project became increasingly limited to restoration archaeology in the strictest form. Whatever ambitions Berge maintained for a comprehensive cultural study of Nauvoo by means of archaeological excavation and artifact analysis rapidly deteriorated under NRI's new organization and interpretative program. Although he conducted sound restoration archaeology at a few additional sites during the summer of 1975, he found little sympathy for his interest in studying the past by analyzing the artifacts he uncovered.

Thus, although changes in the leadership of the LDS Church allowed for additional restoration work in Nauvoo, when Berge returned to the restoration project, NRI was operating under an entirely new set of rules. Previously, archaeological investigations had been seen as a crucial element in the authentic restoration and reconstruction of Nauvoo's historic structures. As the restoration project became less concerned with authenticity, however, and more interested in proselytizing, historical archaeology came to be viewed as less essential to the restoration process. As a result, the number of sites excavated rapidly decreased. Following the limited excavations of 1975, there were only two other times NRI sponsored historical archaeology in Nauvoo, and then only on a very limited scale.[181]

Yet the restoration work continued to move forward. In fact, without conducting any archaeological investigation at all, the new trustees continued to "restore" (rehabilitate) the exteriors of a number of standing historic structures in Nauvoo, while renovating their interiors, so that they could serve as residences or service centers for the missionary guides stationed in the historic city.[182] Given the dismissal of NRI's original professionals, the missionary guides themselves performed much of this "restoration" work. As one guide, a retired airline executive, explained, "Almost none of us who have been restoring the Coolidge House are professional carpenters."[183] In this way, authentic restoration, including historical archaeology, was compromised for the sake of, and as a result of, religious proselytizing.

More recently, this lack of concern for authenticity at Nauvoo has resulted in construction projects that have disregarded professional labor and archaeological investigations altogether. For example, in the summer of 1998, missionary guides began reconstructing a replica of the Patty Sessions log cabin on what was allegedly the site of the original structure. However, no archaeological investigation was conducted to confirm the location, size, or features of the original building. On the contrary, with no professional training in historic preservation or architecture, the missionary guides constructed a replica cabin that appears to resemble more a 1930s NPS log cabin than it does an 1840s log structure of Nauvoo. Since then, at least two additional replica cabins have likewise been constructed, with similar results.[184]

The most recent and perhaps most egregious example of the indifference toward historical archaeology and lack of concern for authenticity in Nauvoo is the "fast-track construction project" that created sixty "historically inspired" apartment units for missionaries assigned to work in the recently reconstructed Nauvoo Temple. Other than their uniform brick facades and conventional stepped gables, the twenty-four modern apartment complexes—complete with garages, in some cases—bear little resemblance to the authentic historic structures that surround them on the Nauvoo flats. Moreover, although they were constructed in the middle of Nauvoo's historic district, there was no effort to archaeologically investigate the ground in which their modern foundations, plumbing, and wiring were buried. Unfortunately, given the historic population density of the city, there can be little doubt that no fewer than twenty-four archaeological sites were severely compromised by their construction. The precedent established by this and other recent construction projects in Nauvoo makes the future of LDS-sponsored historical archaeology and authentic restoration in the restored city highly uncertain.[185]

Robert T. Bray and RLDS Historical Archaeology in Nauvoo

Interestingly, if the 1970s was a period of decline for NRI and its archaeology program, it was also a time of renewed restoration activity for the RLDS Church, including the implementation of its own program of historical archaeology. In reality, the earliest RLDS excavations at Nauvoo were carried out in 1928, when the Church located the unmarked graves of Joseph Smith and his brother Hyrum through archaeological

22. RLDS excavation of the graves of Joseph Smith Jr. and Hyrum Smith, 1928. Courtesy of the Community of Christ Library–Archives, Independence, Missouri.

exploration (figure 22).[186] However, it was not until 1969 that the RLDS officially adopted historical archaeology as part of their restoration work in the historic city.

No doubt stimulated by the tremendous growth and success of NRI during the 1960s, leaders of the RLDS Church decided to step up their restoration efforts as the decade drew to a close. By the summer of 1969, it was clear the RLDS Church was preparing to restore more of its historic Nauvoo properties. Aware of the success of NRI's archaeology program in providing information necessary for the authentic restoration of the LDS sites, the RLDS made archaeological investigations a major element of its restoration plans. Accordingly, it acquired the services of Robert T. Bray (1925–99) (figure 23), an archaeologist from the University of Missouri–Columbia, who, although not a member of the RLDS Church, agreed to lead the RLDS archaeology program in Nauvoo.

23. Robert T. Bray, June 1986. Courtesy of Mrs. Joan Bray.

Like most persons excavating historic sites at this time, Bray was trained in prehistoric archaeology. However, by the time he came to Nauvoo to excavate for the RLDS Church, he had developed a genuine skill and interest in historical archaeology. After receiving his master's degree in anthropology from the University of Missouri–Columbia in 1955, he took an archaeology position with the NPS and was assigned to work at two significant prehistoric sites, Effigy Mounds National Monument in McGregor, Iowa, and Ocmulgee National Monument in Macon, Georgia. Notably, however, while working at Effigy Mounds in 1958, Bray received a special assignment to investigate the Reno-Benteen Battle Site at what was then called the Custer Battlefield National Monument. Although this was his first experience investigating a historic site, the excavation has since been called "a pioneering work in the archaeology of battlefield sites, and one of the earliest applications of historical archaeology" because of the way Bray and his colleague successfully recognized "patterns in the artifacts, not artifacts simply for display."[187] The year after this first encounter with historical archaeology, Bray left the NPS to become the director of the University of Missouri's Lyman Archaeological Research Center. Although he continued to be involved in prehistoric archaeology at this time, additional experiences excavating historic sites solidified his interest in historical archaeology. For example, he excavated at a number of historic sites under contract with the Missouri State Park system, including the Civil War Battle of Lexington State Park and the first Missouri state capital in St. Charles. Likewise, he continued to do work for the NPS on sites in Missouri, including the excavation of Wilson's Creek Battlefield National Park. Thus, by the time he began to manage the RLDS archaeology program in Nauvoo, Bray had acquired considerable experience in historical archaeology.[188]

Although the RLDS plans were still being finalized, some preliminary excavations were conducted during the summer of 1969. For example, a trenching machine was used to locate the foundation of Joseph Smith's Mansion House stable. There were also limited excavations at the Mansion House itself, as well as at the site of Joseph Smith's Red Brick Store. Although these small-scale excavations were nothing more than preliminary explorations, they were clear indications the RLDS was beginning a new phase of restoration in Nauvoo. Upon observing these activities, NRI historian T. Edgar Lyon wrote, "It appears that the RLDS group have decided that they are going to try to meet the NRI competition."[189]

Far from wanting to compete, however, those involved with this new stage of RLDS restoration openly requested the advice and cooperation of their NRI counterparts. Given the improved relations between the two churches at this time and the restoration experience NRI's employees had accumulated over the past several years, it is not surprising the RLDS figures sought the guidance of NRI. Among other things, they were specifically interested in NRI's archaeology program. Thus, in late June 1969, Bray and other members of the RLDS restoration team met with J. C. Harrington, his wife Virginia, and T. Edgar Lyon to discuss the RLDS Church's plans for archaeological excavations. Significantly, Bray and Harrington were already acquaintances. Not only had both men worked for the NPS, but Bray had also attended a special class Harrington had taught at William and Mary College in Williamsburg, Virginia. When their paths crossed again, this time in Nauvoo, Bray remained interested in learning from Harrington. At their request, Harrington advised the group on the logistics of excavating in Nauvoo, providing cost and labor estimates for their proposed excavation of the Mansion House stables. Likewise, Virginia hosted the men to a tour of the NRI excavations, where they saw for themselves the way the NRI archaeology program operated and the interesting results of the excavations. According to Lyon, the men were "very interested when they completed [the tour]," enough so that they "came back to have a second study of the Browning dig" later that day.[190]

Although there was no additional archaeological work on the RLDS properties in 1969, Bray began full-scale excavations at the Mansion House stables the following summer. Unsurprisingly, over the next several years, Bray developed an archaeology program for the RLDS Church that was in many ways patterned after the program established by Harrington for NRI. For example, if the Harringtons' (and Berge's) Nauvoo excavations were exemplary of restoration archaeology, Bray's work in the historic city was likewise specifically oriented toward recovering information needed for the authentic restoration of the RLDS properties. Indeed, it was for this very reason that the RLDS Church acquired his services. Thus, more than anything else, "The questions of where? How large? When was it built? When and why was it demolished? [and] Of what was it made?" guided the RLDS excavations in Nauvoo.[191]

Moreover, because of the emphasis on restoration, the artifacts uncovered during the RLDS excavations were primarily used to illustrate the site being restored and the person(s) who lived there. In the case of the Joseph Smith properties they were restoring, it was the philosophy of RLDS restoration officials that "the life of the Joseph Smith, Jr. family is the central interpretive point of these biographical house museums." Accordingly, "Emphasis should be placed on the items and events that are related to the family."[192] Thus, it is not surprising that the artifact of perhaps the most value to the RLDS Church was a hand-painted presentation mug found in the Mansion House Hotel privy that reads, "J & E Smith / 1840 / Presented by / EB." Although the person (E. B.) who presented this mug to Joseph Smith and his wife Emma remains unknown, the direct association with the Smith family made the artifact ideally suited for the RLDS Church's interpretive philosophy.[193]

This is not to say Bray did not understand or appreciate the academic value of the artifacts uncovered in Nauvoo. On the contrary, he consistently made a conscious effort to include artifact descriptions and analyses in his Nauvoo site reports, something Harrington rarely did in the reports he authored. Artifacts also occupied a good portion of the two peer-reviewed articles Bray published on his Nauvoo excavations.[194] In one of those articles, however, he revealed some of the limitations he faced doing archaeology in connection with a large restoration project. "An overriding objective of research at all historic sites in Nauvoo," he noted, "has been to preserve in place—intact if possible—all significant architectural features." "Thus," he continued, "it happens occasionally . . . that certain investigative procedures which are theoretically sound and which would normally be followed [are] precluded because of a more important consideration—preservation of the architectural remains."[195] Therefore, although as a professionally trained archaeologist Bray understood the greater scientific value of his excavations, he was at times forced to compromise his scholarly tendencies because of the larger goals of the restoration project in which he was engaged.

Finally, much like NRI, the RLDS interpreted their archaeological excavations for the visiting public. Indeed, in the same way NRI originally recruited students from BYU and other Utah schools to act as both diggers and guides on their historic sites, the RLDS utilized students from the University of Missouri–Columbia and its Church-sponsored institution, Graceland College, to staff their archaeological digs. To help recruit, Bray offered archaeology courses, including one entitled "Historical American Archaeology," through which students could earn academic credit for their participation in the Nauvoo excavations.[196] In addition, beginning in 1973, a formal internship in outdoor museum interpretation was developed "to produce more effective interpreters who would also serve as tour guides of the [RLDS] Joseph Smith Historic Center." Students who enrolled in this internship not only received

24. Excavations inside the foundation of Joseph Smith's Red Brick Store, 1972. Photograph by Kenneth Stobaugh. Courtesy of the Community of Christ Library–Archives, Independence, Missouri.

college credit for courses in museum interpretation and history, but also received hands-on experience in archaeological excavation and nineteenth-century craft demonstrations. Beyond participating in the actual excavations, however, student interns were instructed on how to interpret the excavations to the visiting public "so that archaeological investigations can become an interpretive tool." In this way, historical archaeology was formally incorporated into the RLDS interpretive program in Nauvoo.[197]

Although each of the archaeological investigations sponsored by the RLDS Church was oriented toward particular restoration criteria, there were occasions when additional factors also motivated an excavation. For example, in 1973 Bray was asked to excavate the Turley site, the alleged location of the first home built by the Latter-day Saints in Nauvoo. Although interested in locating the foundations of the cabin that once

25. Paul DeBarthe inspecting a prehistoric canine skeleton found in association with three Titterington projectile points in the backyard of the Joseph Smith Mansion House in Nauvoo, 1983. The skeleton was packaged in plaster of paris for safekeeping during its removal from the site. Courtesy of Marvin Crozier.

stood on the property, the RLDS officials were as equally interested in finding a secret cache of Joseph Smith's papers that were purportedly buried beneath a tree growing on the site. Although the cache of papers was never found, a substantial amount of archaeological data was recovered, including the location of the foundations and associated features of a brewery that at one time occupied a portion of the property.[198]

Passing of the Trowel: Paul DeBarthe

All in all, Bray oversaw the excavation of six Nauvoo sites for the RLDS Church between 1970 and 1975, the results of which he described in a series of professional site reports (figure 24).[199] In 1976, however, after six active seasons in Nauvoo, Bray decided to delegate field supervisory duties to a young RLDS archaeologist named Paul DeBarthe (figure 25). Although

Bray remained the primary archaeologist on the project, it was DeBarthe who managed the Nauvoo excavations for the RLDS Church from this time forward.

At the time DeBarthe accepted responsibility for the RLDS excavations in Nauvoo he had limited academic credentials. He graduated from the RLDS Church's Graceland College in Lamoni, Iowa, with a bachelor's degree in sociology and a teaching certificate in 1969. But it was not until 1977, the year after he took over the Nauvoo excavations, that he was awarded a master's degree in anthropology (emphasis in archaeology) from the University of Kansas, Lawrence, after completing a thesis on prehistoric settlement patterns. His prehistoric leanings notwithstanding, DeBarthe was well prepared to manage the Nauvoo excavations. He had participated in Bray's archaeological field school at the Joseph Smith Homestead lot in 1971 and later served as Bray's field assistant in 1975. Thus, when asked to take over the RLDS excavations in 1976, DeBarthe confidently assumed responsibility for the archaeological program.

Historical archaeology as a discipline had substantially matured by this time. Although a number of excavations continued to be oriented toward historic site restoration, as at Nauvoo, others were solidly grounded in a desire to understand past lifeways by means of analyzing surviving material remains. DeBarthe's training in anthropological archaeology, even though focused on the prehistoric past, taught him to approach archaeological sites with cultural questions in mind. Accordingly, he, like Dale Berge, knew of the great potential of archaeology in Nauvoo to study past lifeways. Nevertheless, whereas Berge's Nauvoo reports lacked detailed lists of artifacts and frequently included a disclaimer indicating that the reports were "intended to be used for restoration purpose and . . . not provide an intensive analysis of artifacts,"[200] DeBarthe, following Bray's example, always included detailed artifact descriptions in his Nauvoo reports. However, although both Berge and DeBarthe understood the great potential of artifacts to shed light on past lifeways, when it came to the analysis of the artifacts they excavated at Nauvoo, both were similarly frustrated. Despite their anthropological considerations, they were limited in what they could accomplish, owing to the lack of resources devoted to non-restoration-related objectives. For example, although DeBarthe was aware that careful study of both the floral and faunal deposits in the Mansion House Hotel latrine could "expand our understanding of living conditions in the nineteenth century," his suggestion that specialists be hired to perform such work went unfulfilled.[201] The RLDS Church simply did not have the resources, nor perhaps the interest, to pursue such non-restoration-related concerns. After all, just as for NRI, the primary rationale of the RLDS archaeology program was the discovery of information needed for the restoration or reconstruction of certain historic sites.

DeBarthe was also inhibited by the lack of detailed information on artifacts commonly uncovered at nineteenth-century historic sites. That is, although he knew artifacts represented past cultural systems, he lacked sufficient knowledge about nineteenth-century material culture to adequately interpret what he was finding at Nauvoo. Unlike Berge, who had developed specialized knowledge about historic artifacts during his dissertation research, DeBarthe's graduate training focused on prehistoric sites and artifacts. Thus, he specifically identified the need for information on "the evolution of buttons, the history of suspender buckles, the development of kaolin pipes, [and] historical blueprints or designs of outbuildings of the period" (the nineteenth century). He also observed that, given the large number of ceramic plates and bowls uncovered in Nauvoo, "A history of table settings might provide insight into the eating habits and etiquette of the period."[202]

Significantly, at the same time that DeBarthe issued a plea for assistance by qualified individuals in any of these projects, historical archaeologists around the country were working on these very subjects. Indeed, as the discipline of historical archaeology matured, more and more detailed information relevant to the study of historic sites and artifacts was generated. Dale Berge's dissertation, for example, although never published, was an early attempt to classify historic—nineteenth-and twentieth-century—artifacts from the American Southwest. Most of the published literature at this time, however, focused on artifacts from colonial America and was of little use to someone excavating a nineteenth-century site in the Midwest. For example, in 1969 Ivor Noël Hume, director of the Department of Archaeology at Colonial Williamsburg, published his impressive monograph, *A Guide to Artifacts of Colonial America*, complete with sections on buttons, buckles, and tobacco pipes, among many others.[203] Similarly, in 1977 noted historical archaeologist James Deetz published his insightful archaeological synthesis of early American life, including a cultural analysis of ceramic table settings.[204] Although discussing a time period too early for general utility in studying artifacts from Nauvoo, these books are landmarks in the evolution of artifact studies in historical archaeology and reflect the development of the discipline in the 1970s.

Despite the general lack of institutional support for anthropological objectives and the relative dearth of information about nineteenth-century artifacts, DeBarthe, with Bray's support, made legitimate efforts to go beyond mere artifact lists and descriptions in his Nauvoo archaeological reports. For example, even though the stated goal of the 1976 RLDS excavations at the Joseph Smith Homestead Complex was "to identify and define structures relating to the Smith Homestead," DeBarthe attempted an interpretive approach aimed at understanding social and economic stratification within the historic Nauvoo community. Although again limited by the number of resources at his disposal, the approach, which involved "comparing quantities of artifacts [ceramics] of known relative worth for a historical period," in many ways foreshadowed later work on the economic scaling of historic ceramics that is now widely used among historical archaeologists in America.[205]

DeBarthe continued excavations in Nauvoo through the summer of 1984, after which funding for the RLDS archaeology program was terminated.[206] In the nine years during which he managed RLDS archaeology in Nauvoo, DeBarthe excavated an additional four historic sites.[207] When added to the six sites Bray had previously investigated, the RLDS Church sponsored archaeological excavation at a total of ten of its sites in Nauvoo.[208] Even though most of these excavations were oriented toward historic site restoration, only three of the excavated structures were ultimately reconstructed, mainly because of financial constraints.[209] After all, the RLDS never had the multi-million-dollar budget NRI was afforded by the

LDS Church. Notwithstanding such limitations, however, the RLDS archaeology program in Nauvoo endured twice as many continuous years as NRI's.

Conclusion

More than thirty sites were excavated during the approximately twenty-four years (1961–84) the LDS and RLDS Churches sponsored historical archaeology in Nauvoo. Many of these excavations have significantly contributed to the restorations and reconstructions that constitute the bulk of the Nauvoo landscape today. Most recently, the archaeological data generated and compiled by J. C. and Virginia Harrington were used in the reconstruction of the Nauvoo Temple, which was completed in June 2002. However, in spite of continuing development, archaeological excavations in Nauvoo have all but ceased at present.[210] In fact, it appears that historical archaeology is no longer conceived as playing an integral role in the restoration of Nauvoo.

Nevertheless, the historical archaeology conducted at Nauvoo provides a case study in the history of the discipline at large. In particular, the Nauvoo excavations offer a glimpse into a significant period of transition in the development of the field. During the nearly twenty-five years of excavations in Nauvoo, historical archaeology as a whole emerged from its formal beginnings in restoration archaeology and entered the academic world as a legitimate and professional scholarly discipline. As a result, historical archaeology at Nauvoo highlights important aspects of this significant period of the field's development.

The Nauvoo excavations, for example, illustrate the way

institutions, such as the LDS and RLDS Churches, adopted historical archaeology for the purpose of restoring or reconstructing historic sites they believed held particular interpretive significance. At the same time, the history of historical archaeology at Nauvoo demonstrates not only that excavations contributed to the interpretation of the historic sites being restored, but that the archaeology itself was often publicly interpreted. The Nauvoo excavations also illustrate how such institutionally supported restoration archaeology was often at odds with the scholarly desires of a younger generation of anthropologically trained historical archaeologists that sustained the growth and development of the discipline as it emerged as a professional field of academic study. Finally, the history of the Nauvoo excavations reveals how historical archaeology, by contributing to historic site restorations, has been used in efforts to legitimize and validate the particular theologies of the two churches.

All of these aspects of the Nauvoo excavations reflect similar developments in historical archaeology as a whole at this time. As such, the historical archaeology of Nauvoo reflects broad national patterns in the discipline's development. How the Nauvoo excavations elucidate the sequence of this development is the subject of the final chapter.

Chapter 5

The Nauvoo Excavations and the Development of Historical Archaeology in America

Historical archaeology—the archaeology of the modern world—was born in the American historic preservation movement of the late nineteenth and early twentieth centuries. Its formal beginnings are linked to the institutionally sponsored excavations of famous historic sites in the 1930s. For example, most scholars point to the federally supported excavations at Jamestown, Virginia, in the last half of the 1930s as the origin of what is known today as historical archaeology. The field's professional beginnings, however, are grounded in the 1960s, when historical archaeology emerged as an independent discipline of academic scholarship. A key benchmark in this period of professional development was the organization of the Society for Historical Archaeology in 1967. Since then, historical archaeology has continued to mature as a scholarly discipline devoted to the study and interpretation of the material remains of the modern world, and is now widely practiced by scholars around the globe.

The excavations in Nauvoo took place at the same time historical archaeology was emerging from its institutional roots and finding a place in academia as a professional discipline. Remarkably, J. C. Harrington, the founding father of historical archaeology, was involved in all of this; not only did he play a prominent role in both the early institutional phase of the discipline and its later professional development, but he was also instrumental in establishing historical archaeology at Nauvoo. Consequently, the history of historical archaeology in Nauvoo in many ways highlights this important period of transition in the history of the discipline.

On a broader scale, however, the history of archaeological excavations in Nauvoo serves as a case study in the history of historical archaeology at large. Indeed, precisely because the Nauvoo excavations occurred at a pivotal moment in the history of the discipline, they reflect, either positively or negatively, key aspects of the entire developmental history of the field. A more detailed review of the history of historical archaeology further illustrates this point.

Historical Archaeology in Nauvoo and the History of the Field

Robert L. Schuyler, one of the few scholars who has written about the history of the field, has asserted that historical archaeology, in its development, passed through a series of five broad levels or stages. These stages, as set forth by Schuyler, are:

1. The study of standing monuments and relics

2. Excavation of standing monuments and discovery of associated artifacts
3. Broad excavations and use of artifacts as illustrators
4. Recognition of cultural context and expansion of the range of sites
5. Explanation of recovered cultural context[1]

The history of historical archaeology in Nauvoo follows the first four stages of this sequence remarkably well. For example, the first stage, the study of standing monuments and relics, is seen in the various individuals and groups who expressed early interest in Nauvoo's historic buildings. Throughout the last half of the nineteenth century and into the early twentieth century members of both the LDS and RLDS Churches visited Nauvoo to admire the deteriorating structures and to remember the greatness of what was once the second largest city in Illinois. Although RLDS leaders were the first to purchase and preserve some of the historic Nauvoo buildings in the first decades of the twentieth century, enthusiastic LDS individuals, such as Bryant S. Hinckley and Wilford C. Wood, similarly took early action to preserve the remains of Nauvoo's structures. Lane K. Newberry, although not a member of either church, was also enthralled by the structures of old Nauvoo and did much to encourage leaders from both the State of Illinois and the LDS Church to preserve and restore the city. Even the National Park Service, as directed by key pieces of legislation, took measures to promote the preservation and restoration of the surviving structures at an early date. A final example of such early interest is the work of Dr. J. LeRoy Kimball. It was his fascination with the original Mormon structures that eventually led to the establishment of Nauvoo Restoration, Inc. in 1962. Significantly, all of this initial interest was focused on Nauvoo's surviving architecture, standing or buried, and stimulated by the restoration potential of the historic city.

The great interest in restoring Nauvoo's standing monuments in time led to activities that characterize the second stage of Schuyler's sequence, the excavation of standing monuments and the discovery of associated artifacts. Even before NRI was formally organized, Kimball and others were coordinating the excavation of the Nauvoo Temple site in anticipation of its proposed restoration. Although archaeologists from Southern Illinois University were compelled to stop their excavations before reaching the sloping floor of the Temple's basement, they did successfully locate most of the Temple's foundation walls and, in the process, uncovered thousands of associated artifacts. That only a small sample of these artifacts was ever analyzed supports Schuyler's point that although architecture and artifacts meet in this stage, they do not fuse in any meaningful way. That is, artifacts are unavoidably discovered as foundation walls are followed, but they receive little emphasis in the overall project.[2]

If the 1962 excavation of the Nauvoo Temple was characteristic of stage 2 of the developmental sequence, it was not until NRI acquired the services of J. C. Harrington in 1965 that historical archaeology in Nauvoo reached stage 3, broad excavation and the use of artifacts as illustrators. As Schuyler points out, during this third stage a fusion of architecture and artifacts is reached, as excavation areas are broadened and the quantity and variety of artifacts recovered substantially increase. Yet this combination is "technical and noncultural," the artifacts being "viewed as secondary items appended to architecture and serving the goals of restoration." Moreover, the assemblages recovered through such broadened excavations "are not used so much to interpret the site as to illustrate it," with the result that "The museum case rather than the scholarly monograph is the benefactor."[3]

In Nauvoo, these developments are exemplified by the work of the Harringtons, Dollar, and Berge for NRI, and later that of Bray and DeBarthe for the RLDS Church. In all cases, broadened excavations generated larger quantities of artifacts. In spite of this expansion, however, the artifacts continued to serve a supplementary function to the principal objective of restoration. Harrington recognized this fact in light of the excavations in Nauvoo. He wrote,

> *The [archaeological] report, to a large extent, serves as part of the documentation for the final restoration . . . so it is imperative that the final . . . report be submitted as soon as feasible after the close of the field season. It cannot wait for the supplementary and tangential studies that are normally carried out in connection with an archaeological report (soil analyses, bone identification, etc., etc.), nor can the report be held up until the artifacts are fully studied and readied for illustration in the report. This is the cold reality that archaeologists working on restoration projects must face, although it is counter to their training and to archaeological precedent.*[4]

The "cold reality" that artifact analysis and other scientific aspects of archaeological research are often compromised in restoration projects like that at Nauvoo is why Schuyler contends that "conflict first appears between the excavators and the restoration/preservation committees" in the third stage of the developmental sequence. However, it is not until stage 4, recognition of the cultural context and expansion of the range of sites, that this conflict between the goals of restoration and scholarly research comes to a head. It is during this stage that "the study of artifacts recovered . . . eventually leads to the recognition that a total cultural context is preserved in the site." Consequently, instead of focusing strictly on the structures or monuments under investigation, the goal becomes the reconstruction of past lifeways. As a result, "architecture devolves to one of a wide range of aspects of culture, and . . . the types of sites investigated greatly expands." Ultimately, Schuyler argues, stage 4 is the most crucial, because "it is only at this stage that a separate and autonomous area of scholarship appears."[5]

At Nauvoo, the potential for conflict inherent in these developments was managed in various ways. The RLDS archaeology program, for example, seemingly avoided such conflict. This is partly explained by the fact that neither Bray nor DeBarthe went to Nauvoo in search of strictly academic research opportunities. As trained archaeologists, both men were clearly aware of the anthropological potential of the Nauvoo excavations. Yet at the same time, they understood the reasons for which they were hired. As a result, both willingly and skillfully worked under the limitations imposed by the RLDS restoration program. It helped too that the RLDS respected and supported the full breadth of Bray's and DeBarthes's archaeological research and did not restrict their archaeological activities to uncovering foundation walls alone. Indeed, some of their work with the artifacts they excavated represents a legitimate move toward stage 4 and an attempt to reconstruct past lifeways at Nauvoo.[6] However, despite the fact that both Bray and DeBarthe clearly recognized that an entire cultural context was preserved in the Nauvoo sites, there were few efforts to explain it in terms of larger sociocultural processes. Consequently, the RLDS archaeology program never advanced to stage 5, explanation of the recovered cultural context, before its virtual termination in 1984.

The situation with NRI's archaeology program was slightly different, although it too never reached stage 5 in its development. For example, although Harrington recognized the scholarly potential of the Nauvoo excavations, he freely subscribed to the restoration goals of NRI. After all, his entire professional career prior to excavating at Nauvoo had been devoted to similar "restoration archaeology" projects in the NPS. At the same time, he realized that not all archaeologists would be as willing to sacrifice their scholarly ambitions to accommodate the goals of the restoration project. The conflict inherent in this situation was especially evident during his search for an archaeologist to take over the Nauvoo program. At that time he wrote, "We must recognize at the outset that the kind of archaeology we are committed to at Nauvoo is a very practical kind, relating specifically to restoration. There will be very little, if any, opportunity for a budding young anthropologist to apply his scientific training and dedication. I have found that even those archaeologists working on historic sites feel that they are obliged to look for socio-scientific problems, rather than seeing the objectives as plain history."[7]

Ironically, Dale Berge was just such a "budding young anthropologist" when he started work in Nauvoo. In spite of his anthropological affinity for artifacts, however, Berge was able to mitigate the potentially divisive situation by proposing a collaborative relationship between NRI and Brigham Young University in which both the goals of the restoration project and the objectives of scholarly research could be met. Yet the restoration project was fundamentally altered before these plans were fully realized. Under these circumstances, NRI's program of historical archaeology did not advance past stage 4 in its development. In reality, it devolved to activities characteristic of stage 3, until finally being abandoned altogether, despite continuing restoration projects in Nauvoo. Thus, even though Berge recognized the cultural context preserved in the sites and had the desire to try and explain it scientifically, changes to the restoration project prevented him from pursuing such anthropological interests in Nauvoo.

Faced with such obstacles in Nauvoo, Berge looked elsewhere for opportunities to fulfill his anthropological ambitions. He specifically turned to Mormon-occupied sites outside of Nauvoo that the LDS Church had no interest in restoring. Exemplary of this nonrestoration work was his project at Lower Goshen, Utah, a Mormon pioneer town of the 1860s. Here Berge excavated a number of residential dwellings, identifying the specific floor plans and layouts of different structures while recovering a large quantity of artifacts. Notably, from the beginning this project was conceived in anthropological terms. Indeed, Berge expressed his hope "to reconstruct economic, social and religious conditions at Lower Goshen."[8] Motivating the investigation, therefore, were questions and interests dealing with mid-nineteenth-century Utah history and culture. "For example," Berge proposed, "how large were the log houses? How did the residents build their dugouts? What type of local ceramic or glasswares did the settlers use in their home? What kinds of domestic items did they make themselves?" "Archaeology," he continued, "can help answer many of these questions as well as those relating to human habits and the ways these pioneers coped with life on this remote edge of the American frontier." Finally, reflecting his anthropological background and scholarly desires, he wrote of the potential for artifacts to reveal historical and cultural information about the town and its people:

Not only do the artifacts indicate what was used, but they also suggest certain vital information about the occupants, such as whether they were better off than others in a similar situation or how industrious and innovative they were. The artifacts can also demonstrate the degree of craftsmanship and concern individuals had for their work. Bones, seeds, and other plant materials provide insights into the diet of specific households. In addition, artifacts may help to identify ethnic origins of these pioneer households. Indeed, many clues to the lives of the Lower Goshen inhabitants remain entombed in the ruins.[9]

In reality, Berge's work at Lower Goshen was still characteristic of stage 4, insofar as it was an attempt to reconstruct past lifeways. That is, although he recognized and described the cultural implications of the architectural features and artifacts he discovered, he did not attempt to explain these in terms of larger sociocultural phenomena. His research successfully documented the answers to questions of who, what, when, and where, but never attempted to answer the more elusive questions of stage 5—those of how and why. As Schuyler points out, however, the development to stage 5 is not inevitable, because the goal of stage 4—the reconstruction of past lifeways—is a legitimate scholarly objective in itself.[10] Significantly, it was only outside the constraints of NRI and other restoration-related projects, only after the range of sites was expanded, that Berge was able to achieve this level of analysis.

Similarly, a small number of archaeologists currently working on a broad range of Mormon-occupied sites continue to investigate the Mormon cultural past.[11] Although much of this work continues to focus on the reconstruction of past lifeways and, as such, represents research characteristic of stage 4, there are signs the historical archaeology of the Mormon Domain will ultimately progress to stage 5 in its development. Indeed, as Schuyler has suggested, because many of these historical archaeologists are trained anthropologists, the transition to stage 5, where anthropological explanation of archaeologically recovered data is achieved, may ultimately be predetermined.[12]

Historical Archaeology and Mormon Identity

While some archaeologists are trying to push the boundaries of such scholarship, the LDS Church continues to work comfortably in stages 2 and 3. Although historical archaeology in Nauvoo has ceased, Church-sponsored excavations persist in connection with the restoration of other LDS historic sites. An example is provided by the recent excavations in Kirtland, Ohio, the first gathering place and temple center of the Church. Here, as part of a multi-million-dollar restoration project, Church employees excavated a number of archaeological sites, including a sawmill and ashery, both of which have since been reconstructed. Excavation at Kirtland was swift and massive, with heavy machinery doing most of the digging until foundations or other architectural features were discovered. This was partly due to budget and time constraints, but it also reflects the fact that LDS officials have no apparent interest in the Church's historical archaeology adopting a more anthropological mode of inquiry. In reality, from their institutional perspective, there is no need for the Church-sponsored archaeological investigations to become more anthropological. The restoration-oriented historical archaeology of stages 2 and 3 fulfills the objectives of the LDS Church's interpretive programs quite well.

The key to understanding this phenomenon is summed up nicely by one official of the LDS Church's historical department, who said, "The Church of Jesus Christ of Latter-day Saints is not in the business of historic preservation per se. [But] It is in the business of saving souls."[13] In other words, the reason why the LDS Church is at all interested in its historic places is because these places have the potential to promote belief in the Church's theological tenets. Historical archaeology contributes to this process because of its materiality. As David Lowenthal has correctly stated, "history and memory usually come in the guise of stories which the mind must purposefully filter; physical relics [however] remain directly available to our senses. This existential concreteness explains their evocative appeal."[14] Beyond simply generating interest and appeal, however, material remains also contribute tangibility to an often otherwise distant past. In this way, archaeological remains are useful in creating a heightened sense of reality and authenticity for representations of the past, which ultimately leads to an increased level of credibility granted to such representations.

This helps explain why archaeology is particularly useful in the restoration of historic sites, where authenticity and credibility are primary objectives.

This is particularly true of the historic sites of the LDS Church. Authenticity and credibility are crucial at these places because it is here where LDS theology and history are inextricably intertwined. In other words, because the Church's representation of its own history depicts the events of its past as part of a grand, divinely directed drama, the authentic reconstruction or restoration of the places where these events occurred becomes an essential component in perpetuating and legitimizing the LDS Church's theological tenets, including its status as a divinely inspired institution. Moreover, inasmuch as identity is built on shared interpretations of the past, this process serves to reinforce the perceived identity of LDS Church members, who view themselves as key players in this divine drama. This philosophy is captured nicely in the remarks of one LDS official when discussing the Church's most recent historic site restoration in Kirtland, Ohio. "By restoring Historic Kirtland," he said, "the Church is officially remembering the works of the Lord that were accomplished there through Joseph Smith and others nearly one and three-quarter centuries ago. The Church is also witnessing to the truthfulness of these experiences to its members and to the world." In this sense, the Church's historical sites become three-dimensional witnesses to the supernatural events that underlie Mormon theology and identity.[15]

Take, for example, the appearance of God the Father, Jesus Christ, and the angel Moroni to the young Joseph Smith, prior to the coming forth of the Book of Mormon in 1829. Although these events lie outside the realm of empirical proof, they are of supreme importance for Latter-day Saints insofar as they constitute some of the most fundamental doctrines of their faith. Accordingly, members of the Church view the simple log home in which Joseph Smith lived when these events occurred as more than just the place where the young prophet spent his boyhood years. For them it is a place where sacred and eternally significant events transpired, the actual location where the latter-day restoration of Christ's gospel and church began. Consequently, even though it is a modern replica built by the LDS Church, the log home that sits on the site today at once validates and perpetuates LDS Church members' belief in the supernatural events that transpired there, while solidifying their identity as Latter-day Saints. Significantly, it is the structure's material presence, corroborated by archaeological excavation, that grants it credibility as a tangible witness to the reality of these events.

The same is true for Nauvoo and all the other historic sites developed by the LDS Church. Indeed, precisely because they are actual material places that visitors can see, touch, and otherwise physically experience, the restored and reconstructed buildings that now dot the Nauvoo landscape add a sense of authenticity to the past they represent. As J. LeRoy Kimball observed, "The restoration project makes history a reality. People can come here and see what happened in Nauvoo; it's not a myth." "It does something for people," Kimball continued," to walk on the same dirt, see the same river and travel the same streets as did those early Mormons and the Prophet Joseph Smith."[16]

The ability of the Church's historic sites to authenticate

history and affirm faith is not lost on the current leadership of the LDS Church. In fact, the Church continues to develop its historic sites for these reasons. As John K. Carmack, former executive director of the LDS Church's historical department, recently said, "What is important for you to understand is that these things happened in real places, in the near past. Places and things still exist that . . . let us see and feel . . . [T]hus visitors can personally experience these sacred events and strengthen their testimonies of the Restoration [i.e., the history of the Church] in profound and sensory ways."[17]

The former managing director of the LDS Church History Department has echoed the same sentiment. "The buildings that have been restored or rebuilt," he declared, "the furnishings that have been installed, the events and personalities that are featured in the interpretive tours, the site improvements, and visitor experiences on site combine to testify to the eyes, ears, hands, hearts, and souls of visitors that what happened here . . . has great significance for a religion that now nearly spans the globe."[18]

Thus, it is the physicality of the LDS Church's historic sites that contributes to their ability to confirm belief and verify history. As a result, insofar as historical archaeology can provide data that will help physically reconstruct or restore these places, the LDS Church will likely utilize it to that end. Even in Nauvoo, where recent construction projects have gone ahead without archaeological investigation, excavations could possibly continue for these very reasons, just as they have at Kirtland and at other significant LDS historic sites.[19] However, because of the role historic sites play in validating and promoting LDS theology and identity, historical archaeology in the LDS Church will likely remain in stages 2 and 3 of the developmental sequence, where restoration, not anthropological explanation, is the primary objective.

"The Archaeology of the Mormons Themselves"

Because historical archaeology is the study of the recent past and is concerned with the people and events that shaped the world we live in today, it has great potential to directly influence individuals in the present. Indeed, since the excavations at Jamestown, historical archaeology has been used in restoration projects designed to help mold public ideas, values, and identity.[20] Thus, the historical archaeology employed in the restoration of Nauvoo (and at other LDS historic sites) is but one example of how the discipline has been used to shape the present since its formal beginnings in the 1930s.

The restoration of Nauvoo, however, is more than just an example of the social and political use of historical archaeology in North America. The Nauvoo excavations provide a window onto the history of the discipline as a whole. Occurring as they did in the 1960s—a pivotal moment in the history of the field—the excavations capture the origins and early development of the discipline, including the transition from its formal institutional beginnings to its current professional status in the academic world. Specifically, they reveal historical archaeology emerging from its roots in historic site restoration and its early development as the anthropological study of the modern world. This is significant because historical archaeology, although academically grounded in anthropology, continues to be practiced at various stages of development throughout the globe. Therefore, to know of the origins and growth of the discipline is to ultimately know how to understand and evaluate its current practice in the world today. Accordingly, although excavations in the historic city have ceased at present, the historical archaeology of Nauvoo should not be forgotten.

Appendix

Chronology of Nauvoo Excavations

Site	Year(s)	Sponsor	Director(s)	Result
Nauvoo Temple	1961–62	LDS	M. Fowler and D. F. Green	Reconstructed
	1966–69		V. S. Harrington and J. C. Harrington	
Brigham Young Home	1965–68	LDS	C. Dollar and J. C. Harrington	Reconstructed and restored
Wilford Woodruff Home	1966–67	LDS	J. C. Harrington	Restored
Webb Blacksmith and Wagon Shop	1967–68	LDS	J. C. Harrington and V. S. Harrington	Reconstructed
North Unit of Times and Seasons Complex	1968	LDS	V. S. Harrington	Reconstructed
Jonathon Browning Home and Gun Shop	1968–69	LDS	D. Berge	Reconstructed and restored
Winslow Farr Home	1969	LDS	D. Berge	Restored
Chauncey Webb Home	1970	LDS	D. Berge	Restored
Seventies Hall	1970	LDS	D. Berge	Reconstructed
Lorin Farr Home	1970	LDS	D. Berge	None
Stillman Pond	1970	LDS	D. Berge	None
Alvah Tippets	1970	LDS	D. Berge	None
Daniel Butler Jr.	1970	LDS	D. Berge	Exposed foundation
Joseph Smith Stable	1970	RLDS	R. Bray	Exposed foundation
Joseph Bates Noble–Lucy Mack Smith Home	1971	LDS	D. Berge	Restored
Scovil Bakery	1971	LDS	D. Berge	Reconstructed
Joseph Smith Homestead Summer Kitchen and Bee House	1971	RLDS	R. Bray	Reconstructed

Joseph Smith's Red Brick Store	1972	RLDS	R. Bray	Reconstructed
Theodore Turley	1973	RLDS	R. Bray	None
Hyrum Smith	1974	RLDS	R. Bray and G. Waselkov	None
Masonic Hall	1975	LDS	D. Berge	Reconstructed and restored
Riser Boot and Shoemaker Shop	1975	LDS	D. Berge	Reconstructed
Kimball-Heywood Store	1975	LDS	D. Berge	None
Stoddard Tinsmith Shop	1975	LDS	D Berge	Restored
Times and Seasons Print Shop	1975	RLDS	R. Bray	Exposed foundation
Outbuildings at Joseph Smith Homestead	1976	RLDS	P. DeBarthe	None
Joseph Smith Mansion and Hotel	1977–78 1980–83	RLDS	P. DeBarthe	Exposed foundations
Levi Hancock	1979	RLDS	P. DeBarthe	Exposed foundation
James Brinkerhof	1979	RLDS	P. DeBarthe	Exposed foundation
Windsor P. Lyon Home and Store	1980	LDS	J. T. Walker and R. Stamps	Restored
Sarah Granger Kimball Home	1981	LDS	D. Berge	Restored
William Law Store	1984	RLDS	P. DeBarthe	None

Notes

Abbreviations, Archives and Depositories

LDS Archives	Archives of the Church of Jesus Christ of Latter-day Saints, Salt Lake City, Utah
NRI Corporate Files	Corporate files of Nauvoo Restoration, Inc., housed in the LDS Archives, Salt Lake City, Utah

Introduction

1. Pilling, "Beginnings," 1–22.

2. Pilling, "Beginnings," 21.

3. J. C. Harrington to J. LeRoy Kimball, January 11, 1967, NRI Corporate Files, box 155, folder 7.

4. Schuyler, "The J. C. Harrington Medal," 1–2.

5. For an overview and discussion of some early examples of excavations at historic-period sites, see Schuyler, "Historical Archaeology," 623–24; see also Linebaugh, *The Man Who Found Thoreau*, 9–26.

6. Lee, *The Antiquities Act of 1906*.

7. G. L. Miller, "Memorial: J. C. Harrington, 1901–1998," 1–7; Jelks, "Jean Carl Harrington, 1901–1998," 26.

8. Pykles, "An Early Example of Public Archaeology," 311–49.

9. Harrington, "Historic Site Archaeology in the United States," 295–315; Harrington, "Archaeology as an Auxiliary Science to American History," 1121–30.

10. Schuyler, "The Second Largest City in the English-Speaking World," 156–64; Schuyler, "Historical Archaeology," 626; Schuyler, "Historical Archaeology as an Integral Part of the Anthropological Curriculum," 95–96; Cotter, "Continuity in Teaching Historical Archaeology," 100–101.

11. Schuyler, "Historical Archaeology," 629; Pykles, "A Brief History of Historical Archaeology," 32–34.

12. Michael Coe is a noted Mesoamerican archaeologist who, in a 1973 article, encouraged his peers to give up their efforts to find archaeological evidence of the Book of Mormon and "start digging into the archaeological remains of the Saints themselves." Coe, "Mormons and Archaeology," 47–48.

1. The Origins of the Restoration of Nauvoo

1. Leonard, *Nauvoo*; Flanders, *Nauvoo*; G. W. Givens, *In Old Nauvoo*; Cannon, *Nauvoo Panorama*; Launius and Hallwas, *Kingdom on the Mississippi River*; Colvin, *Nauvoo Temple*.

2. For a comprehensive work on Smith, see Bushman, *Joseph Smith: Rough Stone Rolling*; see also his *Joseph Smith and the Beginnings of Mormonism*. For detailed accounts of the history of the Latter-day Saints, see Arrington and Bitton, *The Mormon Experience*, and Allen and Leonard, *The Story of the Latter-day Saints*.

3. Cross, *The Burned-Over District*.

4. Smith, *History of the Church*, 1:3–4.

5. On the Book of Mormon, see T. Givens, *By the Hand of Mormon*.

6. At first the Church was called the Church of Christ. In 1834 the name was changed to the Church of the Latter-day Saints; in 1838 the name was changed to the Church of Jesus Christ of Latter-day Saints. See Allen and Leonard, *The Story of the Latter-day Saints*, 55.

7. On the Mormons in Ohio, see Backman, *The Heavens Resound*.

8. Smith, *History of the Church*, 3:175.

9. On the Missouri conflict, see Baugh, *A Call to Arms*; see also LeSueur, *The 1838 Mormon War in Missouri*.

10. On the Mormon exodus to Utah, see Bennett, *We'll Find the Place*.

11. Although the Reorganized Church of Jesus Christ of Latter Day Saints has since changed its name to the Community of Christ, I use the earlier name (RLDS), as it is historically accurate, given the time period discussed.

12. See Bitton, "The Ritualization of Mormon History," 67–85; P. L. Anderson, "Heroic Nostalgia," 47–55; Eliason, "Pioneers and Recapitulation," 175–211.

13. Bitton suggests that two of the earliest examples of visits to Palmyra and the Hill Cumorah are recorded in the John S. Carter Diary, September 1833, and the Jonathon H. Hale Diary, May 30, 1835, LDS Archives. See Bitton, "The Ritualization of Mormon History," 76 n. 19.

14. P. L. Anderson, "Heroic Nostalgia," 49–50.

15. See Alexander, *Mormonism in Transition*.

16. See G. O. Larson, *The "Americanization" of Utah*; Gordon, *The Mormon Question*; Lyman, *Political Deliverance*; Moyer, "Dancing with the Devil."

17. See G. O. Larson, *The "Americanization" of Utah*; see also Flake, *The Politics of Religious Identity*.

18. Holzapfel, Cottle, and Stoddard, *Church History in Black and White*, 12.

19. Allen and Leonard, *The Story of the Latter-day Saints*, 453.

20. P. L. Anderson, "Heroic Nostalgia," 50.

21. See P. L. Anderson, "Heroic Nostalgia"; Bitton, "The Ritualization of Mormon History."

22. Erekson, "American Prophet, New England Town"; Erekson, "'Out of the Mists of Memory,'" 30–69.

23. P. L. Anderson, "Heroic Nostalgia," 51; Cannon, *Nauvoo Panorama*, 72.

24. P. L. Anderson, "Heroic Nostalgia," 53.

25. Roberts, *Comprehensive History*, 3:24.

26. See Van Wagoner, *Mormon Polygamy*; Hardy, *Solemn Covenant*; Flake, *The Politics of Religious Identity*.

27. Frederick M. Smith, "Open Letter to All People," *Salt Lake Tribune*, July 1, 1905, cited in Erekson, "'Out of the Mists of Memory,'" 55.

28. "Prayer in Dedication of the Memorial Monument," *Improvement Era* 9 (February 1906): 324–27, cited in Erekson, "'Out of the Mists of Memory,'" 63.

29. Pardoe, *Lorin Farr, Pioneer*, 305, quoted in Cannon, *Nauvoo Panorama*, 69.

30. Heman C. Smith to E. L. Kelley, October 17, 1905, cited in Howard, "Nauvoo Heritage," 49. The derogatory label "Brighamites" referred to the LDS belief in Brigham Young's rightful succession to the presidency of

the Church following Joseph Smith's death. The reciprocal term used by the LDS was "Josephites," highlighting the RLDS's rejection of Brigham Young. Both labels served to accentuate the theological differences between the two groups.

31. Smith to Kelley, October 17, 1905.

32. Bingham, "Packaging the 'Williamsburg of the Midwest,'" 16–18; Shireman, "The Mormon Prophet's Illinois Legacy," 145–60.

33. Bishop C. A. Skinner to the Presiding Bishopric, May 20, 1941, Presiding Bishopric Papers, P54, f217, Community of Christ Archives, Independence MO, cited in Bingham, "Packaging the 'Williamsburg of the Midwest,'" 18.

34. Lane K. Newberry to Bryant S. Hinckley, June 8, 1938, cited in B. S. Hinckley, "The Nauvoo Memorial," 460.

35. Newberry to Hinckley, June 8, 1938.

36. First Presidency (Heber J. Grant and J. Reuben Clark Jr.) to Lane K. Newberry, April 9, 1938, cited in B. S. Hinckley, "The Nauvoo Memorial," 460.

37. B. S. Hinckley, "The Nauvoo Memorial," 458.

38. *Historic Sites Act of 1935*, Public Law 292, 74th Cong., 49 Stat. 666, 16 U.S.C. 461–67, Sect. 462a.

39. U.S. Department of the Interior, *Report on Nauvoo, Illinois*.

40. U.S. Department of the Interior, *Report on Nauvoo, Illinois*, 4.

41. See Greenspan, *Creating Colonial Williamsburg*.

42. U.S. Department of the Interior, *Report on Nauvoo, Illinois*, 6.

43. U.S. Department of the Interior, *Report on Nauvoo, Illinois*, 6.

44. U.S. Department of the Interior, *Report on Nauvoo, Illinois*, 5, emphasis in original.

45. See Bruner, "Abraham Lincoln as Authentic Reproduction," 399–400.

46. See Greenspan, *Creating Colonial Williamsburg*.

47. B. S. Hinckley, "The Nauvoo Memorial," 459.

48. U.S. Department of the Interior, *Report on Nauvoo, Illinois*, 4.

49. See Alexander, *Mormonism in Transition*; G. O. Larson, *The "Americanization" of Utah*; Lyman, *Political Deliverance*; Moyer, "Dancing with the Devil."

50. B. S. Hinckley, "The Nauvoo Memorial," 461.

51. B. S. Hinckley, "The Nauvoo Memorial," 459.

52. For a discussion of the origin and historical development of these doctrinal differences, see Howard, "Nauvoo Heritage," 41–52.

53. Burgess, *Early History of Nauvoo*, 13.

54. Roosevelt to Ickes, March 28, 1942, quoted in U.S. Department of the Interior, *Historic Sites Survey and National Landmarks Program*, 21.

55. Cannon, *Nauvoo Panorama*, 72.

56. Federal Writers' Project of Illinois, *Nauvoo Guide*, 14.

57. For a nice review of the various reasons Church members visited Nauvoo at this time, see Bingham, "Packaging the 'Williamsburg of the Midwest,'" 22–23, 39–44.

58. Stobaugh, "Development of the Joseph Smith Historic Center," 36; see also Bingham, "Packaging the 'Williamsburg of the Midwest,'" 26–27.

59. Cannon, *Nauvoo Panorama*, 72; see also Bingham, "Packaging the 'Williamsburg of the Midwest,'" 29.

60. Bingham, "Packaging the 'Williamsburg of the Midwest,'" 29–30, 36–38; Colvin, *Nauvoo Temple*, 298–300.

61. Cannon, *Nauvoo Panorama*, 71–72.

62. Bingham, "Packaging the 'Williamsburg of the Midwest,'" 34; Cannon, *Nauvoo Panorama*, 71–72.

63. Illinois House of Representatives, Resolution No. 53, April 27, 1949, Illinois State Archives, Springfield.

64. "Two Mormon Churches Eye Temple Project," *The Nauvoo Independent*, May 5, 1949, and "L.D.S. Leaders Deny Nauvoo Temple Plans," *The Nauvoo Independent*, May 12, 1949, both cited in Bingham, "Packaging the 'Williamsburg of the Midwest,'" 21–22.

65. Stobaugh, "Development of the Joseph Smith Historic Center," 38.

66. The plaque is now located in the LDS Relief Society's Monument to Women garden at Nauvoo.

67. "Huge Mormon Billboard Erected East of Nauvoo," *The Nauvoo Independent*, July 23, 1959, cited in Bingham, "Packaging the 'Williamsburg of the Midwest,'" 44.

68. T. Edgar Lyon to J. LeRoy Kimball, July 13, 1964, NRI Corporate Files, box 177, folder 18. See footnote 30 of this chapter for an explanation of the term "Josephites." For a similar account of LDS–RLDS tensions, see also Kennedy, interviews by Gordon Irving, 1:328.

2. The Rise of Nauvoo Restoration, Inc.

1. Mackintosh, *Historic Sites Survey and National Landmarks Program*, 32–33.

2. U.S. Department of the Interior, National Survey of Historic Sites and Buildings, *Westward Expansion*, 107. See also U.S. Department of the Interior, National Park Service, History Branch, *Sites Recommended for Classification of Exceptional Value*.

3. U.S. Department of the Interior, National Survey of Historic Sites and Buildings, *Westward Expansion*, 133.

4. U.S. Department of the Interior, National Survey of Historic Sites and Buildings, *Westward Expansion*. Also quoted in Kimball, "Report of Progress and Development," June 25, 1964, 3, NRI Corporate Files, box 214, folder 5.

5. The RLDS Church also acquired a few additional Nauvoo lots and structures in the early 1960s. See Shireman, "The Mormon Prophet's Illinois Legacy," 154–55.

6. "Record Number of Visitors at Smith Properties," *The Nauvoo Independent*, November 21, 1963, cited in Bingham, "Packaging the 'Williamsburg of the Midwest,'" 62.

7. The changes made to the house at this time are detailed in T. Edgar Lyon's oral history. Specifically, he mentions the addition of bathrooms on the first and second floors, the installation of a furnace, the relocation of doorways, and a modern furnishing arrangement inconsistent with nineteenth-century living standards. See Lyon, interviews by Davis Bitton, 217–18.

8. Ida Blum, "Kimball Home Dedicated on Sunday," *The Nauvoo Independent*, July 7, 1960, cited in Bingham, "Packaging the 'Williamsburg of the Midwest,'" 64–65; Kimball Jr., "J. LeRoy Kimball, Nauvoo Restoration Pioneer," 5–12; R. J. Miller, "A Short History of NRI," NRI Corporate Files, box 197, folder 7; Kimball, "Report of Progress and Development," 1.

9. These events are related in Lyon, interviews with Bitton, 220.

10. David Kennedy, a mutual associate, later commented on this relationship, noting that Clark "was a close friend of Roy Kimball." He continued, "I always kidded Roy about influencing and indoctrinating him. But the relationship there was very close because when he passed away he gave Roy his saddle and a few other things that were very dear to him." Kennedy, interviews by Irving, 1:324.

11. Kimball, "Nauvoo Restoration, Incorporated," January 8, 1974, 1, NRI Corporate Files, box 3, folder 11; Reiser, interviews by William G. Hartley, 3:83–84.

12. Kimball, "Nauvoo Restoration, Incorporated," 1.

13. Kimball, "Report of Progress and Development," 15, 20; see also Lyon, interviews by Bitton, 224.

14. Reiser, interviews by Hartley, 3:84.

15. Reiser, interviews by Hartley, 3:81; see also 3:84.

16. Reiser uses the term "showcase" in describing the way in which President McKay and other leading LDS Church officials thought of Nauvoo's potential utility to publicize the Church. See Reiser, interviews by Hartley, 3:82 and 3:112.

17. W. Glen Fairclough Jr., "Utah Centennial Commission (1947)," Utah History Research Center, http://archives.state.ut.us/research/agencyhistories/180.html (accessed June 23, 2009); Smith-Mansfield, "'This Is The Place' Monument," 555.

18. Reiser, interviews by Hartley, 3:84–88; M. Christensen, "Parks and Recreation in Utah," 416–17; This Is The Place Heritage Park, "Park History," http://www.thisistheplace.org/info/parkhistory.html (accessed June 23, 2009).

19. Kimball, "Report of Progress and Development," 1.

20. Kimball, "Nauvoo Restoration, Incorporated," 1. See also Krohe, "A New City of Joseph," 60; Lyon, interviews by Bitton, 221.

21. Kimball, "Report of Progress and Development," 2. The figure of $350,000 comes from a letter written by J. LeRoy Kimball to President David O. McKay and Counselors, September 20, 1962, NRI Corporate Files, box 214, folder 5. See the financial statement attached to this letter as well.

22. Bingham, "Packaging the 'Williamsburg of the Midwest,'" 67, 71, 80. Other acquisitions authorized by the LDS First Presidency at this time included the Newberry Home, the McCarty Farm, the block on which the Seventies Hall once sat, and an old house north of the Temple lot. Allegedly, at the insistence of J. LeRoy Kimball, Salt Lake City music dealer Hyrum B. Summerhays purchased the Winslow Farr property in January 1960, and later deeded it to the LDS Church as well. See Kimball, "Report of Progress and Development," 17.

23. Lyon, interviews by Bitton, 222.

24. Similar situations arose in connection with the construction of the

LDS Church's Polynesian Cultural Center in Laie, Oahu, and in the acquisition of property on which the Washington DC Temple was later built. See Prince and Wright, *David O. McKay*, 181, 265.

25. T. Edgar Lyon, noted historian of Nauvoo, later attributed the initiation of interaction with President McKay to either J. LeRoy Kimball or Fabian himself. Apparently, there was some confusion and conflict between Fabian and Kimball over whose actions were responsible for the conceptualization of the Nauvoo restoration. See Lyon, interviews by Bitton, 219–20.

26. Fabian's grandfather operated a bank and store in Kanesville (Council Bluffs), Iowa, in the mid-nineteenth century. He came to know and befriend several prominent Latter-day Saints, including Brigham Young, as the Mormon wagon trains passed through the town on the way to the Salt Lake Valley. Presumably, these positive interactions and relationships later compelled the Fabians to move to Utah and make their home among the Latter-day Saints. Subsequently, Fabian's father became a banker in Salt Lake City. See Harold P. Fabian, "Mr. Fabian's Remarks at the Presidential Dinner," April 20, 1965, 2, NRI Corporate Files, box 4, folder 1; see also Texas A&M University, Department of Parks, Recreation and Tourism Sciences, "Harold P. Fabian: Cornelius Amory Pugsley National Medal Award, 1964," http://www.rpts.tamu.edu/pugsley/Fabian.htm (accessed June 23, 2009).

27. One of Fabian's senior partners in the firm was Robert L. Judd, the son-in-law of Heber J. Grant, president of the LDS Church from 1918 until his death in 1945. See Reiser, interviews by Hartley, 3:100–101.

28. Righter, *Crucible for Conservation*, 49.

29. Fabian subsequently served as trustee, treasurer, and executive vice president of this company until 1952. He also served as an officer or trustee for other companies created for the benefit of the project. From 1946 to 1954 he was director of the Grand Teton Lodge and Transportation Company, and from 1946 to 1952 he was treasurer and trustee of Jackson Hole Wildlife Park. See U.S. Department of the Interior, "The Harold P. Fabian Advisory Board Collection (1961–1973)," National Park Service History Collection RG 3, Harpers Ferry Center, Harpers Ferry WV, http://www.nps.gov/hfc/products/library/fabian.htm (accessed June 23, 2009). See also Dan Eagan, "Today Is Anniversary of Much-Hated Park Edict; Expansion of Park Is Now Widely Hailed," *Salt Lake Tribune*, September 14, 2000.

30. Lucinda Dillon, "Utahn Played Role in Secret Teton Deal," *Deseret News*, September 14, 2000.

31. Utah's first four state parks were the old state prison in Sugar House (now Sugarhouse Park), This Is The Place Monument in Salt Lake City, the Territorial Statehouse in Fillmore, and Camp Floyd in Fairfield. See M. Christensen, "Parks and Recreation in Utah," 416–17.

32. Powell, "Utah's First State Park," 19–20.

33. Reiser, interviews by Hartley, 3:72.

34. *Historic Sites Act of 1935*, Sect. 463a.

35. Mackintosh, *The Historic Sites Survey and National Landmarks Program*, 32–41.

36. Fabian, "Mr. Fabian's Remarks at the Presidential Dinner," 4.

37. Fabian, "Mr. Fabian's Remarks at the Presidential Dinner," 6.

38. Fabian, "Mr. Fabian's Remarks at the Presidential Dinner," 7–8.

39. Harold P. Fabian and J. LeRoy Kimball, "Outline for the Restoration of Nauvoo," December 11, 1961, NRI Corporate Files, box 1, folder 16. Also quoted in Kimball, "Report of Progress and Development," 7.

40. Greenspan, *Creating Colonial Williamsburg*, 112; Allaback, *Mission 66 Visitor Centers*.

41. Henry A. Smith, "Church to Study Restoring Nauvoo," *Deseret News and Telegram*, May 3, 1962; Henry A. Smith, "Church Officials Study Historic Nauvoo Sites," *Deseret News and Telegram*, May 5, 1962.

42. Conrad Wirth, "Remarks of Conrad Wirth," May 1962, NRI Corporate Files, box 3, folder 10.

43. Hugh B. Brown, "Remarks of President Hugh B. Brown," May 1962, NRI Corporate Files, box 3, folder 10; see also "Mormon Leaders Study Site: First Step in Restoration Plan," *Quincy Herald-Whig*, May 5, 1962.

44. Henry A. Smith, "Steps Taken to Restore Historic Nauvoo," *Church News*, June 30, 1962; Henry A. Smith, "Church Forms Corporation to Restore Historic Nauvoo," *Deseret News*, June 28, 1962.

45. Reiser, interviews by Hartley, 3:71–72, 3:100–101.

46. One example comes from the LDS Church's involvement in the broadcasting industry; see Prince and Wright, *David O. McKay*, 124–38.

47. Reiser, interviews by Hartley, 3:116.

48. Marriott, "Building a Family Legacy," 4–7.

49. J. Willard Marriott Jr. [by way of Julie Paull] to the Awards Administration of Freedoms Foundation at Valley Forge, August 27, 1986, NRI Corporate Files, box 196, folder 16.

50. O'Brien, *Marriott*.

51. At the time of Marriott's death in 1985, the company was earning more than $4 billion annually, a figure that more than doubled a decade later.

52. Minutes of First Meeting of Board of Directors Named in the Articles of Incorporation, July 27, 1962, 23, NRI Corporate Files, box 214, folder 5.

53. Kennedy, interviews by Irving, 1:320.

54. Hickman, *David Matthew Kennedy*.

55. Kennedy, interviews by Irving, 1:330.

56. John K. Edmunds, a lawyer from Chicago, drafted the articles of incorporation for NRI. In addition to practicing law, Edmunds was president of the LDS Church's Chicago Stake. His legal services for NRI at this time were tied to the fact that David M. Kennedy served as his counselor in the stake presidency. The articles of incorporation and the minutes of this first board meeting are found in NRI Corporate Files, box 214, folder 5.

57. By-Laws of Nauvoo Restoration, Incorporated, Article I, NRI Corporate Files, box 214, folder 5.

58. On Kendrew's career with Colonial Williamsburg, see Hosmer, *Preservation Comes of Age*, vol. 1, chap. 1, especially 50–73.

59. At a special dinner meeting in 1964 during which the Nauvoo project was presented to many members of the LDS Church hierarchy, Fabian publicly identified Kendrew as "one of my best friends." See Fabian, "Mr. Fabian's Remarks at the Presidential Dinner."

60. Fabian, "Mr. Fabian's Remarks at the Presidential Dinner."

61. Fabian, "Mr. Fabian's Remarks at the Presidential Dinner."

62. Kimball, "Report of Progress and Development," 6. See also Minutes of Meeting of the Executive Committee, September 29, 1964, 1, NRI Corporate Files, box 214, folder 5; T. Edgar Lyon, "Historian's Progress Report—May to October, 1964," NRI Corporate Files, box 177, folder 10; Minutes of Meeting Held at the Village Inn, Nauvoo, IL, March 18, 1966, NRI Corporate Files, box 169, folder 1; J. C. Harrington to Rowena J. Miller, October 24, 1966, NRI Corporate Files, box 155, folder 7; Rex Sohm Diary, typescript, August 11, 1967, NRI Corporate Files, box 169, folder 7.

63. See "Memorandum Requested by President Tanner," October 19, 1964, 5, NRI Corporate Files, box 214, folder 5.

64. Louise Hutchinson, "Nauvoo Restoring Old Mormon Scene," *Chicago Tribune*, September 2, 1962. A copy of this article is available in NRI Corporate Files, box 3, folder 14.

65. A. Edwin Kendrew, "Remarks of Kendrew at Presidential Dinner," April 20, 1965, NRI Corporate Files, box 4, folder 1.

66. The "Operational Outline" can be found in Kimball, "Report of Progress and Development," 10.

67. In an earlier presentation of these principles, Kendrew expounded on this point and revealed his own biases in the process. He acknowledged that in the field of preservation and restoration the sentiment is to retain structures of different periods so that all types of buildings that might depict a place are preserved. He continued, however, by saying, "In many instances, i.e., Williamsburg, Old Salem, etc., this theory was not considered desirable. At Nauvoo it would seem rather obvious that the chief historic value of the restoration of the old town lies within the period when it was a flourishing Mormon settlement. Hence, buildings of the 1837–1850 period . . . might be selected." Finally, in reference to the French Icarians, who occupied Nauvoo after the Mormons had evacuated, he added, "It does not appear that the buildings of the later French settlement should be included, as they cannot equal the significance of the earlier settlement." A. Edwin Kendrew, "Notes Concerning Restoration of Nauvoo, Illinois," April 28, 1964, 4, NRI Corporate Files, box 3, folder 15.

68. A. Edwin Kendrew, "General Principles for the Restoration of Nauvoo, Illinois," October 22, 1964, appendix to Board of Trustees Meeting, November 7, 1964, NRI Corporate Files, box 214, folder 5.

69. Kendrew, "General Principles for the Restoration of Nauvoo, Illinois."

70. Kennedy, interviews by Irving, 1:321.

71. Kendrew, "Remarks by A. Edwin Kendrew," Board of Trustees Meeting, Nauvoo Restoration, Incorporated, May 22, 1971, 2, NRI Corporate Files, box 4, folder 13.

72. Kendrew, "Remarks by A. Edwin Kenrew," Board of Trustees Meeting, Nauvoo Restoration, Incorporated, May 22, 1971, 2.

73. Minutes of Meeting of the Board of Directors of Nauvoo Restoration, Incorporated, October 12, 1962, NRI Corporate Files, box 214, folder 5. See also the attached letter from Kimball to President McKay and Counselors, September 20, 1962.

74. Minutes of First Meeting of Board of Directors Named in the Articles of Incorporation of Nauvoo Restoration, Incorporated, July 27, 1962, 22–23, NRI Corporate Files, box 214, folder 5.

75. Minutes of Meeting of the Board of Directors of Nauvoo Restoration, Incorporated, October 12, 1962.

76. An excellent account of the LDS Church's elaborate building program and the resultant financial crisis is given in Prince and Wright, *David O. McKay*, 199–226. The remark about "a real liquidity crunch" comes from Alan Blodgett, an employee in the Church's Financial Department, in Prince and Wright, *David O. McKay*, 210.

77. Prince and Wright, *David O. McKay*, 210.

78. Prince and Wright, *David O. McKay*, 225.

79. Kendrew, "Remarks of Kendrew at Presidential Dinner," April 20, 1965, 5, NRI Corporate Files, box 4, folder 1. J. LeRoy Kimball also remembered this experience with Moyle. He later wrote, "President Henry D. Moyle visited Nauvoo with me and others, and standing on the hill which we have named 'Inspiration Point' and looking over the Mississippi River and Nauvoo, he said, 'Buy a thousand acres!'" Kimball, "Nauvoo Restoration, Incorporated," 1.

80. David M. Kennedy believed the planned area would be ideal for business conventions because "They can go out there and be secluded and yet have something for people to see in their leisure time." Kennedy, interviews by Irving, 1:329.

81. Reiser, interviews by Hartley, 3:100.

82. Kimball, "Report of Progress and Development," 13; Bingham, "Packaging the 'Williamsburg of the Midwest,'" 85.

83. Kennedy, interviews by Irving, 1:321.

84. J. LeRoy Kimball to A. Hamer Reiser, July 15, 1962, NRI Corporate Files, box 3, folder 12.

85. Reiser, interviews by Hartley, 3:100.

86. Kennedy, interviews by Irving, 1:321.

87. Preston W. Kimball to J. LeRoy Kimball, September 17, 1962, NRI Corporate Files, box 6, folder 8.

88. Minutes of Meeting, Board of Trustees of Nauvoo Restoration, Inc., with the First Presidency of the Church of Jesus Christ of Latter-day Saints, April 21, 1965, 5, NRI Corporate Files, box 215, folder 1.

89. J. LeRoy Kimball to David M. Kennedy, November 22, 1966, NRI Corporate Files, box 4, folder 5. The property in question was known as the Mulch property, which consisted of some eighty acres near the river. Apparently Wilford Wood had previously entered into a purchase agree-

ment for a portion of this property and had given Miss Mulch a fur in order to persuade her to sell.

90. Kennedy, interviews by Irving, 1:331. On the same page Kennedy recounts his role in the purchase of the Jonathon Browning Home as well. Kennedy was also to use his influence with the Catholic Church in Chicago during negotiations for certain parcels of land owned by the Catholic Church in Nauvoo. See Minutes of Meeting, Board of Trustees of Nauvoo Restoration, Inc., with the First Presidency of the Church of Jesus Christ of Latter-day Saints, April 21, 1965, 7–8.

91. "Land Acquisition Account," September 6, 1962, attached to Minutes of Meeting of the Board of Directors, October 12, 1962. See also Hutchinson, "Nauvoo Restoring Old Mormon Scene."

92. "Property Acquisition," April 1, 1965, NRI Corporate Files, box 4, folder 1. These figures include the properties acquired prior to the incorporation of NRI, namely those on the Temple block, the Snow-Ashby duplex, the Times and Seasons Building, the Brigham Young Home, the Wilford Woodruff Home, the Seventies Hall lot, and several other properties that Kimball had purchased under the direction of the LDS First Presidency for a total of $156,658.92. See Kimball, "Report of Progress and Development," 17. For a detailed record of properties purchased between January 1 and September 30, 1964, including the names of property owners and purchase prices, in addition to a list of properties not yet purchased and an inventory of Mormon buildings in Nauvoo, see "Property Acquisition, January 1, 1964 to date," NRI Corporate Files, box 4, folder 1.

93. "Property Acquisition," April 1, 1965. Compare this with the summary of property acquisition in Kimball, "Report of Progress and Development," 17–18.

94. First Presidency (David O. McKay, Hugh B. Brown, and N. Eldon Tanner) to J. LeRoy Kimball, April 28, 1965, NRI Corporate Files, box 215, folder 1. This number does not reflect the $156,658.92 spent on properties purchased prior to NRI's inception, which were later deeded to the corporation.

95. Kendrew, "Remarks of Kendrew at Presidential Dinner," April 20, 1965, 6.

96. Kimball, "Nauvoo Restoration, Incorporated," 4.

97. Kimball Jr., "J. LeRoy Kimball," 10.

98. "C. Of C. Endorses Restoration Project," *The Nauvoo Independent*, July

11, 1963, cited in Bingham, "Packaging the 'Williamsburg of the Midwest,'" 72–73.

99. Preston W. Kimball to John K. Edmunds, January 11, 1963, NRI Corporate Files, box 5, folder 20.

100. T. Edgar Lyon to J. LeRoy Kimball, May 24, 1965, NRI Corporate Files, box 158, folder 9.

101. Anonymous memorandum to the First Presidency, December 21, 1977, NRI Corporate Files, box 215, folder 3. In addition to the $6 million spent prior to this time, the LDS First Presidency authorized nearly $600,000 more in the first three months of 1978. This money was to finance various irrigation projects in Nauvoo and the repair or restoration of eight additional historic Mormon structures. See the following four letters, all of which are found in NRI Corporate Files, box 215, folder 3: the First Presidency to Mark E. Petersen, February 10, 1978; the First Presidency to Nauvoo Incorporated, February 27, 1978; The First Presidency to Nauvoo Restoration, Incorporated, March 23, 1978; and the First Presidency to Nauvoo Restoration, Inc., March 31, 1978. In 1990 the *Chicago Tribune* reported that a total of $15 million in LDS Church funds had been expended on the restoration of Nauvoo. See "Restored Nauvoo Tells of Mormon History," *Chicago Tribune*, September 21, 1990.

102. Kendrew, "Remarks of Kendrew at Presidential Dinner," 5.

103. Kendrew, "Remarks of Kendrew at Presidential Dinner," 5.

104. George Cannon Young, "Nauvoo Restoration," October 11, 1962, attached to the Minutes of Meeting of the Board of Directors, October 12, 1962. See also Young, interview by Paul L. Anderson, December 20, 1973.

105. Kimball, "Report of Progress and Development," 23–24.

106. Minutes of the Annual Meeting of the Members and Board of Trustees of Nauvoo Restoration, Incorporated, May 14, 1966, 2, NRI Corporate Files, box 215, folder 1.

107. Minutes of the Annual Meeting of the Members and Board of Trustees of Nauvoo Restoration, Incorporated, May 13, 1967, 6, NRI Corporate Files, box 215, folder 1.

108. In speaking of this $15,000 grant from the NPS, T. Edgar Lyon, a later historian for NRI, reported that NPS officials "would not give the money to Nauvoo Restoration. They said, 'It's obviously the Church.' So they turned the money over to the University of Utah and they took 10 percent for administration or 15 percent." Lyon, interviews by Bitton, 223.

109. NRI's secretary-treasurer, A. Hamer Reiser, recalled that NRI was established as a nonprofit organization because "we were hoping to get—and this is still the hope—grants from individuals who have money and who are interested in the historic properties and sites of the Church and of the country. The Church preferred to have a non-profit corporation organized for that purpose rather than to have contributions given directly to the Church. There's some doubt that the federal government, for example, would have helped with anything if it meant giving money to a church. So it had to be an independent corporation. And the state of Illinois was also to be involved. Rather than a state dealing with a church it would be a non-profit corporation. That was the main reason for the incorporation." Reiser, interviews by Hartley, 3:99–100.

110. *National Historic Preservation Act of 1966*, Public Law 89–665, 80 Stat. 915, 16 U.S.C. 470 et seq. See also Murtagh, *Keeping Time*, 67–74.

111. Minutes of a Special Meeting of the Members and Board of Trustees of Nauvoo Restoration, Incorporated, October 27, 1967, 5–7, NRI Corporate Files, box 215, folder 1.

112. Minutes of a Special Meeting of the Members and Board of Trustees of Nauvoo Restoration, Incorporated, October 27, 1967, 7, NRI Corporate Files, box 215, folder 1.

113. Minutes of a Meeting of the Board of Trustees of Nauvoo Restoration, Incorporated, March 16, 1968, 2, NRI Corporate Files, box 215, folder 1.

114. Minutes of Meeting, Executive Committee of Nauvoo Restoration, Inc. with the First Presidency of the Church of Jesus Christ of Latter-day Saints, April 18, 1968, 3, NRI Corporate Files, box 215, folder 1. See also Minutes of the Annual Meeting of the Members and Board of Trustees of Nauvoo Restoration, Incorporated, May 11, 1968, 1, NRI Corporate Files, box 215, folder 1.

115. Hickman, *David Matthew Kennedy*, 217.

116. Hickman, *David Matthew Kennedy*, 217.

117. Minutes of Meeting, Board of Trustees of Nauvoo Restoration, Inc. with the First Presidency of the Church of Jesus Christ of Latter-day Saints, April 21, 1965, 2–3.

118. Minutes of Meeting, Board of Trustees, Nauvoo Restoration, Inc., April 20, 1965, 3, NRI Corporate Files, box 215, folder 1.

119. Minutes of Meeting, Executive Committee of Nauvoo Restoration,

Inc. with the First Presidency of the Church of Jesus Christ of Latter-day Saints, April 18, 1968, 5, NRI Corporate Files, box 215, folder 1.

120. Minutes of Meeting, Board of Trustees of Nauvoo Restoration, Inc. with the First Presidency of the Church of Jesus Christ of Latter-day Saints," April 21, 1965, 12.

121. Minutes of the Annual Meeting of the Members and Board of Trustees of Nauvoo Restoration, Incorporated, May 23, 1969, 6, NRI Corporate Files, box 215, folder 1.

122. Kennedy, interviews by Irving, 1:323.

123. Kennedy, interviews by Irving, 1:323. Kennedy also shared this story with members of the general LDS Church hierarchy at a dinner hosted by NRI in April 1965. In this setting, he related that McKay had said, "Here is something that is big. It is important and it will be carried on by our successors." See Kennedy, "Remarks of Kennedy at Presidential Dinner," April 20, 1965, 29, NRI Corporate Files, box 4, folder 1.

124. Illinois Department of Conservation, Division of Long Range Planning, Systems Planning and Research Unit, *State of Illinois Historic Preservation Plan*; Hosmer, "Preservation Movement in Illinois," in *Preservation Illinois*, 10–19; Theodore Hild, "State and National Surveys," in *Preservation Illinois*, 75–79.

125. Theodore Hild, Assistant Division Chief and Deputy State Historic Preservation Officer, State of Illinois, personal communication, October 20, 2005.

126. Minutes of Meeting, Board of Trustees of Nauvoo Restoration, Inc., with the First Presidency of the Church of Jesus Christ of Latter-day Saints, April 21, 1965, 7.

127. First Presidency (David O. McKay, Hugh B. Brown, and N. Eldon Tanner) to J. LeRoy Kimball, April 28, 1965, NRI Corporate Files, box 215, folder 1.

128. Minutes of Meeting, Board of Trustees, Nauvoo Restoration, Inc., April 20, 1965, 4.

129. Minutes of the Annual Meeting of the Members and Board of Trustees of Nauvoo Restoration, Incorporated, May 23, 1970, 3, NRI Corporate Files, box 215, folder 1.

130. Larry R. King to J. LeRoy Kimball, October 3, 1973, attached to Minutes of Meeting of Board of Trustees of Nauvoo Restoration, Incorporated, January 2, 1974, NRI Corporate Files, box 215, folder 2. See also, John V.

Browning to J. LeRoy Kimball, November 27, 1972, attached to Minutes of Adjourned Meeting of Board of Trustees of Nauvoo Restoration, Incorporated, January 3, 1973, NRI Corporate Files, box 215, folder 2.

131. Minutes of the Annual Meeting of the Members and Board of Trustees of Nauvoo Restoration, Incorporated, May 23, 1970, 3.

132. Lyon, interviews by Bitton, 222.

133. Reiser, interviews by Hartley, 3:106.

134. J. L. Kimball, "Report of Progress and Development," 5.

135. "Church, Civic Officials Confer in Nauvoo," *Church News*, May 9, 1964. See also Minutes of Meeting of the Members and Board of Trustees of Nauvoo Restoration, Incorporated, May 1, 1964, 7, NRI Corporate Files, box 214, folder 5; "Luncheon for Governor Otto Kerner," May 2, 1964, NRI Corporate Files, box 3, folder 15.

136. Henry A. Smith, "Illinois Governor Lauds Nauvoo Mormons," *Church News*, September 1, 1962.

137. J. L. Kimball, "Report of Progress and Development," 5; "Memorandum Requested by President Tanner," 3–4. See also Minutes of Meeting of Executive Committee, April 2, 1964, 1, NRI Corporate Files, box 214, folder 5; Minutes of Meeting of the Executive Committee, September 29, 1964, 1, NRI Corporate Files, box 214, folder 5; Minutes of Meeting, Board of Trustees, April 20, 1965, 1.

138. J. L. Kimball, "Report of Progress and Development," 5; "Memorandum Requested by President Tanner," 3–4. The State of Illinois did eventually develop a small wharf north of the present-day historic area, which is primarily used by recreational fishermen today.

139. J. L. Kimball, "Report of Progress and Development," 6; "Memorandum Requested by President Tanner," 3. See also Minutes of Meeting of the Executive Committee, August 31, 1965, 1, NRI Corporate Files, box 215, folder 1.

140. The nine structures included the homes of Heber C. Kimball, Wilford Woodruff, Brigham Young, Winslow Farr, and Joseph B. Noble–Lucy M. Smith, in addition to the Seventies Hall, the Times and Seasons print shop, the Webb Wagon and Blacksmith Shop, and the Jonathon Browning Home and Gun Smith Shop. See Todd, "Nauvoo: A Progress Report," 20–24, and "Historic Nauvoo," *Church News*, July 31, 1971. On the partial reconstruction of the Nauvoo Temple, including architectural drawings of the proposed reconstruction, see Todd, "Nauvoo Temple Restoration," 10–16.

141. "A Groundbreaking at Nauvoo," *Church News*, May 3, 1969.

142. Allaback, *Mission 66 Visitor Centers*.

143. "Center to Tell Nauvoo Story," *Church News*, May 24, 1969.

144. J. M. Heslop, "Nauvoo Looks Forward," *Church News*, May 31, 1969.

145. Todd, "Nauvoo: A Progress Report," 24.

3. Interpretive Conflict at Nauvoo

1. Sharon A. Brown, *Administrative History: Jefferson National Expansion Memorial National Historic Site, 1935–1980* ([St. Louis?: s.n.], 1984), http://www.nps.gov/history/history/online_books/jeff/adhit.htm (accessed June 23, 2009).

2. Wirth, "Remarks of Conrad Wirth," May 1962, NRI Corporate Files, box 3, folder 10.

3. See the discussion in chapter one concerning Bryant S. Hinckley, president of the LDS Northern States Mission.

4. Dick Emery, "Nauvoo Takes on a New Look," *Church News*, September 30, 1961; Henry A. Smith, "Interest at Nauvoo," *Church News*, February 8, 1964. See also Cannon, *Nauvoo Panorama*, 72.

5. Eliason, "Pioneers and Recapitulation," 175–211.

6. Wirth, "Remarks of Conrad Wirth," 10, spelling corrected.

7. For a summary of this unprecedented missionary success, see chapter 10, "The Missionary Program," in Prince and Wright, *David O. McKay*, 227–55.

8. Monitor C. Noyce, "Restoring an Historic City," *Church News*, July 22, 1967. This comment was made by J. Byron Ravsten, NRI's resident project manager. Significantly, Ravsten was a former mission president for the LDS Church. Moreover, he was serving on the LDS Church's Priesthood Missionary Committee at this time.

9. Noyce, "Restoring an Historic City."

10. Limerick, *Legacy of Conquest*.

11. See Greenspan, *Creating Colonial Williamsburg*, for a comprehensive analysis of Colonial Williamsburg's evolving interpretive approach.

12. *Colonial Williamsburg Official Guidebook and Map*, xv. See also Greenspan, *Creating Colonial Williamsburg*, and Handler and Gable, *New History in an Old Museum*.

13. Minutes of Meeting, Board of Trustees of Nauvoo Restoration, Inc.

with the First Presidency of the Church of Jesus Christ of Latter-day Saints, April 21, 1965, 1, NRI Corporate Files, box 215, folder 1.

14. Kendrew, "Remarks by A. Edwin Kendrew," May 22, 1971, 1–2, attached to Minutes of the Annual Meeting of the Members and Board of Trustees of Nauvoo Restoration, Incorporated, May 22, 1971, NRI Corporate Files, box 215, folder 2.

15. Harold P. Fabian and J. LeRoy Kimball, "Outline for the Restoration of Nauvoo," December 11, 1961, NRI Corporate Files, box 1, folder 16. Also quoted in Kimball, "Report of Progress and Development," June 25, 1964, 7, NRI Corporate Files, box 214, folder 5.

16. Fabian, "Mr. Fabian's Remarks at the Presidential Dinner," April 20, 1965, 4, NRI Corporate Files, box 4, folder 1.

17. For insight into this perspective, see Lyon, interviews by Bitton, 222.

18. Fabian, "Mr. Fabian's Remarks at the Presidential Dinner," 7–8.

19. Henry A. Smith, "Church Forms Corporation to Restore Historic Nauvoo," *Church News*, June 30, 1962.

20. Articles of Incorporation, Nauvoo Restoration, Incorporated, July 27, 1962, NRI Corporate Files, box 214, folder 5.

21. J. L. Kimball, "Report of Progress and Development," 7.

22. J. L. Kimball "Dr. J. LeRoy Kimball's Comments at the President's Dinner," April 20, 1965, 6–7, NRI Corporate Files, box 4, folder 1.

23. J. L. Kimball, "Dr. J. L. Kimball's Comments at the President's Dinner," 6.

24. Kennedy, "Remarks of Kennedy at Presidential Dinner," April 20, 1965, 30–31, NRI Corporate Files, box 4, folder 1.

25. J. LeRoy Kimball, Memorandum, April 27, 1965, NRI Corporate Files, box 215, folder 1; the First Presidency to Dr. J. LeRoy Kimball, April 28, 1965, NRI Corporate Files, box 215, folder 1.

26. Rowena J. Miller to Rex Sohm, April 26, 1967, NRI Corporate Files, box 169, folder 5.

27. T. Edgar Lyon, "Historian's Progress Report—May to October, 1964," 4, NRI Corporate Files, box 177, folder 10; Minutes of Meeting, Board of Trustees of Nauvoo Restoration, Inc., April 20, 1965, 1–2, NRI Corporate Files, box 215, folder 1.

28. Arta to T. Edgar Lyon, April 5, 1969, NRI Corporate Files, box 177, folder 15.

29. Clement P. Hilton, "Guidelines for Interpreting Nauvoo," [1969], NRI Corporate Files, box 177, folder 15.

30. Hilton, "Guidelines for Interpreting Nauvoo."

31. Clement P. Hilton, "A Sample NRI Tour of Nauvoo," [1969], 1, NRI Corporate Files, box 177, folder 15.

32. Hilton, "A Sample NRI Tour of Nauvoo," 10.

33. T. Edgar Lyon to J. LeRoy Kimball, July 13, 1964, NRI Corporate Files, box 177, folder 18.

34. "The Era Asks About Nauvoo Restoration," 16.

35. Reiser, interviews by Hartley, 3:106.

36. Reiser, Memorandum of a meeting with the First Presidency, November 17, 1967, 3, NRI Corporate Files, box 215, folder 1.

37. Minutes of a Meeting of the Board of Trustees of Nauvoo Restoration, Incorporated, March 16, 1968, 2, NRI Corporate Files, box 215, folder 1.

38. Minutes of Meeting, Board of Trustees of Nauvoo Restoration, Inc. with the First Presidency of the Church of Jesus Christ of Latter-day Saints, April 21, 1965, 1–2.

39. Prince and Wright, *David O. McKay*, 181.

40. Prince and Wright, *David O. McKay*, 265–66.

41. Lyon, interviews by Bitton, 222.

42. Church of Jesus Christ of Latter-day Saints, *Church History*, 566.

43. Lyon, interviews by Bitton, 223.

44. Kennedy, interviews by Irving, 1:323. See also J. M. Heslop, "Nauvoo Looks Forward," *Church News*, May 31, 1969, and "Nauvoo Information Center Groundbreaking," official program of the ceremony, copy in author's possession.

45. Lyon, interviews by Bitton, 222.

46. First Presidency (Joseph Fielding Smith, Harold B. Lee, and N. Eldon Tanner) to J. LeRoy Kimball, March 30, 1971, NRI Corporate Files, box 1, folder 23. This letter is also reproduced in the Minutes of the Annual Meeting of the Members and Board of Trustees of Nauvoo Restoration, Incorporated, May 22, 1971, 2.

47. Church of Jesus Christ of Latter-day Saints, *Church History*, 562. See also Prince and Wright, *David O. McKay*, 139–58.

48. Church of Jesus Christ of Latter-day Saints, *Church History*, 563.

49. First Presidency to J. LeRoy Kimball, March 30, 1971.

50. "Nauvoo Mission Unique; Tells Dramatic Story," *Church News*, September 11, 1971.

51. First Presidency to J. LeRoy Kimball, March 30, 1971; First Presidency to Wilford W. Kimball, April 21, 1971, NRI Corporate Files, box 1, folder 23; First Presidency to Mark E. Petersen, Delbert L. Stapley, John H. Vandenberg, and J. LeRoy Kimball, March 21, 1974, NRI Corporate Files, box 215, folder 2; First Presidency to Mark E. Petersen, Delbert L. Stapley, John H. Vandenberg, and J. LeRoy Kimball, April 22, 1974, NRI Corporate Files, box 215, folder 2.

52. Kimball Jr., "J. LeRoy Kimball, Nauvoo Restoration Pioneer," 11–12.

53. "Nauvoo Visitors Center, Exhibition Buildings in Nauvoo, Old Carthage Jail," September 16, 1973, attached to Minutes of Meeting of Board of Trustees of Nauvoo Restoration, Inc., January 2, 1974, NRI Corporate Files, box 215, folder 2.

54. Nauvoo Committee (Spencer W. Kimball, Mark E. Petersen, and Delbert L. Stapley), "Nauvoo: Our Recommendations for the Future," March 1971, NRI Corporate Files, box 1, folder 23.

55. First Presidency to All Members of the Board of Directors of Nauvoo Restoration, Incorporated, May 13, 1971, NRI Corporate Files, box 214, folder 5.

56. Minutes of the Annual Meeting of the Members and Board of Trustees of Nauvoo Restoration, Incorporated, May 22, 1971, 3.

57. Minutes of the Annual Meeting of the Members and Board of Trustees of Nauvoo Restoration, Incorporated, May 22, 1971 3.

58. Kendrew, "Remarks by A. Edwin Kendrew," May 22, 1971, 3, 8–9.

59. Kendrew, "Remarks by A. Edwin Kendrew," May 22, 1971, 6.

60. Kendrew, "Remarks by A. Edwin Kendrew," May 22, 1971, 6–7.

61. Minutes of the Annual Meeting of the Members and Board of Trustees of Nauvoo Restoration, Incorporated, May 22, 1971, 3.

62. Minutes of Meeting of the Executive Committee of Nauvoo Restoration, Incorporated, September 16, 1967, 1, NRI Corporate Files, box 215, folder 1.

63. Minutes of Meeting, Executive Committee of Nauvoo Restoration, Inc. with the First Presidency of the Church of Jesus Christ of Latter-day Saints, April 18, 1968, 2–3, NRI Corporate Files, box 215, folder 1.

64. Mark E. Petersen to Delbert L. Stapley, July 7, 1970, 1, NRI Corporate Files, box 177, folder 8.

65. Petersen to Stapley, July 7, 1970, 1.

66. Petersen to Stapley, July 7, 1970, 1.

67. Petersen to Stapley, July 7, 1970, 3.

68. Petersen to Stapley, July 7, 1970, 3.

69. Petersen to Stapley, July 7, 1970, 2.

70. Petersen to Stapley, July 7, 1970, 2, 3.

71. Kennedy, interviews by Irving, 1:323.

72. Dell Van Orden, "New Center Dedicated," *Church News*, September 11, 1971.

73. Van Orden, "New Center Dedicated."

74. On the morning of December 20, 1972, Harold Boyer of the LDS Church's Law Department called the office of NRI to discuss the possible dissolution of NRI. Items discussed included the corporation's indebtedness and its property holdings. Typed notes of this telephone conversation are found in NRI Corporate Files, box 4, folder 14 ("Possible dissolution of Nauvoo Restoration, Incorporated"). Although it appears LDS Church leaders were considering dissolving NRI at this time, these efforts were never fulfilled, leaving NRI's status as a nonprofit corporation intact.

75. First Presidency (Harold B. Lee, N. Eldon Tanner, and Marion G. Romney) to Nauvoo Restoration, Inc., September 12, 1972, NRI Corporate Files, box 215, folder 2.

76. 2005 *Church Almanac*, 93.

77. The five structures dedicated at this time were the Brigham Young Home, the Jonathon Browning Home and Gun Shop, the Webb Blacksmith and Wagon Shop, the Seventies Hall, and the Joseph Bates Noble–Lucy Mack Smith Home. Work on all but the last had been initiated and mostly completed before the major reorganization of NRI's board of trustees in 1971.

78. David Johnston, "5 Restored Buildings Dedicated in Nauvoo," *Church News*, June 2, 1973; "Church Officials Dedicate 5 Restored Nauvoo Buildings," *Deseret News*, May 26, 1973.

79. See J. LeRoy Kimball to Spencer W. Kimball, N. Eldon Tanner, and Marion G. Romney, January 7, 1974, NRI Corporate Files, box 3, folder 11.

80. J. L. Kimball to Spencer W. Kimball et al., January 7, 1974.

81. T. Edgar Lyon, NRI's historian, had the following to say about the

genealogical relationship of President Spencer W. Kimball and Dr. J. LeRoy Kimball: "Now Dr. Kimball is a great grandson of Heber C. Kimball by the first wife Vilate, and Spencer W. Kimball is a grandson, one generation closer, but he comes from one of the Gheen girls, I think Ann Alice Gheen—two girls of Pennsylvania Dutch stock whose house is up the street a couple of blocks from the Kimball house, still standing. These two girls Heber C. Kimball married I think in 1845 or 1846 before they left Nauvoo. So in between the oldest family there could be quite a gap, as you see in this case of one being the great-grandson and yet he's several years younger than Spencer W. Kimball, a grandson." Lyon, interviews by Bitton, 217.

82. Memorandum of Meeting with the First Presidency, June 5, 1974, NRI Corporate Files, box 215, folder 2. This money was used to renovate and landscape the Nauvoo Temple block, reconstruct the Scovil Bakery, and restore both the Print Shop and the Hiram Clark Store. A surplus of more than $200,000 from this fund was also used to restore the Masonic Hall in Nauvoo. See Rowena J. Miller to J. LeRoy Kimball, "Special Projects-Balances," August 23, 1976, NRI Corporate Files, box 215, folder 2. See also Minutes of Meeting of Board of Trustees of Nauvoo Restoration, Incorporated, August 28, 1976, 2, NRI Corporate Files, box 215, folder 2.

83. These monies were used to (1) install an irrigation system that would service the Nauvoo Temple Block, the Visitors Center Block, and NRI's farm lands; (2) repair four historic buildings—the Vinson Knight House, the Erastus Snow-Nathaniel Ashby duplex, the William Weeks House, and the William A. Gheen House; and (3) renovate the Times and Seasons Building, the Ivins-Smith House (John Taylor's Home), and the Windsor Lyon Store and Carriage House. See First Presidency to Mark E. Petersen, February 10, 1978; First Presidency to Nauvoo Incorporated, February 27, 1978; First Presidency to Nauvoo Restoration, Incorporated, March 23, 1978; and First Presidency to Nauvoo Restoration, Incorporated, March 31, 1978, all of which are found in NRI Corporate Files, box 215, folder 3. See also Memorandum to the First Presidency, December 21, 1977, NRI Corporate Files, box 215, folder 3.

84. Gerry Avant, "Nauvoo Tested Faith, Says Leader at Rites," *Church News*, August 21, 1982; Johnson, "17 Historical Sites Dedicated in Nauvoo"; "Pres. Hinckley Dedicates 16 Sites in Nauvoo," *Deseret News*, August 14, 1982; "11 Nauvoo Buildings Regain Early Luster," *Church News*, July 10, 1982.

85. Gerry Avant, "Sarah's House in Nauvoo Will Again Welcome Visi-

tors," *Church News*, June 20, 1981; Kathleen Lubeck, "Relief Society Turns 140," *Church News*, March 20, 1982; Kathleen Lubeck, "Sarah M. Kimball's Nauvoo Home Is Dedicated"; "LDS Dedicate Birthplace of Relief Society," *Deseret News*, March 11, 1982; "Restored Homes, Buildings, Bring Back the 1840s," *Church News*, August 21, 1982.

86. Nauvoo Committee, "Nauvoo: Our Recommendations for the Future," March 1971, NRI Corporate Files, box 1, folder 23.

87. "Pres. Hinckley Dedicates 16 Sites in Nauvoo," *Deseret News*, August 14, 1982.

88. Gerry Avant, "Nauvoo's Impact," *Church News*, August 27, 1977.

89. Jack Mabley, "Mormons of Nauvoo Did What They Had to Do," *Chicago Tribune*, March 5, 1977.

90. Gerry Avant, "Play Beckons, 'Walk My Quiet Roads,'" *Church News*, August 21, 1982.

91. Roger Hughes, "Restoration of Mormon Buildings Nauvoo: A Williamsburg of West," *The Courier* [Urbana IL], August 18, 1974, cited in Bingham, "Packaging the 'Williamsburg of the Midwest,'" 96–97.

92. Program for the Joseph Smith Historic Center Service of Dedication, May 3, 1980, Joseph Smith Historic Center Archives, Joseph Smith Historic Center, Nauvoo IL, cited in Bingham, "Packaging the 'Williamsburg of the Midwest,'" 141.

93. "RLDS Historic Center Internationally Recognized," *Nauvoo Grapevine*, February 23, 1978, cited in Bingham, "Packaging the 'Williamsburg of the Midwest,'" 96.

94. Wallace B. Smith to Kenneth E. Stobaugh, March 3, 1980, Joseph Smith Historic Center Archives, Joseph Smith Historic Center, Nauvoo IL, as cited in Bingham, "Packaging the 'Williamsburg of the Midwest,'" 140.

95. Janet Brigham, "Nauvoo Today: Building Again the City Beautiful," *Ensign* 47.

96. Program for the Joseph Smith Historic Center Service of Dedication, May 3, 1980, cited in Bingham, "Packaging the 'Williamsburg of the Midwest'," 141.

97. Launius and McKiernan, *Joseph Smith, Jr.'s Red Brick Store*, 31–32.

98. "Nauvoo's History Coming Back to Life," *Salt Lake Tribune*, March 1, 1983.

99. T. Edgar Lyon to J. LeRoy Kimball and J. Byron Ravsten, Memorandum,

June 27, 1969, "Re: RLDS Archaeological Activities et Restoration plans et Nauvoo, June 23rd–28, 1969," NRI Corporate Files, box 176, folder 23.

100. Kimball Jr., "J. LeRoy Kimball, Nauvoo Restoration Pioneer," 10.

101. This was elder Loren C. Dunn of the First Quorum of the Seventy. See "Four Restored Nauvoo Projects Dedicated," 66.

102. Shireman, "The Mormon Prophet's Illinois Legacy," 155–57.

103. Daniel M. Larsen, "At Last a Wish Fulfilled: New Face for Historic Nauvoo Cemetery," *Restoration Trail Forum*, no. 17 (Spring 1991): 3–4; Dan Booz, "Commentary," *Restoration Trail Forum*, no. 17 (Spring 1991): 2, cited in Bingham, "Packaging the 'Williamsburg of the Midwest,'" 176.

104. Sheridan R. Sheffield, "Cemetery Dedication a Fulfillment of Dreams," *Church News*, August 10, 1991. See also Sheridan R. Sheffield, "Cemetery Project Increases Fellowship, Unity," cited in Bingham, "Packaging the 'Williamsburg of the Midwest,'" 177.

105. "He Saved Old Nauvoo from the Ruin of Time," *Church News*, January 31, 1987.

106. R. Scott Lloyd, "Nauvoo: City on Banks of Mississippi River Was Forged from Fire of Adversity," *Church News*, May 20, 1989.

107. Dell Van Orden, "'Hallowed, Sacred Site Made Beautiful' Out of Respect, Love," *Church News*, July 8, 1989.

108. "A Message of 'Healing' to Be Gained from Restored Nauvoo and Carthage," *Church News*, September 30, 1989.

109. R. Scott Lloyd, "Era of Restoration Ends in Nauvoo," *Church News*, October 6, 1990.

110. John L. Hart, "Nauvoo Restoration Now Complete; 'Hallowed' Burial Ground Dedicated," *Church News*, October 14, 1989; and "LDS Leader to Dedicate 4 Projects in Nauvoo," *Deseret News*, October 6, 1989.

111. The Pendleton log cabin was reconstructed in 1990, while the Patty Sessions log cabin was "replicated" in 1998. See Lloyd, "Era of Restoration Ends in Nauvoo," and Loren and Annette Burton, "Patty Sessions' Nauvoo Home Being Replicated on Original Site," *Church News*, August 22, 1998. Since then, two additional log cabins have been erected in the historic area. The historic Newel K. Whitney frame home was also renovated in 1997 to house the Nauvoo Lands and Records Office, in which visitors can look up information about the Nauvoo pioneers. See R. Scott Lloyd, "Early Nauvoo Home to be Research Facility," *Church News*, June 28, 1997. Unfortunately, many of these more recent constructions are historically inauthentic. See

Don Enders to President Hinckley, September 22, 1999, copy in author's possession.

112. Ann Whiting Orton, "60 Historically Inspired Housing Units in Nauvoo," *Church News*, April 20, 2002. See also John L. Hart, "Nauvoo, Illinois Temple: Most Well-Built," *Church News*, May 4, 2002. For a plea to stop the construction of these modern buildings, see Don Enders to President Gordon B. Hinckley, June 8, 2001, copy in author's possession.

113. G. B. Hinckley, "Thanks to the Lord for His Blessings," 89.

114. G. B. Hinckley, "'O That I Were an Angel," 4.

115. Gardner, "Making Nauvoo Beautiful Again," 24.

4. Historical Archaeology at Nauvoo

1. Stephens, *Incidents of Travel*. Stephens's traveling companion, Frederick Catherwood, created the book's detailed illustrations.

2. Smith, *History of the Church*, 5:44.

3. On Joseph Smith and the origins of Book of Mormon archaeology, see Norman, "Joseph Smith"; Clark, "Archaeological Trends," 83–104; and Evans, *Romancing the Maya*, 88–102.

4. R. T. Christensen, *Some Views on Archaeology*; Dahl, "Mormons and American Archaeology," 128–34.

5. S. Larson, *Quest for the Gold Plates*; Wilkinson and Arrington, *Brigham Young University*, 3:120–25; Wilkinson and Skousen, *Brigham Young University*, 739–41; Rudolph, "Walking a Sacred Tightrope"; Dahl, "Mormons and American Archaeology."

6. Coe, "Mormons and Archaeology," 47.

7. Coe, "Mormons and Archaeology," 47.

8. Coe, "Mormons and Archaeology," 48.

9. W. A. R. Goodwin had conducted early amateur archaeology underneath Williamsburg's Bruton Parish Church before its 1905 renovation. However, Prentice Duell, an archaeological draftsman from the University of Pennsylvania, conducted the first archaeology associated with the Colonial Williamsburg restoration project. On early archaeology at Colonial Williamsburg, see Hosmer, *Preservation Comes of Age*, 1:16–17, 60; and Noël Hume, "When Tut Went Phut."

10. Harold P. Fabian and J. LeRoy Kimball, "Outline for the Restoration of Nauvoo," December 11, 1961, NRI Corporate Files, box 1, folder 16.

11. A. Edwin Kendrew, "General Principles for the Restoration of Nau-

voo, Illinois," October 22, 1964, Appendix to Board of Trustees Meeting, November 7, 1964, NRI Corporate Files, box 214, folder 5.

12. With respect to the early desire of the LDS Church to reconstruct the Nauvoo Temple and early negotiations with the RLDS Church over this prospect, see especially Preston W. Kimball to J. LeRoy Kimball, January 4, 1962, NRI Corporate Files, box 166, folder 3; and Preston W. Kimball to J. LeRoy Kimball, January 31, 1962, NRI Corporate Files, box 166, folder 4.

13. Jesse D. Jennings to Melvin L. Fowler, December 6, 1961, NRI Corporate Files, box 166, folder 3. In this letter Jennings explains Fowler's assignment "to discover through archaeological techniques the *foundation outlines* of the Mormon Temple itself . . . [and] immediately submit a brief illustrated report including recommendations as to appropriate additional excavation" (emphasis in original).

14. Fowler, "Preliminary Archaeological Excavation at the Nauvoo Temple Site," 2–3. Copy also available in NRI Corporate Files, box 166, folder 8.

15. Although Fowler believed he had uncovered some of the piers underlying the temple's south wall, future excavations revealed that these piers were really interior supports, some of which had been constructed by the French Icarians, who had refitted the temple for their own purposes following the Mormon exodus from Nauvoo. See Green and Bowles, "Excavation of the Mormon Temple Remains at Nauvoo," 78–79.

16. Fowler, "Preliminary Archaeological Excavation," 7–9. Fowler reported that a cursory examination of the skeleton indicated that the individual was probably a mature male and that a belt buckle was found in association with the bones. Preston Kimball speculated the skeleton could have been that of a "saloon victim," as there were two taverns on the east side of the temple block in the late nineteenth century. See Preston W. Kimball to J. LeRoy Kimball, December 17, 1961, NRI Corporate Files, box 166, folder 4. The other artifacts found during these preliminary investigations were mostly items relating to the architecture or construction of the temple. Fowler reported finding objects such as pieces of cut stone, nails, broken and melted glass, a brass handle, and an iron wedge. Charles Snelgrove, an LDS missionary in Nauvoo who bulldozed a portion of the temple site in May 1959 in an attempt to locate the northeast corner of the building's foundation, created the large area of disturbed earth noted by Fowler. At the time, Preston Kimball wrote, "I hope they find it [the temple's foundation] and make a careful excavation and it would really be interesting and attract

people to see just where the temple stood and to see the basement" (Preston W. Kimball to J. LeRoy Kimball, May 28, 1959, NRI Corporate Files, box 166, folder 4). See also T. Edgar Lyon to J. Earl Arrington, February 3, 1965, NRI Corporate Files, box 8, folder 1.

17. Fowler, "Preliminary Archaeological Excavation," 9–11.

18. A copy of the contract between the LDS Church and SIU for the 1962 excavation season is enclosed with a letter from J. LeRoy Kimball to John O. Anderson, April 10, 1962, NRI Corporate Files, box 166, folder 4. With respect to Green serving as the field supervisor for the 1962 excavation season, Fowler told Fabian, "We have an advanced graduate student who is a very competent field archaeologist an[d] very interested in working on this project. His name is *Dee F. Green* and I recommend him very highly as the man to do the actual field excavations" (Melvin L. Fowler to Harold P. Fabian, January 15, 1962, NRI Corporate Files, box 166, folder 3, emphasis in original). See also John O. Anderson to Jay M. Heslop, June 7, 1962, enclosed with John O. Anderson to J. LeRoy Kimball, June 8, 1962, NRI Corporate Files, box 166, folder 3.

19. "Memorandum of Agreement," 1, enclosed with a letter from J. LeRoy Kimball to John O. Anderson, April 10, 1962, NRI Corporate Files, box 166, folder 4.

20. Dee F. Green, Journal of the Nauvoo Temple Excavation, entry for July 28, 1962, 41–42, copy in author's possession.

21. Green, Journal, August 4, 1962, 48–49.

22. Green, Journal, August 25, 1962, 65–66

23. For the results of the 1962 excavation of the Nauvoo Temple site, see Green, "Nauvoo Excavation Field Report" (copy also available in NRI Corporate Files, box 163, folder 9). Other summaries of this excavation are available in Dee F. Green, "End of the Season Report," September 25, 1962, NRI Corporate Files, box 166, folder 9; Green and Bowles, "Excavation of the Mormon Temple Remains at Nauvoo," 77–81; and Green, "Excavations at the Nauvoo Temple Site, 1962 Season," 1–6 (a copy of the latter is available in NRI Corporate Files, box 166, folder 7).

24. Green, "Nauvoo Excavation Field Report."

25. J. LeRoy Kimball to John O. Anderson, January 7, 1963, NRI Corporate Files, box 166, folder 3.

26. Richard W. Maycock to Howard W. Hunter, December 21, 1961, NRI Corporate Files, box 166, folder 4.

27. First Presidency to Richard W. Maycock, December 22, 1961, NRI Corporate Files, box 166, folder 4.

28. J. LeRoy Kimball to Dee F. Green, December 13, 1962, NRI Corporate Files, box 166, folder 3.

29. J. LeRoy Kimball to John O. Anderson, January 7, 1963, NRI Corporate Files, box 166, folder 3.

30. John O. Anderson to Bishop John H. Vandenberg, August 20, 1963, NRI Corporate Files, box 166, folder 3.

31. "Memorandum of Agreement," 1, enclosed with a letter from Kimball to Anderson, April 10, 1962 (emphasis added).

32. John O. Anderson to Bishop John H. Vandenberg, August 20, 1963, NRI Corporate Files, box 166, folder 3.

33. Melvin L. Fowler to J. LeRoy Kimball, November 7, 1963, NRI Corporate Files, box 166, folder 3.

34. Melvin L. Fowler, "A Discussion of the Artifacts from the Nauvoo Temple Site," June 1964, 2, 5, NRI Corporate Files, box 167, folder 3.

35. Fowler, "Discussion of the Artifacts," 3–5.

36. J. LeRoy Kimball to T. Edgar Lyon, June 26, 1964, NRI Corporate Files, box 177, folder 18.

37. The approximately 150 cardboard boxes of carved temple stone uncovered during the 1962 season remained in Nauvoo following the excavation. This material was still in Nauvoo as late as 2004, when I saw it stored in a maintenance building of the old Catholic St. Mary's Academy, then owned by the LDS Church. That building has since been torn down, however, and the location and status of the temple stone are currently unknown. The more than 1,200 bags of other artifacts excavated during the 1962 season were taken to SIU for processing. These were returned to Nauvoo in 1966. See T. Edgar Lyon, "Historian's Activity Report," July 16–31, 1966, NRI Corporate Files, box 177, folder 9. Dee Green remained interested in studying these artifacts and even offered to conduct an analysis free of charge. See Dee F. Green, "Nauvoo Temple Research Project," April 20, 1966, NRI Corporate Files, box 163, folder 5. NRI officials, however, were wary of letting the artifacts out of their possession and believed their own employees could undertake the analysis. Yet as late as 1969 they remained unsorted and uncatalogued. It is unclear what happened to the artifacts after this time, although NRI employees in 1969 said much of the material would be discarded. See J. C.

Harrington to Byron Ravsten, March 31, 1969, NRI Corporate Files, box 160, folder 11. The present location of these artifacts is currently unknown.

38. T. Edgar Lyon to J. LeRoy Kimball, 20 June 1964, typed excerpt, NRI Corporate Files, box 166, folder 2.

39. Minutes of Meeting of the Executive Committee of Nauvoo Restoration, Incorporated, February 5, 1963, NRI Corporate Files, box 214, folder 5.

40. Ernest L. Wilkinson to A. Hamer Reiser, September 29, 1962, NRI Corporate Files, box 5, folder 10.

41. Wilkinson and Skousen, *Brigham Young University*, 740.

42. Minutes of Meeting of the Executive Committee of Nauvoo Restoration, Incorporated, January 29, 1963, NRI Corporate Files, box 214, folder 5.

43. Minutes of Meeting of the Executive Committee of Nauvoo Restoration, Incorporated, May 26, 1964, and June 2, 1964, NRI Corporate Files, box 214, folder 5.

44. J. LeRoy Kimball to T. Edgar Lyon, June 26, 1964, NRI Corporate Files, box 177, folder 18.

45. Minutes of Meeting of the Executive Committee of Nauvoo Restoration, Incorporated, June 2, 1964, NRI Corporate Files, box 214, folder 5.

46. Lyon Jr., *T. Edgar Lyon*, 128.

47. T. Edgar Lyon to J. LeRoy Kimball, June 20, 1964, typed excerpt, NRI Corporate Files, box 166, folder 2.

48. On these small-scale excavations, see Kevin R. Watts, Daily Journal, NRI Corporate Files, box 168, folder 9. See especially the following entries: June 23, 1964 (11), June 24, 1964 (12), June 25, 1964 (14), July 1, 1964 (22), July 3, 1964 (25), July 8, 1964 (30–31), July 9, 1964 (32), September 3, 1964 (77), September 22, 1964 (91). See also T. Edgar Lyon to J. LeRoy Kimball, July 11, 1964, NRI Corporate Files, box 177, folder 18; and Lyon, "Historian's Progress Report—May to October, 1964," NRI Corporate Files, box 177, folder 10.

49. J. LeRoy Kimball to T. Edgar Lyon, July 8, 1964, NRI Corporate Files, box 177, folder 18.

50. Lyon, "Historian's Progress Report—May to October, 1964," 3. Two years earlier, NRI's trustees also visited Colonial Williamsburg and were scheduled to tour the Archaeological Laboratory with chief archaeologist Ivor Noël Hume. See "Proposed Itinerary for the visit of Directors and Officers of Nauvoo Restoration, Inc. to Colonial Williamsburg, September 1962," NRI Corporate Files, box 5, folder 15.

51. T. Edgar Lyon, "[1965] Budget," 2–4, NRI Corporate Files, box 177, folder 10.

52. Minutes of Meeting of the Executive Committee of Nauvoo Restoration, Incorporated, February 23, 1965, 2, NRI Corporate Files, box 215, folder 1. See also T. Edgar Lyon to Richard Ambler (Department of Anthropology, University of Colorado), January 22, 1965, NRI Corporate Files, box 5, folder 3; T. Edgar Lyon to Dr. Lewis Binford (Department of Anthropology and Archaeology, University of Chicago), January 22, 1965, NRI Corporate Files, box 5, folder 7; and T. Edgar Lyon to Ross T. Christensen (Chairman, Department of Archaeology, BYU), February 11, 1965, NRI Corporate Files, box 5, folder 13.

53. T. Edgar Lyon to Evan I. DeBloois, March 12, 1965, and March 22, 1965, NRI Corporate Files, box 5, folder 18.

54. A. Edwin Kendrew to J. LeRoy Kimball, April 27, 1965, NRI Corporate Files, box 158, folder 9. The nickname "Pinky" came from his red hair and the color of his skin when exposed to the sun. See G. L. Miller, "Memorial: J. C. Harrington, 1901–1998," 1.

55. Jelks, "Jean Carl Harrington, 1901–1998," 26.

56. J. C. Harrington and Virginia Harrington, interview by Charles B. Hosmer Jr., May 18, 1970, 20.

57. J. C. Harrington, "From Architraves to Artifacts," 3.

58. J. C. and Virginia S. Harrington, interview by S. Herbert Evison, March 15, 1971, 4.

59. J. C. Harrington and V. S. Harrington, interview by Hosmer, May 18, 1970, 26.

60. J. C. Harrington, "From Architraves to Artifacts," 4.

61. J. C. Harrington and V. S. Harrington, interview by Evison, March 15, 1971, 2; Miller, "Memorial: J. C. Harrington, 1901–1998," 2–3.

62. J. C. Harrington, "From Architraves to Artifacts," 3.

63. G. L. Miller, "Memorial: J. C. Harrington, 1901–1998," 3; J. C. Harrington and V. S. Harrington, interview by Hosmer, May 18, 1970, 35–36; J. C. Harrington and V. S. Harrington, interview by Evison, March 15, 1971, 45–48.

64. A copy of this award is found in NRI Corporate Files, box 159, folder 7.

65. J. C. Harrington and V. S. Harrington, interview by Evison, March 15, 1971, 42.

66. J. C. Harrington, "From Architraves to Artifacts," 6.

67. The term is Harrington's as used in his "Nauvoo Restoration Incorporated, Proposed Archaeological Program, 1966–1970," February 17, 1966, 3, NRI Corporate Files, box 159, folder 4.

68. J. LeRoy Kimball to A. Edwin Kendrew, May 26, 1965, NRI Corporate Files, box 4, folder 2.

69. J. C. Harrington to J. LeRoy Kimball, May 21, 1965, NRI Corporate Files, box 154, folder 6.

70. Minutes of the Adjourned Annual Meeting of the Board of Trustees of Nauvoo Restoration, Inc., September 18, 1965, 12, transcript, NRI Corporate Files, box 4, folder 3.

71. Minutes of the Adjourned Annual Meeting of the Board of Trustees of Nauvoo Restoration, Inc., September 18, 1965, 2.

72. J. C. Harrington to Clyde Dollar, May 21, 1965, NRI Corporate Files, box 154, folder 6.

73. A. Edwin Kendrew to J. LeRoy Kimball, March 26, 1965, NRI Corporate Files, box 158, folder 9.

74. J. C. Harrington, "Prospectus for Archaeological Investigations, Summer of 1965," 1, NRI Corporate Files, box 154, folder 8.

75. J. C. Harrington, "Nauvoo Restoration Incorporated, Proposed Archaeological Program, 1966–1970," February 17, 1966, 3.

76. J. C. Harrington, "Archaeological Excavations at the Brigham Young Site (126–2), Nauvoo, Illinois, 1965–1968," 1969, 1, Nauvoo Restoration, Inc. Copy available in NRI Corporate Files, box 162, folder 2.

77. Harrington, "Prospectus for Archaeological Investigations," 3–4.

78. For a good example of how artifacts were limited to their use in dating recovered architectural features, see J. C. Harrington, "Archaeological Excavations at the Brigham Young Site," 13–17.

79. J. C. Harrington, "Archaeological Excavations at the Brigham Young Site," 1.

80. J. C. Harrington and V. S. Harrington, interview by Evison, March 15, 1971, 10–12.

81. For a detailed summary and analysis of the public archaeology in Nauvoo, see Pykles, "An Early Example of Public Archaeology," 311–49.

82. Harrington, "Prospectus for Archaeological Investigations," 4.

83. Harrington, "Archaeological Excavations at the Brigham Young Site," 1.

84. J. C. Harrington to A. Edwin Kendrew, June 20, 1965, NRI Corporate Files, box 158, folder 9.

85. A. Edwin Kendrew to J. C. Harrington, July 9, 1965, NRI Corporate Files, box 158, folder 9.

86. For biographical background and an analysis of Dollar's career, see Pykles, "Do You Remember Clyde Dollar?"

87. Clyde D. Dollar, "Long Range Plans for Nauvoo Historic Archaeology Research Program," September 22, 1965, 1, NRI Corporate Files, box 154, folder 11.

88. J. C. Harrington to Clyde Dollar, May 21, 1965, NRI Corporate Files, box 154, folder 6.

89. Clyde Dollar, "Interim Report of the Historic Archaeological Excavation Conducted by Nauvoo Restoration, Incorporated On the Brigham Young Site (126–2), First Season's Work (June 15–October 20, 1965)," March 1966, Nauvoo Restoration, Inc. Copy available in NRI Corporate Files, box 154, folder 13.

90. A. Edwin Kendrew to Andrew Hepburn and Ed Bullerjahn, July 30, 1965, NRI Corporate Files, box 158, folder 9.

91. Dollar, "Interim Report," 8.

92. Dollar, "Interim Report," 23.

93. Dollar, "Interim Report," 26.

94. Dollar, "Interim Report," 17.

95. Dollar, "Interim Report," 25. See also Dollar, "The Stone Lined Shaft in Brigham Young's Backyard (Nauvoo, Illinois)"; V. S. Harrington, "Mysterious Staffordshire—and the Mormons?"; and J. C. Harrington, "Archaeological Excavations at the Brigham Young Site," 63–72. Interestingly, more than a decade after Dollar excavated the Brigham Young site, RLDS archaeologists also discovered similar "Poonah" ceramics during the excavations of the latrine behind Joseph Smith's Mansion Hotel. See DeBarthe, "The Smith Mansion Hotel Latrine" (copy available at the Community of Christ Library, Independence MO.)

96. George L. Miller, who was responsible for the laboratory work at Nauvoo from 1966 to 1968, prepared a complete catalogue of the materials found in the stone-lined vault and demonstrated that most of the objects were from the post-Mormon occupation of the site, a time period of little relevance to NRI's broader restoration goals. Miller's catalogue was supposedly deposited in the archaeological files of NRI. Unfortunately,

however, I did not encounter such a catalogue during my research. See the footnote in J. C. Harrington, "Archaeological Excavations at the Brigham Young Site," 66.

97. J. C. Harrington, "Proposed Archaeological Program, 1966–1970," 2. A small number of artifacts from the Brigham Young site are on display with other Nauvoo objects on the second floor of the reconstructed Seventies Hall in Nauvoo. Significantly, these artifacts have been divorced from their original location partly because their purpose was to simply illustrate objects from "old" Nauvoo.

98. This extended to the archaeology as well. "The possibility of uncovering something built or used by Brigham Young," wrote Harrington, "added a zest to the digging, which was sometimes quite routine (J. C. Harrington, "Archaeological Excavations at the Brigham Young Site," iii).

99. Minutes of the Adjourned Annual Meeting of the Board of Trustees of Nauvoo Restoration, Inc., September 18, 1965, 13.

100. J. C. Harrington to J. LeRoy Kimball, August 11, 1965, NRI Corporate Files, box 158, folder 9.

101. Harrington to Kimball, August 11, 1965.

102. Clyde Dollar to Pinky Harrington, September 18, 1965, NRI Corporate Files, box 158, folder 9. See also Clyde Dollar to J. C. Harrington, November 30, 1965, NRI Corporate Files, box 158, folder 9.

103. J. C. Harrington to Clyde Dollar, September 30, 1965, NRI Corporate Files, box 158, folder 9.

104. Clyde Dollar to Pinky Harrington, September 18, 1965, NRI Corporate Files, box 158, folder 9. See also Clyde Dollar to J. C. Harrington, November 30, 1965, NRI Corporate Files, box 158, folder 9.

105. J. C. Harrington to Clyde Dollar, September 30, 1965, NRI Corporate Files, box 158, folder 9.

106. Dollar, "Long Range Plans for Nauvoo Historic Archaeology Research Program."

107. A. Edwin Kendrew to J. LeRoy Kimball, November 1, 1965, NRI Corporate Files, box 158, folder 9.

108. Kendrew to Kimball, November 1, 1965, 5.

109. Clyde D. Dollar to T. Edgar Lyon, December 1, 1965, NRI Corporate Files, box 158, folder 9.

110. J. LeRoy Kimball to J. C. Harrington, October 15, 1965, NRI Corporate Files, box 158, folder 9.

111. A. Edwin Kendrew to J. LeRoy Kimball, November 1, 1965, NRI Corporate Files, box 158, folder 9; and J. C. Harrington to A. Edwin Kendrew, November 15, 1965, NRI Corporate Files, box 154, folder 7.

112. A. Edwin Kendrew to J. LeRoy Kimball, November 1, 1965, NRI Corporate Files, box 158, folder 9.

113. Later the following year, Harrington and others concluded that Dollar had indeed taken his field notes and excavation records from Nauvoo, although he adamantly denied it when confronted about the situation. See Clyde D. Dollar to J. C. Harrington, September 14, 1966, NRI Corporate Files, box 155, folder 7; and J. C. Harrington to J. LeRoy Kimball, November 2, 1966, NRI Corporate Files, box 155, folder 7. See also the draft copy of a letter from J. LeRoy Kimball to Clyde Dollar, November 2, 1966, NRI Corporate Files, box 155, folder 7, in which Dollar is accused of retaining materials related to the 1965 excavation.

114. J. C. Harrington to J. LeRoy Kimball, January 8, 1966, NRI Corporate Files, box 155, folder 8.

115. J. C. Harrington to Clyde Dollar, February 23, 1966, NRI Corporate Files, box 155, folder 7.

116. Clyde D. Dollar to J. LeRoy Kimball, January 24, 1967, NRI Corporate Files, box 161, folder 11.

117. J. C. Harrington to A. Edwin Kendrew, November 15, 1965, NRI Corporate Files, box 158, folder 9.

118. J. C. Harrington to J. LeRoy Kimball, February 15, 1966, NRI Corporate Files, box 159, folder 1.

119. J. C. Harrington to J. LeRoy Kimball, November 4, 1966, NRI Corporate Files, box 159, folder 17.

120. J. C. Harrington and V. S. Harrington, interview by Evison, March 15, 1971, 12.

121. See untitled biographical sketch of Virginia in NRI Corporate Files, box 160, folder 9. See also Paid Death Notices, *Richmond Times Dispatch* (Virginia), June 21, 2003.

122. Minutes of the Adjourned Annual Meeting of the Board of Trustees of Nauvoo Restoration, Inc., September 18, 1965, 11.

123. V. S. Harrington, "Why Archaeology at Nauvoo."

124. Ida Blum, "Why Archaeology at Nauvoo," *Nauvoo Independent*, August 8, 1968, copy available in NRI Corporate Files, box 160, folder 9.

125. V. S. Harrington, "Why Archaeology at Nauvoo," 732, 737.

126. See J. C. Harrington "Archaeological Excavations at the Brigham Young Site"; J. C. Harrington, "Archaeological Excavations at the Wilford Woodruff Site (106–1) Nauvoo, Illinois, 1966," January 1967, Nauvoo Restoration, Inc., copy available in NRI Corporate Files, box 155, folder 13; J. C. Harrington, "Archaeological Excavations at the Webb Blacksmith & Wagon Shop (127–4), Nauvoo, Illinois, 1967–1968," March 1969, Nauvoo Restoration, Inc., copy available in NRI Corporate Files, box 163, folder 1; Virginia S. Harrington, "Report on the Excavation of the North Building, Times and Seasons Complex, Nauvoo, Illinois," December 1968, Nauvoo Restoration, Inc., copy available in NRI Corporate Files, box 168, folder 1, or box 161, folder 12. See also the following summary reports: J. C. Harrington, "Report on Archaeological Program, 1966 Field Season," November 12, 1966, NRI Corporate Files, box 156, folder 12; J. C. Harrington, "Summary Report on the 1967 Field Season," November 10, 1967, NRI Corporate Files, box 159, folder 18; J. C. Harrington, "Annual Report for the 1968 Fiscal Year," November 22, 1968, NRI Corporate Files, box 160, folder 7; and J. C. Harrington, "Annual Report for the 1969 Fiscal Year," October 28, 1969, NRI Corporate Files, box 160, folder 14.

127. J. C. Harrington, "Report on Archaeological Program, 1966 Field Season," 3, 5.

128. J. C. Harrington, "Report on Archaeological Program, 1966 Field Season," 5.

129. J. C. Harrington, "Report on Archaeological Program, 1966 Field Season," 10.

130. J. C. Harrington and Virginia S. Harrington, "The Nauvoo Temple Site: Site Renovation, Excavation of the Temple Well, Proposed Future Archaeological Work," January 1967, 3, NRI Corporate Files, box 163, folder 8.

131. J. C. Harrington and V. S. Harrington, "The Nauvoo Temple Site," 4.

132. J. C. Harrington and V. S. Harrington, "The Nauvoo Temple Site," sections 2 and 3. See also J. C. Harrington, "Report on Archaeological Program, 1966 Field Season," 6.

133. Virginia S. Harrington, "Archaeological Excavations in the Temple Basement—1967," December 15, 1967 (copy in author's possession); and Virginia S. Harrington, "Archaeological Excavations in the Temple Basement—1968," March 1969, NRI Corporate Files, box 163, folder 8. See also J. C. Harrington, "Summary Report on the 1967 Field Season," 5–6;

J. C. Harrington, "Annual Report for the 1968 Fiscal Year," 4; and J. C. Harrington, "Annual Report for the 1969 Fiscal Year," 3.

134. V. S. Harrington and J. C. Harrington, *Rediscovery of the Nauvoo Temple.*

135. J. C. Harrington, "Proposed Archaeological Program for the Temple Site," December 10, 1967, 3, NRI Corporate Files, box 163, folder 14.

136. J. C. Harrington to J. LeRoy Kimball, December 16, 1967, NRI Corporate Files, box 159, folder 14.

137. Virginia S. Harrington, "Report on Interpretation at the Temple Site," December 16, 1967, 1, NRI Corporate Files, box 159, folder 14.

138. J. C. Harrington, "Statement Relative to the Proposed Archaeological Work at the Nauvoo Temple Site," February 6, 1967, 1, NRI Corporate Files, box 163, folder 13.

139. V. S. Harrington, "Report on Interpretation at the Temple Site," 2.

140. V. S. Harrington and J. C. Harrington, *Rediscovery of the Nauvoo Temple,* 2.

141. V. S. Harrington, "Report on Interpretation at the Temple Site," 2.

142. A. Edwin Kendrew to J. C. Harrington, April 19, 1967, NRI Corporate Files, copy in author's possession.

143. J. C. Harrington to J. LeRoy Kimball, May 8, 1967, NRI Corporate Files, box 159, folder 14.

144. J. C. Harrington to J. LeRoy Kimball, May 8, 1967, NRI Corporate Files, box 159, folder 14.

145. Ray T. Matheny to T. Edgar Lyon, February 19, 1968, NRI Corporate Files, box 160, folder 5.

146. Dale LeRoy Berge, "Historical Archaeology in the American Southwest," (Ph.D. dissertation, University of Arizona, 1968).

147. Dale Berge, interview by Benjamin C. Pykles, December 22, 2000, transcript, copy in author's possession.

148. Ed. (T. Edgar Lyon) to Dr. Kimball (J. LeRoy Kimball), Memorandum, "Re: Dale Borge [sic]," March 5, 1968, NRI Corporate Files, box 160, folder 5.

149. J. C. Harrington to J. LeRoy Kimball, March 17, 1968, NRI Corporate Files, box 160, folder 13. See also J. C. Harrington to T. Edgar Lyon, March 17, 1968, NRI Corporate Files, box 177, folder 4.

150. J. C. Harrington, "Semi-monthly Report—June 1 to 15, 1968," NRI Corporate Files, box 155, folder 9.

151. See the published abstract of Berge's dissertation in NRI Corporate Files, box 160, folder 5.

152. Harrington, "Semi-monthly Report—June 1 to 15, 1968."

153. Lyon, interviews by Bitton, 1974–1975, typescript, 228, Oral History Program, Archives of the Church of Jesus Christ of Latter-day Saints, Salt Lake City, Utah.

154. Lyon, interviews by Bitton, 1974–1975, 229.

155. Lyon, interviews by Bitton, 1974–1975, 229.

156. Lyon, interviews by Bitton, 1974–1975, 229.

157. See the entry for July 3 in Rex Sohm Diary, 1–10 July 1968, NRI Corporate Files, box 169, folder 7.

158. See the entry for July 3 in Rex Sohm Diary, 1–10 July 1968, NRI Corporate Files, box 169, folder 7. For the official report of these excavations see, Dale L. Berge, "Archaeological Investigations at the Jonathan Browning Site (tract 118–2), Nauvoo, Illinois, 1968 and 1969," 1970, Nauvoo Restoration, Inc., copy available in NRI Corporate Files, box 158, folder 5.

159. Berge, interview by Pykles, 18.

160. J. C. Harrington to J. LeRoy Kimball, May 15, 1969, NRI Corporate Files, box 160, folder 10.

161. Dale L. Berge, "Archaeology of the Winslow Farr Home, Nauvoo, Illinois," 1979, Nauvoo Restoration, Inc., copy available in NRI Corporate Files, box 157, folder 4.

162. Pinky Harrington to Ed Kendrew, Memorandum on "Nauvoo archaeological program," August 2, 1969, NRI Corporate Files, box 160, folder 10.

163. For an example of this, see J. C. Harrington, "Semi-monthly Report—August 1 to 15, 1968," NRI Corporate Files, box 157, folder 11.

164. J. C. Harrington to Dale Berge, August 12, 1970, NRI Corporate Files, box 160, folder 17.

165. Berge, interview by Pykles, 18.

166. Dale Berge, personal communication, December 22, 2000.

167. J. C. Harrington to J. LeRoy Kimball, May 15, 1969, NRI Corporate Files, box 160, folder 10.

168. T. Edgar Lyon, "Summary of Meeting held July 4, 1969, 9:00 A.M. to 12:00 noon at Dr. Kimball's Residence, Nauvoo, Illinois," NRI Corporate Files, box 177, folder 4.

169. J. C. Harrington to J. LeRoy Kimball, May 15, 1969, NRI Corporate Files, box 160, folder 10.

170. Lyon, "Summary of Meeting held July 4, 1969."

171. For a detailed explanation and justification of the artifact proposal see, Dale L. Berge to J. LeRoy Kimball, November 4, 1968, NRI Corporate Files, box 160, folder 5; Dale L. Berge to J. LeRoy Kimball, April 15, 1969, NRI Corporate Files, box 160, folder 10; and Dale L. Berge, "Annual Report for the 1970 Fiscal Year," December 7, 1970, NRI Corporate Files, box 161, folder 4.

172. J. C. Harrington, "Annual Report for the 1969 Fiscal Year," 5.

173. The six sites were those of Lorin Farr, Alvah Tippets, Stillman Pond, Chauncey Webb, Daniel Butler Jr., and the site of the Seventies Hall. See Berge, "Annual Report for the 1970 Fiscal Year," 3–8; see also the reports for these excavations: Dale L. Berge, "Preliminary Archaeological Explorations at the Lorin Farr, Alvah L. Tippets, and Stillman Pond Sites, Block 106, Lot 4, Nauvoo, Illinois, 1970," 1971, Nauvoo Restoration, Inc., copy available in NRI Corporate Files, box 157, folder 6; Berge, "Archaeology of the Daniel Butler, Jr. Property, Nauvoo, Illinois," 1979, Nauvoo Restoration, Inc., copy available in NRI Corporate Files, box 154, folder 3; Berge, "Archaeology of the Seventies Hall, Nauvoo, Illinois," 1979, Nauvoo Restoration, Inc., copy available in NRI Corporate Files, box 161, folder 14; Berge, "Archaeological Excavations at the Chauncey Webb House, Nauvoo, Illinois," 1983, Nauvoo Restoration, Inc., copy available in personal library of Dale Berge, Provo UT. On the Chauncey Webb site, see also Richard L. Hansen, "Archaeological Excavations at the Chauncey Webb Site (127–4), Nauvoo, Illinois, 1970" (master's thesis, Brigham Young University, 1973).

174. Berge, "Annual Report for the 1970 Fiscal Year," 9.

175. On Berge's struggle to balance his various responsibilities with both NRI and BYU, see Dale L. Berge, "Recommendations for Report Writing at BYU," enclosed with a letter from Berge to J. LeRoy Kimball, February 11, 1969, NRI Corporate Files, box 160, folder 10.

176. Berge, "The Jonathon Browning Site," 201–29.

177. Berge excavated two sites during the summer of 1971: the Noble-Smith home and the Scovil Bakery. See Dale L. Berge, "Archaeology of the Joseph Bates Noble–Lucy Mack Smith Home, Block 124, Lot 2, Nauvoo, Illinois," 1983, Nauvoo Restoration, Inc., copy available in NRI Corporate Files, box 154, folder 2, and Berge, "Archaeological Investigations of the

Lucius N. Scovil Bakery, Nauvoo, Illinois," 1978, Nauvoo Restoration, Inc., copy available in NRI Corporate Files, box 156, folder 9.

178. J. C. Harrington to Rowena Miller, July 29, 1971, NRI Corporate Files, box 161, folder 10.

179. J. C. Harrington to Rowena Miller, Memorandum on "Nauvoo archaeology, etc.," July 30, 1971, NRI Corporate Files, box 161, folder 10. See also, Dale L. Berge to T. Edgar Lyon, January 4, 1972, and T. Edgar Lyon to Dale L. Berge, January 7, 1972, both of which are found in NRI Corporate Files, box 161, folder 9.

180. Berge excavated the following four sites during the summer of 1975: the Nauvoo Masonic Hall, the Riser Shoe Shop, the Kimball-Heywood Store, and the Stoddard Home and Tin Shop. Berge later reported that the popularity of the reconstructed Webb Blacksmith and Wagon Shop, where historic blacksmithing and wagon wheel making were demonstrated to visitors, motivated similar restorations and reconstructions at this time. Hence, the four sites Berge excavated during the summer of 1975 were selected because of their potential to interpret historic arts and crafts and, thus, entertain visitors (Dale L. Berge, personal communication, May 12, 2006). Accordingly, visitors today can learn about historic boot- and shoemaking at the Riser Shoe Shop and historic tinsmithing at the Stoddard Tin Shop, and can watch theatrical performances in the restored Masonic Hall (now called the Cultural Hall). The Kimball-Heywood Store has never been reconstructed. For the archaeological reports of these four sites, see Berge, "Archaeological Investigation of the Masonic Hall, Nauvoo, Illinois," 1976, Nauvoo Restoration, Inc., copy available in NRI Corporate Files, box 156, folder 1; Berge, "Archaeology of the George C. Riser Shoe Shop and the Kimball-Heywood Store, Nauvoo, Illinois," 1978, Nauvoo Restoration, Inc., copy available in NRI Corporate Files, box 161, folder 14; and Berge, "Preliminary Archaeological Investigations at the Sylvester Stoddard Site, Nauvoo, Illinois," 1980, Nauvoo Restoration, Inc., copy available in NRI Corporate Files, box 157, folder 13.

181. In May 1980, two former archaeology graduate students at BYU—J. Terry Walker of Bountiful, Utah, and Richard B. Stamps of Oakland University, Michigan—conducted small-scale excavations at the site of Windsor P. Lyon's house and store prior to the restoration of this structure. The following year the Women's Relief Society of the LDS Church commissioned Berge to conduct preliminary archaeological work at the Sarah Granger Kimball

Home prior to its restoration in commemoration of the 140th anniversary of the women's organization. See J. Terry Walker and Richard B. Stamps, "Archaeological Investigations at the Lyon House and Store, Nauvoo, Illinois, 1980," November 1980, Nauvoo Restoration, Inc., copy available in NRI Corporate Files, box 157, folder 9; Dale L. Berge, "Preliminary Archaeological Excavations at the Sarah Granger Kimball Home, Nauvoo (Commerce), Illinois," 1981, Nauvoo Restoration, Inc., copy available in NRI Corporate Files, box 158, folder 6. See also Gerry Avant, "Sarah's House in Nauvoo Will Again Welcome Visitors," *Church News*, June 20, 1981; and Kathleen Lubeck, "Relief Society Turns 140," *Church News*, March 20, 1982.

182. "Pres. Hinckley Dedicates 16 Sites in Nauvoo," *Deseret News*, August 14, 1982; Dell Van Orden, "Nauvoo of Today: A Window to the Majesty of the Past," *Church News*, September 3, 1994; R. Scott Lloyd, "Early Nauvoo Home to be Research Facility," *Church News*, June 28, 1997. Dale Berge later commented on how he was particularly upset with the lack of archaeology during the restoration of the nearby Carthage Jail, where Joseph Smith and his brother Hyrum were shot and killed in 1844 (Dale Berge, personal communication, May 12, 2006).

183. Kathleen Lubeck, "Old Skills Make New Friends for Couples in Nauvoo," *Church News*, May 22, 1982.

184. Loren and Annette Burton, "Patty Sessions' Nauvoo Home Being Replicated on Original Site," *Church News*, August 22, 1998.

185. Ann Whiting Orton, "60 Historically Inspired Housing Units in Nauvoo," *Church News*, April 20, 2002. See also John L. Hart, "Nauvoo, Illinois Temple: Most Well-Built," *Church News*, May 4, 2002.

186. Bernauer, *Still "Side by Side."* The first edition of this work also appears under the same title in the *John Whitmer Historical Association Journal* 11 (1991): 17–33. See also Mackay, "A Brief History of the Smith Family Nauvoo Cemetery," 241–52.

187. Richard A. Fox, quoted in Wood, "In Memoriam: Robert Taylor Bray," 5. See also Bray, "Archaeological Investigations at the Reno-Benteen Battle Site," 58–95.

188. Wood, "In Memoriam, Robert Taylor Bray," 4–7.

189. T. Edgar Lyon to J. LeRoy Kimball and Byron J. Ravsten, Memorandum on "RLDS Archaeological activities et Restoration plans et Nauvoo, June 23rd–28, 1969," June 27, 1969, NRI Corporate Files, box 176, folder 23.

190. Lyon to Kimball and Ravsten, Memorandum on "RLDS Archaeo-

logical activities et Restoration plans et Nauvoo, June 23rd–28, 1969," June 27, 1969.

191. "Questions Are Answered by Digging," 10.

192. F. Mark McKiernan, "Preserving and Interpreting our Physical Heritage: A Master Plan of the Historic Properties of the Reorganized Church of Jesus Christ of Latter-day Saints," Reorganized Church of Jesus Christ of Latter Day Saints, Independence MO, 1977, 90. Copy available at the Community of Christ Library, Unpublished Collection, Independence, MO.

193. On the presentation mug, see Paul DeBarthe, "Archaeology at the Smith Center," 18–19.

194. Bray, "Times and Seasons," 53–118; Bray, "Archaeology of the First Home in Nauvoo," 93–113.

195. Bray, "Times and Seasons," 108.

196. Bray, "Archaeology of the First Home in Nauvoo," 93–94.

197. McKiernan, "Preserving and Interpreting Our Physical Heritage," 113–15.

198. Bray, "The Turley Site."

199. The six sites were the Joseph Smith Stable site (excavated in 1970), the Joseph Smith Homestead Lot (1971), Joseph Smith's Red Brick Store (1972), the Turley site (1973), the Hyrum Smith site (1974), and the Times and Seasons site (1975). See Bray, "Archaeology at the Joseph Smith Stable"; Bray, "Archaeology at the Joseph Smith Homestead"; Bray, "Archaeological Investigations at the Joseph Smith Red Brick Store"; Bray, "The Turley Site"; Waselkov, Bray, and Waselkov, "Archaeological Investigations of the Hyrum Smith Site"; Bray, "Times and Seasons." Copies of these reports are available in the Unpublished Collection of the Community of Christ Library in Independence MO and the Community of Christ Visitors Center in Nauvoo.

200. Dale L. Berge, "Archaeology of the Winslow Farr Home, Nauvoo, Illinois," 1979, 1, NRI, copy available in NRI Corporate Files, box 157, folder 4.

201. [Paul DeBarthe], "Archaeology at the Smith Mansion, 1978," 2, typescript in author's possession.

202. [DeBarthe], "Archaeology at the Smith Mansion, 1978."

203. Noël Hume, *A Guide to Artifacts of Colonial America*.

204. Deetz, *In Small Things Forgotten*.

205. DeBarthe, "The Joseph Smith Homestead Complex, Nauvoo, Illi-

nois," 2, 78; see also DeBarthe, "The 1977 Project at the Mansion House (N 147–3)." For examples of later work on historic ceramics, see G. L. Miller, "Classification and Economic Scaling of 19th Century Ceramics," 1–40; and G. L. Miller, "A Revised Set of CC Index Values for Classification and Economic Scaling of English Ceramics," 1–25.

206. Oakes, "I Can 'Dig' It!," 3.

207. The excavations were as follows: 1976—searching for the outbuildings of Joseph Smith's Homestead; 1977—excavation at the site of Joseph Smith's Mansion House and Hotel; 1978—further excavation of the Mansion House and Hotel site; 1979—excavation of the Levi Hancock and James Brinkerhof sites; 1980–1983—further excavation of the Mansion Hotel site; 1984—excavation of the William Law Store. See the following reports related these excavations: DeBarthe, "The Joseph Smith Homestead Complex"; DeBarthe, "The 1977 Project at the Mansion House"; DeBarthe, "The Smith Mansion Hotel Latrine and Other Discoveries of the 1978 Archaeological Project"; DeBarthe, "The 1979 Archaeological Projects at Nauvoo, Illinois"; DeBarthe, "The Joseph Smith Mansion Hotel"; DeBarthe, "Archaeology at the William Law Store." Copies of the first three reports are available in the Unpublished Collection of the Community of Christ Library, Independence MO and at the Community of Christ Visitors Center in Nauvoo.

208. DeBarthe was also involved in some prehistoric archaeology in Nauvoo. In 1976, while searching for outbuildings associated with the Joseph Smith Homestead, DeBarthe and his crew uncovered a Late Woodland–period (ca. 500–1000 CE) burial consisting of a tomb, partially faced and capped with limestone slabs, in which eleven human skeletons were deposited. Three years later, in 1979, the RLDS cut a trench to carry electrical cables to the site of Joseph Smith's Red Brick Store and, in the process, cut through a Middle Woodland–period (ca. 1–500 CE) tomb in which the remains of fourteen human skeletons and an associated funeral offering were uncovered. Among the objects salvaged by DeBarthe and others at this time were oval bifaces, a turtle shell rattle, and two bird effigy pieces. Finally, in 1983, while digging in the backyard of the Joseph Smith Mansion House, DeBarthe and his crew uncovered a canine burial and associated projectile points from the Titterington phase of the Late Archaic period (4200–3800 BP) (see figure 25). See DeBarthe, "The Joseph Smith Homestead Complex," and DeBarthe, "The 1979 Archaeological Projects." For the bioarchaeological analyses of these two prehistoric tombs and the human remains uncovered therein,

see Buikstra and Pistono, "N-155–3: A Bio-Archaeological Analysis of a Prehistoric Mortuary Structure"; Baker, "A Bioarchaeological Analysis of N155–2"; and DeBarthe, "The Joseph Smith Mansion Hotel."

209. The three RLDS reconstructions are the Joseph Smith Red Brick Store, the Joseph Smith Homestead's summer kitchen, and a small outbuilding on the homestead lot under which the bodies of Joseph and Hyrum Smith were initially buried.

210. As recently as July 2005, Paul DeBarthe conducted a small-scale excavation on the lot of Joseph Smith's Homestead in connection with the RLDS (now called the Community of Christ) summer camp held to commemorate the 200th anniversary of Joseph Smith's birth. This is the only incident of a Church-sanctioned excavation after 1984 of which I am aware. Mark Scherer (historian for the Community of Christ), personal communication, November 10, 2005.

5. The Nauvoo Excavations and the Development of Historical Archaeology in America

1. Schuyler, "Parallels in the Rise of the Various Subfields of Historical Archaeology," 2.

2. Schuyler, "Parallels in the Rise of the Various Subfields of Historical Archaeology," 3.

3. Schuyler, "Parallels in the Rise of the Various Subfields of Historical Archaeology," 3–4.

4. J. C. Harrington, "Report on Archaeological Program, 1966 Field Season," November 12, 1966, 11, NRI Corporate Files, box 156, folder 12.

5. Schuyler, "Parallels in the Rise of the Various Subfields of Historical Archaeology," 4.

6. See, for example, DeBarthe, "The Joseph Smith Homestead Complex," 66–76.

7. J. C. Harrington to J. LeRoy Kimball, May 8, 1967, NRI Corporate Files, box 159, folder 14.

8. Berge, "Lower Goshen: A Historic Mormon Community in Central Utah," 184.

9. Berge, "Lower Goshen: Archaeology of a Mormon Pioneer Town," 67–68.

10. Schuyler, "Parallels in the Rise of the Various Subfields of Historical Archaeology," 4.

11. Take, for example, the papers presented at the symposium organized by the author, Historical Archaeology of the Mormon Domain, at the 37th Annual Conference of the Society for Historical Archaeology in January 2004, and the papers presented at a companion symposium, Historical Archaeology of, by, and about the Mormons, held at the 70th Annual Meeting of the Society for American Archaeology, March–April 2005.

12. Schuyler, "Parallels in the Rise of the Various Subfields of Historical Archaeology," 4.

13. Olsen, "A History of Restoring Historic Kirtland," 120.

14. Lowenthal, *The Past Is a Foreign Country*, 245.

15. Olsen, "A History of Restoring Historic Kirtland," 121.

16. Gerry Avant, "Nauvoo's Impact," *Church News*, August 27, 1977.

17. John L. Hart, "Sites Connect Visitors with Events of Past," *Church News*, February 20, 1999.

18. Olsen, "A History of Restoring Historic Kirtland," 121.

19. The excavations at Kirtland took place in 2000 and 2001. More recently, in 2004 the LDS Church hired Hartgen Archeological Associates, a private cultural resource management firm, to excavate the foundations of a structure in Harmony (now Oakland), Pennsylvania, where Joseph Smith and his wife lived from late 1827 to August 1830, while he was working on the manuscript of the Book of Mormon.

20. See Schuyler, "Images of America," 27–37.

Bibliography

2005 *Church Almanac*. Salt Lake City UT: Deseret News, 2004.

Alexander, Thomas G. *Mormonism in Transition: A History of the Latter-day Saints, 1890–1930*. Illini Books. Urbana: University of Illinois Press, 1996.

Allaback, Sara. *Mission 66 Visitor Centers: The History of a Building Type*. Washington DC: Government Printing Office, 2000.

Allen, James B., and Glen M. Leonard. *The Story of the Latter-day Saints*. 2nd ed. Salt Lake City UT: Deseret Book Co., 1992.

Anderson, Paul L. "Heroic Nostalgia: Enshrining the Mormon Past." *Sunstone* 5, no. 4 (1980): 47–55.

Arrington, Leonard J., and Davis Bitton. *The Mormon Experience: A History of the Latter-day Saints*. 2nd ed. Urbana: University of Illinois Press, 1992.

Backman, Milton V. *The Heavens Resound: A History of the Latter-day Saints in Ohio, 1830–1838*. Salt Lake City UT: Deseret Book Co., 1983.

Baker, Brenda J. "A Bioarchaeological Analysis of N155–2: A Prehistoric Mortuary Structure from Nauvoo, Illinois." In Paul DeBarthe, "The 1979 Archaeological Projects at Nauvoo, Illinois: The Hancock Site, N146; The Brinkerhoff Site, N146; Middle Woodland Burials, N155." Columbia: University of Missouri, 1982.

Baugh, Alexander L. *A Call to Arms: The 1838 Mormon Defense of Northern Mis-*

souri. Provo UT: Joseph Fielding Smith Institute for Latter-day Saint History and BYU Studies, 2000.

Bennett, Richard E. *We'll Find the Place: The Mormon Exodus, 1846–1848*. Salt Lake City UT: Deseret Book Co., 1997.

Berge, Dale L. "Archaeological Excavation of the Masonic Hall, Nauvoo, Illinois." [Nauvoo IL]: Nauvoo Restoration, Inc., 1976.

———. "Archaeological Excavations at the Chauncey Webb House, Nauvoo, Illinois." [Nauvoo IL]: Nauvoo Restoration, Inc., 1983. Copy in personal library of Dale L. Berge.

———. Archaeological Investigations at the Jonathan Browning Site (Tract 118–2), Nauvoo, Illinois, 1968 and 1969." [Nauvoo IL]: Nauvoo Restoration, Inc., 1970.

———. Archaeological Investigations of the Lucius N. Scovill Bakery, Nauvoo, Illinois." [Nauvoo IL]: Nauvoo Restoration, Inc., 1978.

———. "Archaeology of the Daniel Butler, Jr. Property, Nauvoo, Illinois." [Nauvoo IL]: Nauvoo Restoration, Inc., 1979.

———. "Archaeology of the George C. Riser Shoe Shop and the Kimball-Heywood Store, Nauvoo, Illinois." [Nauvoo IL]: Nauvoo Restoration, Inc., 1979.

———. "Archaeology of the Joseph Bates Noble–Lucy Mack Smith Home, Block 124, Lot 2, Nauvoo, Illinois. [Nauvoo IL]: Nauvoo Restoration, Inc., 1983.

———. "Archaeology of the Seventies Hall, Nauvoo, Illinois." [Nauvoo IL]: Nauvoo Restoration, Inc., 1979.

———. "Archaeology of the Winslow Farr Home, Nauvoo, Illinois." [Nauvoo IL]: Nauvoo Restoration, Inc., 1979.

———. "Historical Archaeology in the American Southwest." PhD diss., University of Arizona, 1968.

———. Interview by Benjamin C. Pykles. December 22, 2000. Provo UT. Transcript. In possession of interviewer.

———. "The Jonathon Browning Site: An Example of Archaeology for Restoration in Nauvoo, Illinois." *BYU Studies* 19, no. 2 (1979): 201–29.

———. "Lower Goshen: Archaeology of a Mormon Pioneer Town." *BYU Studies* 30, no. 2 (1990): 67–89.

———. "Lower Goshen: A Historic Mormon Community in Central Utah." In *Forgotten Places and Things: Archaeological Perspectives on American His-*

tory, edited by Albert E. Ward, 173–84. Albuquerque NM: Center for Anthropological Studies, 1983.

———. "Preliminary Archaeological Explorations at the Lorin Farr, Alvah H. Tipetts, and Stillman Pond Sites, Block 106, Lot 4, Nauvoo, Illinois." [Nauvoo IL]: Nauvoo Restoration, Inc., 1971.

———. "Preliminary Archaeological Investigations at the Sarah Granger Kimball Home, Nauvoo (Commerce), Illinois." Salt Lake City UT: Relief Society, the Church of Jesus Christ of Latter-day Saints, 1981.

———. "Preliminary Archaeological Investigations at the Sylvester Stoddard Site, Nauvoo, Illinois." [Nauvoo IL]: Nauvoo Restoration, Inc., 1980.

Bernauer, Barbara Hands. "Still 'Side by Side': The Final Burial of Joseph and Hyrum Smith." *John Whitmer Historical Association Journal* 11 (1991): 17–33.

———. *Still "Side by Side": The Final Burial of Joseph and Hyrum Smith*. 2nd ed. Kansas City MO: Author, 2001.

Bingham, Justin Hall. "Packaging the 'Williamsburg of the Midwest': Nauvoo, Illinois, 1950–2000." Master's thesis, University of Illinois at Urbana-Champaign, 2002.

Bitton, Davis. "The Ritualization of Mormon History." *Utah Historical Quarterly* 43, no. 1 (1975): 67–85.

Booz, Dan. "Commentary." *Restoration Trail Forum* 17 (Spring 1991): 2.

Bray, Robert T. "Archaeological Investigations at the Joseph Smith Red Brick Store, Nauvoo, Illinois." Columbia: University of Missouri, 1973.

———. "Archaeological Investigations at the Reno-Benteen Battle Site, Little Bighorn Battlefield, Montana." *The Missouri Archaeologist* 57 (1996): 58–95.

———. "Archaeology at the Joseph Smith Homestead, Nauvoo, Illinois." Columbia: University of Missouri, 1972.

———. "Archaeology at the Joseph Smith Stable: Southwest Corner Water and Carlin Streets, Nauvoo, Illinois." Columbia: University of Missouri, 1971.

———. "Archaeology of the First Home in Nauvoo of the Parents of Joseph Smith, Jr." *The Missouri Archaeologist* 56 (1995): 93–113.

———. "Times and Seasons: An Archaeological Perspective on Early Latter Day Saints Printing." Columbia: University of Missouri, 1976.

———. "Times and Seasons: An Archaeological Perspective on Early Latter Day Saints Printing." *Historical Archaeology* 13 (1979): 53–118.

———. "The Turley Site (Block 147 Lot 4): An Account of the 1973 Archaeological Work at Nauvoo, Illinois." Columbia: University of Missouri, 1974.

Brigham, Janet. "Nauvoo Today: Building Again the City Beautiful." *Ensign*, March 1980, 44–47.

Brown, Sharon A. *Administrative History: Jefferson National Expansion Memorial National Historic Site, 1935–1980*. St. Louis?: s.n., 1984. http://www.nps.gov/history/history/online_books/jeff/adhit.htm.

Bruner, Edward M. "Abraham Lincoln as Authentic Reproduction: A Critique of Postmodernism." *American Anthropologist* 96, no. 2 (1994): 397–415.

Buikstra, Jane E., and Tina L. Pistono. "N-155–3: A Bio-Archaeological Analysis of a Prehistoric Mortuary Structure from the Joseph Smith Properties, Nauvoo, Illinois." In Paul DeBarthe, "The Joseph Smith Homestead Complex, Nauvoo, Illinois: A Focus on the Outbuildings 1976," 91–126. Columbia: University of Missouri, 1977.

Burgess, S. A. *The Early History of Nauvoo*. Independence MO: Reorganized Church of Jesus Christ of Latter-day Saints, 1938.

Bushman, Richard L. *Joseph Smith and the Beginnings of Mormonism*. Illini Books. Urbana: University of Illinois Press, 1988.

———. *Joseph Smith: Rough Stone Rolling*. New York: Alfred A. Knopf, 2005.

Cannon, Janath. *Nauvoo Panorama: Views of Nauvoo Before, During, and After Its Rise, Fall, and Restoration*. Salt Lake City UT: Nauvoo Restoration, Inc., 1991.

Christensen, Michael. "Parks and Recreation in Utah." In *Utah History Encyclopedia*, edited by Allan Kent Powell, 416–17. Salt Lake City: University of Utah Press, 1994.

Christensen, Ross T. *Some Views on Archaeology and Its Role at Brigham Young University, Miscellaneous Papers of the University Archaeological Society*, no. 19. Provo UT: University Archaeological Society, 1960.

Church of Jesus Christ of Latter-day Saints. *Church History in the Fullness of Times*. Salt Lake City UT: Author, 1989.

Clark, John E. "Archaeological Trends and the Book of Mormon Origins." *BYU Studies* 44, no. 4 (2006): 83–104.

Coe, Michael. "Mormons and Archaeology: An Outside View." *Dialogue: A Journal of Mormon Thought* 8, no. 2 (1973): 40–48.

Colonial Williamsburg Official Guidebook and Map. Williamsburg VA: Colonial Williamsburg Foundation, 1983.

Colvin, Don F. *Nauvoo Temple: A Story of Faith*. American Fork UT: Covenant Communications, 2002.

Cotter, John L. "Continuity in Teaching Historical Archaeology." In *Teaching and Training in American Archaeology: A Survey of Programs and Philosophies*, edited by William P. McHugh. Carbondale: University Museum and Art Galleries, Southern Illinois University, 1977.

Cross, Whitney R. *The Burned-Over District: The Social and Intellectual History of Enthusiastic Religion in Western New York, 1800–1850*. New York: Harper and Row, 1950.

Dahl, Bruce R. "Mormons and American Archaeology: A Brief History." Master's thesis, California State University, Northridge, 1994.

DeBarthe, Paul. "The 1977 Project at the Mansion House (N 147–3)." Columbia: University of Missouri, 1977.

———. "The 1979 Archaeological Projects at Nauvoo, Illinois: The Hancock Site, N146; The Brinkerhoff Site, N146; Middle Woodland Burials, N155." Columbia: University of Missouri, 1982.

———. "Archaeology at the Smith Center." *Saints Herald*, May 1979, 18–19.

———. "Archaeology at the Smith Mansion, 1978." [n.d., n.p.] Copy in author's possession.

———. "Archaeology at the William Law Store (N-148–3)." Columbia: University of Missouri, 1988.

———. "The Joseph Smith Homestead Complex, Nauvoo, Illinois: A Focus on the Outbuildings, 1976." Columbia: University of Missouri, 1977.

———. "The Joseph Smith Mansion Hotel." Columbia: University of Missouri, 1984.

———. "The Smith Mansion Hotel Latrine and Other Discoveries of the 1978 Archaeological Project." Columbia: University of Missouri, 1979.

Deetz, James. *In Small Things Forgotten: The Archaeology of Early American Life*. New York: Anchor Press/Doubleday, 1977.

Dollar, Clyde D. "The Stone Lined Shaft in Brigham Young's Backyard (Nauvoo, Illinois) and Its Contents." In *The Conference on Historic Site Archaeology*

Papers 1965–1966, edited by Stanley South, 74–91, Columbia: University of South Carolina, 1967.

Eliason, Eric A. "Pioneers and Recapitulation in Mormon Popular Historical Expression." In *Usable Pasts: Traditions and Group Expressions in North America*, edited by Tad Tuleja, 175–211. Logan: Utah State University Press, 1997.

Enders, Don. Letter to President Gordon B. Hinckley. June 8, 2001. Copy in author's possession.

———. Letter to President Hinckley. September 22, 1999. Copy in author's possession.

"The Era Asks About Nauvoo Restoration." *The Improvement Era* 70, no. 7 (July 1967): 16.

Erekson, Keith A. "American Prophet, New England Town: The Memory of Joseph Smith in Vermont." Master's thesis, Brigham Young University, 2002.

———. "'Out of the Mists of Memory': Remembering Joseph Smith in Vermont." *Journal of Mormon History* 32, no. 2 (2005): 30–69.

Evans, R. Tripp. *Romancing the Maya: Mexican Antiquity in the American Imagination*. Austin: University of Texas Press, 2004.

Federal Writers' Project of Illinois. *Nauvoo Guide*. Works Progress Administration, *American Guide Series*. Chicago: A. C. McClurg & Co., 1939.

Flake, Kathleen. *The Politics of Religious Identity: The Seating of Senator Reed Smoot, Mormon Apostle*. Chapel Hill: University of North Carolina Press, 2004.

Flanders, Robert Bruce. *Nauvoo: Kingdom on the Mississippi*. Illini Books. Urbana: University of Illinois Press, 1975.

"Four Restored Nauvoo Projects Dedicated." *Ensign*, December 1989, 66.

Fowler, Melvin L. "Preliminary Archaeological Excavation at the Nauvoo Temple Site." Center for Archaeological Investigations, Southern Illinois University, Carbondale, January 1962.

Gardner, Marvin K. "Making Nauvoo Beautiful Again: Just What the Doctor Ordered." *Ensign*, October 1987, 20–25.

Givens, George W. *In Old Nauvoo: Everyday Life in the City of Joseph*. Salt Lake City UT: Deseret Book Co., 1990.

Givens, Terryl. *By the Hand of Mormon: the American Scripture that Launched a New World Religion*. Oxford: Oxford University Press, 2002.

Gordon, Sarah Barringer. *The Mormon Question: Polygamy and Constitutional*

Conflict in Nineteenth-Century Utah. Chapel Hill: University of North Carolina Press, 2002.

Green, Dee F. "Excavations at the Nauvoo Temple Site, 1962 Season." *U. A. S. Newsletter* 84 (December 1, 1962): 1–6.

———. Journal of the Nauvoo Temple Excavation. 1962. Copy in author's possession.

———. "Nauvoo Excavation Field Report." Foreword by Stanley Kimball. Center for Archaeological Investigations, Southern Illinois University, Carbondale, 1962.

Green, Dee F., and Larry Bowles. "Excavation of the Mormon Temple Remains at Nauvoo, Illinois: First Season." *The Florida Anthropologist* 17, no. 2 (1964): 77–81.

Greenspan, Anders. *Creating Colonial Williamsburg*. Washington DC: Smithsonian Institution Press, 2002.

Handler, Richard, and Eric Gable. *The New History in an Old Museum: Creating the Past at Colonial Williamsburg*. Durham NC: Duke University Press, 1997.

Hansen, Richard L. "Archaeological Excavations at the Chauncey Webb Site (127–4), Nauvoo, Illinois, 1970." Master's thesis, Brigham Young University, 1973.

Hardy, B. Carmon. *Solemn Covenant: The Mormon Polygamous Passage*. Urbana: University of Illinois Press, 1992.

Harrington, J. C. "Archaeological Excavations at the Brigham Young Site (126–2), Nauvoo, Illinois: 1965–1968." Salt Lake City UT: Nauvoo Restoration, Inc., 1969.

———. "Archaeological Excavations at the Edwin D. Webb Site, South Half of Southeast Quarter, Lot 4, Block 127, Nauvoo, Illinois." [Nauvoo IL]: Nauvoo Restoration, Inc., 1969.

———. "Archaeological Excavations at the Webb Blacksmith & Wagon Shop (127–4), Nauvoo, Illinois: 1967–1968. Salt Lake City UT: Nauvoo Restoration, Inc., 1969.

———. "Archaeological Excavations at the Wilford Woodruff Site (106–1), Nauvoo, Illinois." [Nauvoo IL]: Nauvoo Restoration, Inc., 1966.

———. "Archaeology as an Auxiliary Science to American History." *American Anthropologist* 57, no. 6 (1955): 1121–30.

———. "From Architraves to Artifacts: A Metamorphosis." In *Pioneers in*

Historical Archaeology: Breaking New Ground, edited by Stanley South, 1–14. New York: Plenum Press, 1994.

———. "Historic Site Archaeology in the United States." In *Archaeology of Eastern United States*, edited by James B. Griffin, 295–315. Chicago: University of Chicago Press, 1952.

Harrington, J. C., and Virginia S. Harrington. Interview by Charles B. Hosmer, Jr. May 18, 1970. Transcript. Oral History Collection, National Park Service, Harpers Ferry Center, Harpers Ferry WV.

———. Interview by S. Herbert Evison. March 15, 1971. Transcript. Oral History Collection, National Park Service, Harpers Ferry Center, Harpers Ferry WV.

Harrington, Virginia S. "Archaeological Excavations in the Temple Basement-1967." December 15, 1967. Copy in author's possession.

———. "Mysterious Staffordshire—and the Mormons?" *Antiques* 93, no. 2 (1968): 238–39.

———. "Report on the Excavation of the North Building Times and Seasons Complex, Nauvoo, Illinois. [Nauvoo IL]: Nauvoo Restoration, Inc., 1968.

———. "Why Archaeology at Nauvoo." *Relief Society Magazine* 55, no. 10 (1968): 731–37.

Harrington, Virginia S., and J. C. Harrington. *Rediscovery of the Nauvoo Temple: Report on Archaeological Excavations*. Salt Lake City UT: Nauvoo Restoration, Inc., 1971.

Hickman, Martin Berkeley. *David Matthew Kennedy: Banker, Statesman, Churchman*. Salt Lake City UT: Deseret Book Co., 1987.

Hild, Theodore. "State and National Surveys." In *Preservation Illinois: A Guide to State and Local Resources*, edited by Ruth Eckdish Knack, 75–79. Springfield: Illinois Department of Conservation, Division of Historic Sites, 1977.

Hinckley, Bryant S. "The Nauvoo Memorial." *The Improvement Era* 41, no. 8 (1938): 458–61, 511.

Hinckley, Gordon B. "'O That I Were an Angel, and Could Have the Wish of Mine Heart'." *Ensign*, November 2002, 4–6.

———. "Thanks to the Lord for His Blessings." *Ensign*, May 1999, 88–89.

Holzapfel, Richard Neitzel, T. Jeffery Cottle, and Ted D. Stoddard, eds. *Church History in Black and White: George Edward Anderson's Photographic Mission to Latter-day Saint Historical Sites*. Provo UT: Religious Studies Center, Brigham Young University, 1995.

Hosmer, Charles B., Jr. *Preservation Comes of Age: From Williamsburg to the National Trust*. 2 vols. Charlottesville: University Press of Virginia, 1981.

———. "Preservation Movement in Illinois." In *Preservation Illinois: A Guide to State and Local Resources*, edited by Ruth Eckdish Knack, 10–19. Springfield IL: Illinois Department of Conservation, Division of Historic Sites, 1977.

Howard, Richard P. "The Nauvoo Heritage of the Reorganized Church." *Journal of Mormon History* 16 (1990): 41–52.

Illinois Department of Conservation. Division of Long Range Planning, Systems Planning and Research Unit. *State of Illinois Historic Preservation Plan*. Springfield IL: Author, 1970.

Illinois House of Representatives. Resolution No. 53. April 27, 1949. Bills, Resolutions, and Related General Assembly Records, Record Series 600.001, Illinois State Archives, Springfield.

Jelks, Edward B. "Jean Carl Harrington, 1901–1998." *SAA Bulletin* 16, no. 5 (1998): 26.

Johnson, Randy. "17 Historical Sites Dedicated in Nauvoo." *Ensign*, October 1982, 74–76.

Kennedy, David M. Interviews by Gordon Irving. 1981–1987. Transcript, 3 vols. Salt Lake City UT. The James Moyle Oral History Program, Archives of the Church of Jesus Christ of Latter-day Saints, Salt Lake City UT

Kimball, James L., Jr. "J. LeRoy Kimball, Nauvoo Restoration Pioneer: A Tribute." *BYU Studies* 32, no. 1, 2 (1992): 5–12.

Krohe, James, Jr. "A New City of Joseph." *Americana* 8, no. 1 (1980): 56–61.

Larson, Gustive O. *The "Americanization" of Utah for Statehood*. San Marino CA: Huntington Library, 1971.

Larson, Stan. *Quest for the Gold Plates: Thomas Stuart Ferguson's Archaeological Search for the Book of Mormon*. Salt Lake City UT: Freethinker Press in association with Smith Research Associates, 1996.

Launius, Roger D., and John E. Hallwas, eds. *Kingdom on the Mississippi Revisited: Nauvoo in Mormon History*. Urbana: University of Illinois Press, 1996.

Launius, Roger D., and F. Mark McKiernan. *Joseph Smith, Jr.'s Red Brick Store*. Macomb: Western Illinois University, 1985.

Lee, Ronald F. *The Antiquities Act of 1906*. Washington DC: Office of History and Historic Architecture, Eastern Service Center, 1970.

Leonard, Glen M. *Nauvoo: A Place of Peace, A People of Promise*. Salt Lake City and Provo UT: Deseret Book Co. and Brigham Young University Press, 2002.

LeSueur, Stephen C. *The 1838 Mormon War in Missouri*. Columbia: University of Missouri Press, 1987.

Limerick, Patricia Nelson. *The Legacy of Conquest: The Unbroken Past of the American West*. New York: W. W. Norton, 1987.

Linebaugh, Donald W. *The Man Who Found Thoreau: Roland W. Robbins and the Rise of Historical Archaeology in America*. Durham NH: University of New Hampshire Press, 2005.

Lowenthal, David. *The Past Is a Foreign Country*. Cambridge: Cambridge University Press, 1985.

Lubeck, Kathleen. "Sarah M. Kimball's Nauvoo Home Is Dedicated." *Ensign*, May 1982, 109–11.

Lyman, E. Leo. *Political Deliverance: The Mormon Quest for Utah Statehood*. Urbana: University of Illinois, 1986

Lyon, T. Edgar. Interviews by Davis Bitton. 1974–1975. Transcript. Salt Lake City UT. Oral History Program, Archives of the Church of Jesus Christ of Latter-day Saints, Salt Lake City UT

Lyon, T. Edgar, Jr. *T. Edgar Lyon: A Teacher in Zion*. Provo UT: Brigham Young University Press, 2002.

Mackay, Lachlan. "A Brief History of the Smith Family Nauvoo Cemetery." *Mormon Historical Studies* 3, no. 1 (2002): 241–52.

Mackintosh, Barry. *The Historic Sites Survey and National Landmarks Program: A History*. Washington DC National Park Service, 1985.

Marriott, Richard E. "Building a Family Legacy: The Marriott Story." *Marriott Alumni Magazine*, Winter 2003, 4–7.

McKiernan, F. Mark. "Preserving and Interpreting our Physical Heritage: A Master Plan of the Historic Properties of the Reorganized Church of Jesus Christ of Latter-day Saints." Independence MO: Reorganized Church of Jesus Christ of Latter Day Saints, 1977.

Miller, George L. "Classification and Economic Scaling of 19th Century Ceramics: 1770–1881." *Historical Archaeology* 14 (1980): 1–40.

———. "Memorial: J. C. Harrington, 1901–1998." *Historical Archaeology* 32, no. 4 (1998): 1–7.

———. "A Revised Set of CC Index Values for Classification and Economic

Scaling of English Ceramics from 1787 to 1880." *Historical Archaeology* 25, no. 1 (1991): 1–25.

Moyer, Jonathan H. "Dancing with Devil: The Making of the Mormon-Republican Pact." PhD diss., University of Utah, Salt Lake City, 2009.

Murtagh, William J. *Keeping Time: The History and Theory of Preservation in America*. Rev. ed. New York: John Wiley and Sons, Inc., 1997.

"Nauvoo Information Center Groundbreaking." Nauvoo IL: Nauvoo Restoration, Inc., 1969. Copy in author's possession.

Nauvoo Restoration, Inc. (NRI). Corporate Files. Archives of the Church of Jesus Christ of Latter-day Saints, Salt Lake City. Various dates.

Noël Hume, Ivor. *A Guide to Artifacts of Colonial America*. New York: Alfred A. Knopf, 1969.

———. "When Tut Went Phut; or The Day Mr. Junior Changed His Mind." *Colonial Williamsburg*. Spring 2002.

Norman, V. Garth. "Joseph Smith and the Beginning of Book of Mormon Archaeology." *Meridian Magazine*. http://www.ldsmag.com/ideas/030930joseph.html.

Oakes, Cindy. "I Can "Dig" It!" *Restoration Trail Forum* 10, no. 3 (1984): 3.

O'Brien, Robert. *Marriott: The J. W. Marriott Story*. Salt Lake City: Deseret Book Co., 1977.

Olsen, Steven L. "A History of Restoring Historic Kirtland." *Journal of Mormon History* 30, no. 1 (2004): 120–28.

Pardoe, T. Earl. *Lorin Farr, Pioneer*. Provo UT: Brigham Young University Press, 1953.

Pilling, Arnold R. "Beginnings." *Historical Archaeology 1967* 1 (1967): 1–22.

Powell, Allan Kent. "Utah's First State Park." *History Blazer: News of Utah's Past from the Utah State Historical Society* (November 1996): 19–20.

Prince, Gregory A., and William Robert Wright. *David O. McKay and the Rise of Modern Mormonism*. Salt Lake City: University of Utah Press, 2005.

Pykles, Benjamin C. "A Brief History of Historical Archaeology in the United States." *SAA Archaeological Record* 8, no. 3 (2008): 32–34.

———. "Do You Remember Clyde Dollar?" Paper presented at the annual meeting of the Society for Historical Archaeology, Sacramento CA, January 11–15, 2006.

———. "An Early Example of Public Archaeology in the United States: Nauvoo, Illinois." *North American Archaeologist* 27, no. 4 (2006): 311–49.

"Questions Are Answered by Digging." *Saints Herald*, April 1982, 10, 13–14.

Reiser, A. Hamer. Interviews by William G. Hartley. 1974. Transcript, 4 vols. Salt Lake City, Utah. The James Moyle Oral History Program, Archives of the Church of Jesus Christ of Latter-day Saints, Salt Lake City UT

Righter, Robert W. *Crucible for Conservation: The Creation of Grand Teton National Park*. Boulder: Colorado Associated University Press, 1982.

Roberts, B. H. *A Comprehensive History of the Church of Jesus Christ of Latter-day Saints*. 6 vols. Provo UT: Brigham Young University Press, 1965.

Rudolph, Nathanael J. "Walking a Sacred Tightrope: Archaeology, Geography and the Evolution of Belief in the Church of Jesus Christ of Latter-day Saints." Master's thesis, Eastern Washington University, 2002.

Schuyler, Robert L. "Historical Archaeology." In *Encyclopedia of Archaeology: History and Discoveries*, edited by Tim Murray, 623–30. Santa Barbara CA: ABC-CLIO, 2001.

———. "Historical Archaeology as an Integral Part of the Anthropological Curriculum." In *Teaching and Training in American Archaeology: A Survey of Programs and Philosophies*, edited by William P. McHugh. Carbondale: University Museum and Art Galleries, Southern Illinois University, 1977.

———. "Images of America: The Contribution of Historical Archaeology to National Identity." *Southwestern Lore* 42, no. 4 (December 1976): 27–37.

———. "The J. C. Harrington Medal in Historical Archaeology." *Historical Archaeology* 17, no. 1 (1983): 1–2.

———. "Parallels in the Rise of the Various Subfields of Historical Archaeology." In *The Conference on Historic Site Archaeology Papers*, edited by Stanley South, 2–10. Columbia: University of South Carolina, 1975.

———. "The Second Largest City in the English-Speaking World: John L. Cotter and the Historical Archaeology of Philadelphia, 1960–1999." In *Philadelphia and the Development of Americanist Archaeology*, edited by Don D. Fowler and David R. Wilcox. Tuscaloosa: University of Alabama Press, 2003.

Shireman, Joyce A. "The Mormon Prophet's Illinois Legacy as Revealed in the Community of Christ's Historic Restoration in Nauvoo." *The Journal of the John Whitmer Historical Association* 25 (2005): 145–60.

Smith, Joseph, Jr. *History of the Church of Jesus Christ of Latter-day Saints*, edited by B. H. Roberts. 2nd rev. ed. 7 vols. Salt Lake City: Deseret Book Co., 1980.

Smith-Mansfield, Tricia. "'This is the Place' Monument." In *Utah History Encyclopedia*, edited by Allan Kent Powell, 555. Salt Lake City: University of Utah Press, 1994.

Stephens, John Lloyd. *Incidents of Travel to Central America, Chiapas, and Yucatan*. New York: Harper and Brothers, 1841.

Stobaugh, Kenneth E. "The Development of the Joseph Smith Historic Center in Nauvoo." *BYU Studies* 32, no. 1, 2 (1992): 32–40.

Todd, Jay M. "Nauvoo: A Progress Report." *The Improvement Era* 73, no. 7 (July 1970): 20–24.

———. "Nauvoo Temple Restoration." *The Improvement Era* 71, no. 10 (October 1968): 10–16.

U. S. Department of the Interior. National Park Service, History Branch. *Report on Nauvoo, Illinois*. Nauvoo Historic District National Historic Landmark file. Washington DC, November 19, 1940. Copy in author's possession.

———. National Park Service, History Branch. *Sites Recommended for Classification of Exceptional Value*. Nauvoo Historic District National Historic Landmark file. Washington DC. Copy in author's possession.

———. National Park Service. The National Survey of Historic Sites and Buildings. Theme XV, *Westward Expansion and Extension of the National Boundaries to the Pacific, 1830–1898: Overland Migrations West of the Mississippi River*. Washington DC: U.S. Government Printing Office, 1959.

Van Wagoner, Richard S. *Mormon Polygamy: A History*. 2nd ed. Salt Lake City UT: Signature Books, 1989.

Walker, J. Terry, and Richard B. Stamps. "Archaeological Investigations at the Lyon House and Store, Nauvoo, Illinois, 1980." [Nauvoo IL]: Nauvoo Restoration, Inc.

Waselkov, Gregory, Robert T. Bray, and Linda Waselkov. "Archaeological Investigations of the Hyrum Smith Site, 1974." Columbia: University of Missouri, 1975.

Wilkinson, Ernest L., and Leonard J. Arrington, eds. *Brigham Young University: The First One Hundred Years*. 4 vols. Provo UT: Brigham Young University Press, 1975–76.

Wilkinson, Ernest L., and W. Cleon Skousen. *Brigham Young University: A School of Destiny*. Provo UT: Brigham Young University Press, 1976.

Wood, W. Raymond. "In Memoriam: Robert Taylor Bray, 1925–1999." *Missouri Archaeological Society Quarterly* 16, no. 2 (1999): 4–7.

Young, George Cannon. Interview by Paul L. Anderson. 1973. Transcript. Salt Lake City, Utah. The James Moyle Oral History Program. Archives of the Church of Jesus Christ of Latter-day Saints, Salt Lake City UT.

INDEX

Page numbers in italic refer to illustrations

In the Critical Studies in the History of Anthropology series

Invisible Genealogies: A History of Americanist Anthropology
Regna Darnell

The Shaping of American Ethnography: The Wilkes Exploring Expedition, 1838–1842
Barry Alan Joyce

Ruth Landes: A Life in Anthropology
Sally Cole

Melville J. Herskovits and the Racial Politics of Knowledge
Jerry Gershenhorn

Leslie A. White: Evolution and Revolution in Anthropology
William J. Peace

Rolling in Ditches with Shamans: Jaime de Angulo and the Professionalization of American Anthropology
Wendy Leeds-Hurwitz

Irregular Connections: A History of Anthropology and Sexuality
Andrew P. Lyons and Harriet D. Lyons

Ephraim George Squier and the Development of American Anthropology
Terry A. Barnhart

Ruth Benedict: Beyond Relativity, Beyond Pattern
Virginia Heyer Young

Looking through Taiwan: American Anthropologists' Collusion with Ethnic Domination
Keelung Hong and Stephen O. Murray

Visionary Observers: Anthropological Inquiry and Education
Jill B. R. Cherneff and Eve Hochwald
Foreword by Sydel Silverman

Anthropology Goes to the Fair: The 1904 Louisiana Purchase Exposition
Nancy J. Parezo and Don D. Fowler

The Meskwaki and Anthropologists: Action Anthropology Reconsidered
Judith M. Daubenmier

The 1904 Anthropology Days and Olympic Games: Sport, Race, and American Imperialism
Edited by Susan Brownell

Lev Shternberg: Anthropologist, Russian Socialist, Jewish Activist
Sergei Kan

Contributions to Ojibwe Studies: Essays, 1934–1972
A. Irving Hallowell
Edited and with introductions by Jennifer S. H. Brown and Susan Elaine Gray

Excavating Nauvoo: The Mormons and the Rise of Historical Archaeology in America
Benjamin C. Pykles
Foreword by Robert L. Schuyler

Cultural Negotiations: The Role of Women in the Founding of Americanist Archaeology
David L. Browman

Homo Imperii: A History of Physical Anthropology in Russia
Marina Mogilner

American Anthropology and Company: Historical Explorations
Stephen O. Murray

Racial Science in Hitler's New Europe, 1938–1945
Edited by Anton Weiss-Wendt and Rory Yeomans

Cora Du Bois: Anthropologist, Diplomat, Agent
Susan C. Seymour

Before Boas: The Genesis of Ethnography and Ethnology in the German Enlightenment
Han F. Vermeulen

American Antiquities: Revisiting the Origins of American Archaeology
Terry A. Barnhart

An Asian Frontier: American Anthropology and Korea, 1882–1945
Robert Oppenheim

Theodore E. White and the Development of Zooarchaeology in North America
R. Lee Lyman

Declared Defective: Native Americans, Eugenics, and the Myth of Nam Hollow
Robert Jarvenpa

Glory, Trouble, and Renaissance at the Robert S. Peabody Museum of Archaeology
Edited and with an introduction by Malinda Stafford Blustain and Ryan Wheeler

Race Experts: Sculpture, Anthropology, and the American Public in Malvina Hoffman's Races of Mankind
Linda Kim

The Enigma of Max Gluckman: The Ethnographic Life of a "Luckyman" in Africa
Robert J. Gordon

www.ingramcontent.com/pod-product-compliance
Lightning Source LLC
LaVergne TN
LVHW050917080826
845145LV00001B/114

* 9 7 8 1 4 9 6 2 0 2 2 4 6 *